A Guide Through the
New Testament

P9-CLD-853

Also by Celia B. Sinclair
and published by Westminster/John Knox Press

A Guide Through the Old Testament

A Guide Through the New Testament

Celia B. Sinclair

Westminster John Knox Press
LOUISVILLE • LONDON

© 1994 Celia Brewer Marshall

All rights reserved. No part of this book may be reproduced or transmitted in any form or by any means, electronic or mechanical, including photocopying, recording, or by any information storage or retrieval system, without permission in writing from the publisher. For information, address Westminster/John Knox Press, 100 Witherspoon Street, Louisville, Kentucky 40202-1396.

Unless otherwise indicated, scripture quotations are from the New Revised Standard Version of the Bible, copyright © 1989 by the Division of Christian Education of the National Council of the Churches of Christ in the U.S.A., and are used by permission.

Acknowledgment is given to publishers and copyright holders for permission to reprint excerpts or adaptations from the following:

Maps from *The Westminster Historical Atlas to the Bible,* edited by George Ernest Wright and Floyd Vivian Filson. Copyright 1956, by W. L. Jenkins. Published by The Westminster Press.

"John," by Gail R. O'Day, in *The Women's Bible Commentary,* ed. Carol A. Newsom and Sharon H. Ringe. © 1992 Westminster/John Knox Press.

The discussion of New Testament ethics according to Paul, by the Rev. Dr. Leslie Weber, is reprinted by permission of Dr. Weber.

"The World of Paul," by Justo González and Catherine G. González, in *Adult Bible Studies Teaching Helps,* September–November 1984. Copyright 1984 by Graded Press.

The Art of Loving, by Erich Fromm. Copyright © 1956 by Erich Fromm. Reprinted by permission of HarperCollins Publishers, Inc.

The Brothers Karamazov, by Fyodor Dostoevsky, A Norton Critical Edition; the Constance Garnett translation revised by Ralph E. Matlaw, edited by Ralph E. Matlaw. Copyright © 1976 by W. W. Norton & Company, Inc. Reprinted by permission of W. W. Norton & Company.

Albrecht Dürer: Master Printmaker, edited by Boston Museum Fine Arts staff. Hacker Art Books, 1987.

Faith, Religion, and Theology, copyright 1990 by Brennan Hill, Paul Knitter, William Madges. Published by Twenty-Third Publications, P.O. Box 180, Mystic, CT 06355.

Cover design by Drew Stevens

First edition

Published by Westminster/John Knox Press
Louisville, Kentucky

This book is printed on acid-free paper that meets the American National Standards Institute Z39.48 standard. ∞

PRINTED IN THE UNITED STATES OF AMERICA

14 13 12 11 10 9 8 7

Library of Congress Cataloging-in-Publication Data

Marshall, Celia Brewer, 1954–
    A guide through the New Testament / Celia Brewer Marshall. — 1st ed.
        p.   cm.
        ISBN-13: 978-0-664-25484-1 (alk. paper)
        ISBN-10: 0-664-25484-5 (alk. paper)
        1. Bible.   N.T.—Textbooks.   I. Title.
BS2535.2.M37   1994
225.6—dc20   93-45517

To my parents,
Nancy Sorrells Brewer and
Spencer Spainhour Brewer, Jr.

Thanks be to God!

Contents

Preface

A newsletter from my church recently announced an upcoming series titled "Living in a Post-Christian World." While I cannot speak of the decline in memberships of Protestant and Catholic churches (numbers baffle me) nor of the rise in Eastern, New Age, and sectarian groups in this country (fascinating, but likewise beyond my scope), I still have a sense of what this newsletter meant. Biblical illiteracy is the norm today. Public schools are not teaching Bible; when high schools do find someone qualified to teach and do offer Bible as an elective, the course rarely makes it, due to low interest. Sunday schools that teach Bible find, at least by the high school level, attendance dropping off as students go elsewhere for fun, friends, and fellowship (and no nagging Bible study). Young adults, given the choice of Sunday school classes on politics or parenting or classes on the Bible, will most often attend those classes that give direct, practical advice or deal with pressing contemporary issues. It is probably the older generation who know the Bible best. They come from a time when verses and passages were memorized, when daily devotionals were a given, when biblical literacy was part of what it meant to be educated. This is simply not the case anymore. I do not see conditions where Bible study is actively discouraged. Rather, I see biblical studies passed like a hot potato from schools to churches to families, and finally tossed from the present to some future time when we may have the opportunity, or when our children get enough sense to know what's best for them.

However, I have seen firsthand the remarkable work being done in programs such as Education for Ministry and Disciples of Christ in Community (EFM and DOCC, both sponsored by the Episcopal Church), and the *Disciple* series (United Methodist Church). These programs are not for everybody. The coursework demands daily commitment to study and weekly meetings of the group for a year (DOCC and *Disciple*) or four years (EFM). But in spite of (or maybe it's because of) the commitment involved, folks love these programs and respond to them with great enthusiasm. They learn to read, study, and know the Bible as a text for themselves. As laypersons they are empowered to do their work of discipleship and ministry. The combination of disciplined Bible study and small-group process is a powerful one. With the drought of biblical illiteracy comes a mighty thirst for reading the Bible with understanding.

When Walt Sutton asked me to think about writing a companion to *A Guide Through the Old Testament*, this time on the New Testament, I thought long and hard for about ten seconds before I said yes. I love the idea of bringing the text to the reader in a way that's fun and interactive and (I pray, in some way) true to the text. I love the idea of you, the reader, picking up a copy of this guidebook, saying "Hmmm," and making a commitment to work through at least one of the chapters. And when I picture who you are, who this audience is, I have in mind people (from teenagers to adults) who are tired of being biblically illiterate, who refuse to be intimidated anymore by arcane scholarship, who wish to struggle with and perhaps befriend scripture, who believe that "faith in search of understanding" will empower them in their lives. If any one of these descriptions applies to you, you have found a good place to begin. You have a lifetime for this process, provided you don't keep postponing it into the future!

I wish to thank Turley Howard and Les Weber, both first-rate New Testament teachers, for allowing me to rummage through their files (more precious than gold!) and borrow many of their ideas. William Berman provided expert counsel. I also wish to thank Lisa Saunders for her graciousness and helpfulness.

Finally I wish to thank Alfred, Anna, and Sally for bearing with me as I worked on this at home. While none of my family was particularly patient with the demands of this project, they were always persistent in their love.

Celia Brewer Marshall

CHAPTER 1

Introduction to the New Testament

WHAT IS THE NEW TESTAMENT?

The New Testament is a collection of twenty-seven books written in Koine Greek, the Greek of the common folk in the Roman Empire. The earliest books were the letters of Paul. These letters were written to give guidance to new churches in a pagan, Greek-speaking world. Four Gospels and a church history (Acts) were written as the eyewitnesses of Jesus' ministry began to die off and a new generation arose who did not know Jesus or the apostles firsthand. Jesus and his apostles spoke Aramaic, a variant of Hebrew. The Gospel writers probably used early written collections or "notes" on the sayings of Jesus (in Aramaic) and unwritten traditions (which circulated orally in the early years of the young church) as sources for their books. Still later, two great threats appeared: persecution from Rome and heresies, or wrong teachings, within the congregations. The need arose for still more spiritual guidance; thus even more letters were written. The point is that the New Testament did not appear all at once and in one piece. The writings arose in bits and pieces as the generations after Jesus saw particular needs to fill and history to transmit. While scholars vary on the dates they assign to these books, we will use the following timeline for our study.

Approximate Chronology of the New Testament Writings

50–51	First and Second Letters of Paul to the Thessalonians
c. 55	Letter of Paul to the Galatians
54–55	The Corinthian correspondence, probably four letters now combined in 1 and 2 Corinthians
57–58	Letter of Paul to the Romans
56–61	Letters of Paul to the Colossians, to Philemon, and to the Philippians
c. 70	Gospel according to Mark
80–90	Letter to the Hebrews
80–90	Gospel according to Matthew
80–90	Gospel according to Luke and the Acts of the Apostles
c. 90	Letter of Paul to the Ephesians
c. 95	Book of Revelation
c. 96	First Letter of Peter
c. 100	Letter of James
c. 100	Gospel according to John and the three letters of John
c. 100	Letters to Titus and the two letters to Timothy, with earlier portions from Paul included
c. 125	Letter of Jude
c. 150	Second Letter of Peter

WAYS OF LOOKING AT THE NEW TESTAMENT

Two metaphors come to mind as I think of the ways of looking at the New Testament. One is an oil well: narrow at the top, extraordinarily deep below. Plumbing the depths of this small collection of books is the task of a lifetime; it has been twenty centuries in the making. The source is bottomless and inexhaustible. This oil well simply will not run dry.

The other image is from Genesis 32—Jacob's eerie night with the angel. Some might simply have shaken hands with the angel, saying, "Nice to meet you," and many might have walked away from the angel saying, "Later," but Jacob wrestled with the angel all night long and would not let go until he had received a blessing. "What is your name? Who are you? Bless me!" Jacob cried as he struggled.

Those who simply shake hands with the New Testament often do so because they think that doubts, questions, and wrestling matches are inappropriate. However, I do not think either the complexity of life or the complexity of the New Testament is addressed this way. The many who walk away from the angel are perhaps more honest; they simply do not want to get involved. (They hear those who say, "The Bible is the Word of God, take it or leave it, all or nothing," and so they leave.)

But what the Genesis story shows us is real involvement, real struggle, real engagement. It was hard work—Jacob's hip went out in the fight—but he was blessed by the angel at daybreak and renamed "Israel," or "he who struggles with God." This image is an appropriate one for what we do, with fear and trembling perhaps, with tenacity and boldness certainly, when we examine the New Testament texts.

We will look at methodology later, but right now brief mention needs to be made of the many interpretive theories that abound in the second half of the twentieth century. The historical-critical method (which dominated the first half of this century) cast Jacob's struggle with the angel in the form of this question: What did the original author mean? Biblical scholars got at meaning by paying attention to the original language, by examining the original historical setting, by trying to get to the original words of Jesus and/or the situation in which these words were first preserved. Their struggle was for objectivity, for leading meaning out of the text (exegesis) rather than reading meaning into the text (eisegesis). While this historical-critical method is extremely important, it is no longer the dominant method as other voices, approaches, and perspectives are being heard in the second half of this century.

Objectivity, once regarded as possible and desirable, is in fact neither. Each of us brings presuppositions to the text; no one reads the Bible (or anything at all) objectively, without a perspective or point of view. The reader has knowledge and experiences that prepare the reader for interpretation. We read with our own eyes, perceive with our own minds. Who would have it any other way?

Experience shows us that the same text offers different interpretations within an individual's own lifetime. The Lord's Prayer means something different to the ten-year-old than it does to this same person later when away at school, than it does to this person when she is teaching her own ten-year-old the Lord's Prayer. More dramatically, we can say that the New Testament is heard and understood anew with each generation. Past events and texts "change" in that they are continually being understood. Every age enters the text with new questions and receives new meaning. Thus the past is not fixed, but flows in a continuum into the present. There is a "surplus of meaning" which goes beyond what the author originally intended and speaks to us in our specific situations.

For example, Abraham Lincoln was aware that slavery was a given in the Old Testament (the patriarchs owned slaves) and the New Testament (slaves were obliged to be obedient to their masters). He knew that the Bible does not contain a single overt condemnation of human slavery. Contemporary tracts such as *Slavery Ordained by God* (1857) made this clear. But as Lincoln struggled to understand the will of God in his time, he saw the Bible's emphasis on justice and mercy and helping those in need. On the deepest level of interpretation, he saw that the Bible really undermines slavery. We are all created in the image of God (Gen. 1:27); no person is a mere thing to be bought and sold. Lincoln's struggle with the text went beyond what was *meant* at the time, when slavery was presupposed, to what it could *mean* for his day and for the future.

There are three elements in interpretation: the author, the text, and the reader. In our time a variety of approaches have arisen, each with an emphasis on one or another of these elements. We will briefly examine the strengths and weaknesses of each as the primary focus for biblical interpretation.

1. *The author.* Here is the primary concern of the historical-critical method. This method yields rich data on the historical setting of the author, the problems that author addressed, the search for the original words, the meaning of the original words, and the way the author put sources together to form the document we study today. It calls us to investigate in a scientific fashion the historical origins, text, composition, and transmission of the document. However, it assumes an objective, unbiased, scientific approach that is simply not possible. It optimistically assumes that we can get at the author's intent and know exactly what the original author actually meant to say. It fears that the text is "at risk" of being understood in ways different from those intended by the author.

Taken to an extreme, the historical-critical method ignores the reader and questions of what is relevant to the reader. It separates what the Bible originally meant from what it means. Finally, it ignores the literary quality, the texture of biblical literature. The text is treated as a static, frozen document.

2. *The text.* Here is the primary concern of literary criticism. The strengths of literary criticism are apparent as we see how words work, how stories are told, how phrases and sentences work together, how themes are played out. Literary criticism asks not what was the author's perspective, but what shines forth in the text. An extreme emphasis on the text is found in the "New Criticism" of the 1940s and 1950s, which maintained that we have no need to know either the author's intent or the historical setting. New Critics say stylistic analysis of narratives is fitting and proper. In fact it is the only way to look at these narratives, because they have self-contained value. Historical questions are irrelevant; what we have is what we have—the words on the page—and the text is autonomous.

As classics, the documents certainly speak to all time. But they also spoke to a concrete situation and spoke of

Jesus in a particular place and time. Focus on the text alone ignores the historical character of biblical religion.

3. *The reader.* The important thing in this emphasis is that, finally, the reader *is* the target of biblical interpretation. The text does not simply make a difference; it makes a difference to some*one.* In struggling to interpret the text, we find the text interprets us! What the reader hears and understands is the point of the reading. Reader-response theory stresses the importance of this element in interpretation.

But in its extreme form, this theory says that the role of the reader is the only thing that really matters. What the reader sees, reads, understands is finally what counts. The reader actually generates new meaning and thus creates a new text. Truth in interpretation is (almost) a matter of personal taste, and wildly arbitrary interpretations must be allowed.

We must acknowledge all three elements, all three points in this triangle, keeping dynamic interaction between the elements in play. Meaning is not limited to the author's intention exclusively, the text is not limited to its literary qualities exclusively, and what you or I get out of a particular reading on a particular day is not the sole aim of interpretation. All are necessary elements.

The same Holy Spirit who inspired the scriptures is the one who brings understanding to the reader, and their primary purpose is to communicate a message that requires a response. In this *Guide*, you will be asked to struggle with the text, to hear what it has to say, and to be open to the possibility that the struggle brings with it a blessing.

THE NEW TESTAMENT CANON

Not one of the twenty-seven books in our New Testament came with a set of instructions: "This is Holy Scripture. Place in set with other books marked same, toward the end of your Bibles, after those labeled Old Testament or Apocrypha." The way these books came to be included in the New Testament was instead a slow process, which took centuries to jell. In fact a large library of gospels, letters, and apocalypses, all claiming apostolic authorship, were winnowed out during this process, which was not completed until A.D. 397.

"Canon" was originally a Greek word meaning a standard of measurement, like a yardstick or meterstick. The term canon is now used for the standard that measures religious belief. The books which made it into the New Testament canon were accepted as sacred by the early church. In other words, over time, they came to be upheld as Holy Scripture or the written rule of faith.

Working backward from the Council of Carthage in 397, when the list was set and closed at the twenty-seven books we now have, we can trace a few steps in this process. Athanasius, bishop of Alexandria, wrote a festal letter in 367 which lists the same books as the Carthage Council. Origen asked that certain books be acknowledged as scripture, including all in our present New Testament except James and Jude, in 254.

Irenaeus, bishop of Lyons in Gaul (modern France), wrote *Against Heresies,* c. 185. He was the first to say that there is a limited number of books that contain the authoritative word of God, and that sacred texts must have apostolic origins. (Matthew and John were apostles, Mark and Luke were disciples of apostles.) He argued that the number of gospels be limited to four.

Irenaeus also relied on the authority of Paul as an apostle and Peter as founder of the most important church, that of Rome. Irenaeus quoted from every document now in the New Testament except Philemon, the Third Letter of John, and Jude. He also quoted from an apocalyptic writing called the Shepherd of Hermas. (Another list from this same period, the Muratorian list, includes the Shepherd of Hermas and the Revelation of Peter, but not 1 and 2 Peter, Hebrews, James, or 3 John.) Furthermore, Irenaeus insisted on two major divisions in the canon: the Hebrew scriptures and the Christian scriptures. Both are authoritative for the church.

The first century A.D. was fluid in terms of religious writings. The Jews did not officially set the canon of Hebrew scriptures until A.D. 90 at the Council of Jamnia. The Bible for Jesus, the apostles, and the early church was the Hebrew Scripture (Torah, Prophets, and Writings), but we cannot imagine this being the *established* set of authoritative writings until some sixty years after Jesus' death. In fact, one reason for the Council of Jamnia's work was the rise of Christianity and the proliferation of Christian writings which the rabbis could not condone!

The first Christians were permitted to speak in local synagogues, where they interpreted the readings of the Hebrew scriptures (later called the Old Testament) in light of their faith in Jesus. After A.D. 85, Christians were no longer permitted to speak in the synagogues or they withdrew from them, reading their "new" writings in Christian gatherings. Again, the times were fluid in terms of religious writings. As we have already noted, there were many more gospels, letters, and writings circulating then than we have now. What principles did the early church use in deciding which books to include in the canon?

Some unwritten rules were at work in the process of canonization. Can a particular book be traced to an apostle or a follower of an apostle? Is the book in harmony with accepted teaching? Is the book widely accepted in the churches? Does it have practical usage within the church? The two key principles were apostolicity (of authorship) and catholicity (or universal use). Of these two, by far the more important was the second. Irenaeus, Origen, and other leaders of early churches recognized that authorship on occasion is known by God alone, but their churches "voted with their feet" (i.e., by practical use and widespread acceptance) on inclusion of the documents now in the New Testament canon. If it were proved beyond the shadow of a doubt that Paul did not write, say, the letter to the Romans, the authority of that book would nevertheless be intact because of practical usage. Conversely, if an indisputably Pauline letter were discovered today, it would not be canonical for the same reason. It would be of great interest to the church, but it would not be part of the canon.

We call those gospels "apocryphal" that were excluded from the canon. Many apocryphal writings have only recently been rediscovered. The Gospel of Thomas, for instance, was known to the early church but lost for centuries. In 1945, a bedouin found a large clay jar near the town of Nag Hammadi in upper Egypt. Inside the jar were fifty-two documents, part of a library that had once belonged to a church or monastery. These documents were written in the Coptic language (Egyptian with a Greek alphabet) after being translated from Greek originals, most of which have been lost. The Gospel of Thomas, found at Nag Hammadi, is a collection of 114 sayings of Jesus. Some are familiar to us:

> "Blessed are the poor, for yours is the kingdom of heaven." (54)

> "He who seeks shall find, and he who knocks, to him it shall be opened." (94)

Some sound a bit "fractured":

> "He who blasphemes against the Father will be forgiven, and he who blasphemes against the Son will be forgiven, but he who blasphemes against the Holy Spirit will not be forgiven, either on earth or in heaven." (44)

> "Blessed are they that hunger, that they may fill the belly of him who desires." (69b)

Some are troubling and downright absurd:

> "Where there are three gods, they are gods; where there are two or one, I am with him." (30)

> "Simon Peter said to them: Let Mary go forth among us, for women are not worthy of the life. Jesus said: Behold, I shall lead her, that I may make her male, in order that she also may become a living spirit like you males. For every woman who makes herself male shall enter the kingdom of heaven." (114)

The Infancy Gospel of Thomas (c. 150) was translated into several languages and appeared in a number of collections in the ancient period. It is a collection of popular stories about the early years of Jesus' life, from ages five to twelve. He made clay sparrows on the Sabbath and they flew away when he clapped his hands. A child fell off the roof of a house and died; Jesus revived his playmate from death. When the carpenter Joseph cut a board too short, Jesus stretched it to its proper length.

The Book of James (also called Protevangelium of James; c. 100–150) gives the events leading up to the birth of Mary and ends with the birth of Jesus. It tells the story of Joachim and Anna (descendants of David), a childless couple. While Joachim was in the wilderness fasting for forty days, an angel appeared to Anna and she conceived a child, Mary. Mary was taken to the Temple at age three and brought up by priests. Joseph, a widower with sons, was chosen to be her husband when she was twelve. However, Joseph saw himself as Mary's guardian and did not have intercourse with her. When Mary became pregnant (with Jesus), Joseph was afraid that she had been seduced by another man. They survived a trial by bitter water showing their innocence and went to Bethlehem, where Jesus was born in a cave. Thus Jesus' brothers were actually stepbrothers, Mary remained a virgin forever, and *her* birth was divine in origin. The Immaculate Conception of Mary was proclaimed to be dogma for Roman Catholics in 1854.

DOING AN EXEGESIS

"Exegesis" is the term students of the New Testament use to describe what they are doing when they try to see what a New Testament passage meant when it was first written. The term comes from the Greek word meaning "to lead out." Exegesis is a reading of the text that attempts to draw out the meaning intended by the author.

At some point in your study you will want to stop and closely examine a passage in a disciplined, scholarly way. Use this section to guide your inquiry. You may simply do research and take notes, or you may wish to compose your findings in a formal written piece. Either way, you will find that you learn plenty about the New Testament; you will also learn much about yourself.

Exegesis seeks to be objective, even while recognizing that total objectivity is impossible. Anyone who reads the New Testament brings to that reading personal preoccupations as well as theological preconceptions. A good exegete is one who becomes aware of, and reflectively critical of, these factors in his or her search for meaning.

Types of Criticism

First off, by "criticism" we do not mean finding fault or censuring the text! Criticism comes out of our need for interpretation and understanding. It means asking every question that can reasonably be asked of any text. (In so doing we find that the New Testament is *not* like any other text.) Criticism is the first step, the basis for understanding. But it is the first step. *Applicatio* follows *explicatio*, that is, application flows out of explication. Here are some types of biblical criticism; later we will see how these types might apply to your work.

Textual criticism: We have no autographs or original copies of any part of the New Testament. Instead, there exist many thousands of manuscripts in the Greek. Adding to the confusion, no two manuscripts are exactly alike. Textual criticism (called "lower criticism" because it is the foundation for all other studies) addresses these problems. Over time we have come to know more about these variations and also more about ways of comparing them, thus the many versions of the New Testament that exist today. For example, the Authorized or King James Version of 1611 was based on a form of the Greek New Testament that was thought to be closer to the autographs (originals) than the English versions that preceded it. (At the time, those translators were attacked for using what was then modern knowledge about the text.) Revisions of the Authorized Version were made in the 1880s (the Revised Version), in

the 1940s (the Revised Standard Version), and again in our time, with the New Revised Standard Version appearing in 1989. In doing your own textual criticism, compare your passage in a variety of English translations. Keep an eye on the margin and/or footnotes of your Bible(s). Pay attention to the notes that show that "other ancient authorities" say something different, using a different word or omitting the word altogether. You might not solve the mystery, but you will do some interesting detective work.

Source criticism: In reading the Gospels of Matthew, Mark, and Luke, you will be struck by the similarities between these three. They share much of the same material. Who wrote first? Who drew material from whom? What common sources did they have? These are the questions addressed by source criticism, which is concerned with the relationship between these three Gospels. Source critical theories are just that—hypotheses that may or may not be helpful to you in comparing the Gospels (sources are not really an issue in any other New Testament books).

Form criticism: Form critics also focus on the Gospels. They are aware that Jesus spoke in Aramaic whereas the Gospels are all written in Greek. The exact words of Jesus, then, cannot be the exact words of the Gospel writers. Form critics are concerned with the preliterary, oral stage, when the sayings of Jesus were preserved. Form criticism tries to go back behind the written documents and see what the individual units might have been in their preliterary form. These individual units, called *pericopes* (per-*ik*-uh-peez), fall into four main groups in the Gospels: pronouncement stories, sayings, miracle stories, and stories about Jesus. In searching for the oldest, most original material (closest to the authentic words of Jesus), form critics make assumptions with which you may or may not agree. For instance, some think that the rougher and wordier pericopes are oldest, with roughness and details being smoothed away later. The source critic tries to look beneath the skin and musculature to find the bones of the skeleton.

Redaction criticism: A redactor is an editor. Redaction criticism looks at the Gospel writers as redactors, or editors. The Gospel writers were not simply stenographers or scribes. They had a job to do, putting together material, and redaction criticism takes the evangelists seriously as theologians in their own right. They wrote for a reason and they organized their materials accordingly. Redaction criticism looks at the way the evangelists edited their sources and put frameworks around the pericopes. It asks what the writers did with the oral tradition they knew and what special interests they had.

Source, form, and redaction criticism apply almost exclusively to the Gospels. The best way to get at some of these issues on your own is through skillful use of *Gospel Parallels: A Synopsis of the First Three Gospels.* If you don't own a copy, consider getting one. (See the Bibliography at the end of this book.) Along with a good concordance, it is a must for your own bookshelves.

Literary criticism: You might breathe a sigh of relief to know that literary criticism is not concerned with the historical setting or process behind the text. Literary criticism does not ask how a text came about or how we can use material outside the text to understand it. It looks at what can be learned from the text itself, standing alone and apart from any other considerations. The most helpful tool here (besides good diagramming skills) is your concordance.

Method

Picking a passage is up to you, but keep in mind that a passage, or pericope, is *not* a chapter, but a unit of roughly five to fifteen verses that has a clear beginning and a clear end.

1. Once you have picked your passage, read the text from as many versions of the Bible as possible. As you read, keep track of the words and/or phrases that vary consistently from version to version. Read footnotes and marginalia looking for points where manuscripts differ ("other ancient authorities say . . ."). You will come back to these words later. (Here you are doing textual criticism.)

2. Determine the context. Where is the passage set in time and space? Where has the author placed the unit in the framework of the narrative? For instance, a particular miracle account will be influenced by where the author has placed the unit. How has the author led up to it? How does he follow it? The placement of your passage within the document helps determine its significance. (Here you are doing redaction criticism.)

3. Determine the literary form. Is your unit a parable, a miracle account, a prayer, preaching, an argument, a narrative? What does the particular genre (form) seek to do? What are the rules governing the literary form of your passage? You may need to use a commentary here; some suggestions are found below. (Here you are doing form criticism.)

4. Determine the life-setting of the passage. While you have a commentary handy, use it to find out the audience the author was addressing and the problems or issues it faced. The New Testament documents were addressed to concrete historical and religious situations. The stories and sayings gain a new dimension when we know, or at least can make an educated guess as to, what the original life-setting was.

5. Now you are ready to do your own literary criticism.

A. *Determine the mood.* Is the passage ironic in mood? Is the tone one of anger? Is it emotionally charged, or simply a statement of fact? Read the passage aloud, many times, preferably with a friend. Have it read to you. Try out different inflections and stresses. Different emphases yield different meanings.

B. *Determine the structure of the passage.* This is one of the most important considerations in exegesis. What we speak of here is the way a passage is put together. How are the sentences arranged to make a certain point? Where is that point to be found in the passage? If the passage presents an argument, what are the essential steps in the argument, and what are simply asides? If the passage is a narrative, what is the climax of the story, what is its denouement, and what is the connection between them? It frequently helps to diagram all, or at least some, of the more complex sentences in the passage. Another helpful practice is to write out the passage in sense lines, using various degrees of indentation to indicate the importance of successive points. This aspect of exegesis resembles thinking along with the author.

C. *Determine the meaning of sentences.* By means of grammatical analysis the exegete is able to discern the relationship between parts of a sentence, the importance of different word order, the effect of certain clauses, and how the sentences are joined together into larger units of meaning. Here, attention to connecting words (*and, but, or, for, because, so,* etc.) is important. The employment of various connecting words indicates whether the author wishes to express opposition, contrast, continuity, result, consequence, or purpose.

D. *Determine the meaning of words.* We move from the larger context to the smallest units of meaning in a passage: the words. Here, we cannot blithely assume that we understand the full meaning of the words an author uses. Often words gain certain theological connotations over time and need to be redefined. Pick out what you think are some key words in your passage, and ask these questions of each:

1. How was the word employed in the Hebrew scriptures? These texts were available to the authors of the New Testament.
2. How is the word used elsewhere in the New Testament?
3. Finally, and most importantly, how is the word used elsewhere in the author's own writings, and/or within the same document?

Skillful use of a concordance is your tool here. Theological dictionaries are helpful if you wish to dig deeper.

6. If your passage is from one of the Gospels, see if the same or similar material is used in the other Gospels or if the material is unique to your writer. Use *Gospel Parallels* for this. Compare and contrast the passages, noting differences in word use and emphasis. (Here you are doing form criticism.)

A final note. Don't be afraid to pose dumb questions to the text, or seemingly obvious ones. Questions like "What in the world does this mean?" or "Why was this passage included?" often cut to the heart of the matter.

Research Suggestions

COMMENTARIES

The Anchor Bible. Garden City, N.Y.: Doubleday & Co., 1964–.

Black, Matthew, ed. *Peake's Commentary on the Bible.* New York: Thomas Nelson & Sons, 1962.

Brown, Raymond E., Joseph Fitzmeyer, and Roland Murphy, comps. *The Jerome Bible Commentary.* Englewood Cliffs, N.J.: Prentice-Hall, 1968.

The New Interpreter's Bible. Nashville: Abingdon Press. (To be published soon.)

DICTIONARIES

Buttrick, George Arthur, ed. *The Interpreter's Dictionary of the Bible.* Nashville: Abingdon Press, 1962.

Leon-Dufour, Xavier. *Dictionary of the New Testament.* Trans. by Terrence Prendergast. San Francisco: Harper & Row, 1980.

Richardson, Alan, ed. *A Theological Word Book of the Bible.* New York: Macmillan Co., 1962.

For concordances and other reference tools, see the "Bibliography" at the back of this book.

NEW TESTAMENT BACKGROUND: ROME AND JUDEA

The birthplace of Christianity was Judea; the time of birth was during the Roman Empire. In this section we will note the *social* and *political* conditions that are important for you to know before you begin your study of the New Testament documents. In the next section we will note the *religious* and *philosophical* undercurrents peculiar to the Greco-Roman world. You will find many topics and terms introduced in these sections; be aware that this background material is introductory in nature. You are encouraged to do further research on those topics which interest you.

I. The Roman Empire

A. *The Pax Romana.* The turbulent years of the Roman Republic ended with the crowning of Augustus as Caesar, or emperor (ruled from 31 B.C. to A.D. 14). Augustus initiated a time of peace, the Pax Romana, which lasted well into the second century A.D. The extent of this peace was geographically vast. It included all of Europe to the Rhine and Danube Rivers, and all of the ancient Near East. You might picture Rome as a peacock with feathers extending out to Hispania (Spain), Gaul (France), Britain, the Germanies, Macedonia and Greece, Asia Minor (Turkey), Syria, Judea, Egypt, and northern Africa. The empire was united under one ruler and at peace.

B. *Roads and communication.* If the Greeks before them were philosophers, the Romans were engineers. They built a system of paved roads with Rome at the hub, connecting the ends of the empire to its center.

Travel became speedier and safer. Couriers were able to cover ground at fifty miles a day. While piracy on the seas was harder to control, the Roman police were able to keep roads relatively safe. Never before had the exchange of goods and the spread of ideas been so easy. Latin was the language of the West and of legal affairs, but Greek was the language of international affairs and commerce. Koine (koy-nay) Greek, a development from classical Greek, was the common tongue for most in the East as well as many in the West. Latin did not fully replace Greek as the common tongue until the third century A.D. The New Testament was written in Koine Greek.

C. *Cities.* Urbanization was at its height during the empire. Rome, Antioch, Alexandria, Caesarea, the Decapolis, and Corinth reemerged as new large cities with bustling populations. Outside of Rome, where the senatorial aristocracy was determined by birth, social mobility (both upward and downward) was a feature of urban life. Roman citizenship was a birthright for children of recognized (freeborn) Roman marriages. Citizens had the right to vote, to hold office, and to appeal to the emperor in legal disputes. Many who were not born citizens were granted citizenship as a gift from the emperor in recognition of their local leadership or talent. Cities were populated not only by citizens, but by emancipated slaves (freedmen and freedwomen), many of whom became quite wealthy and powerful, and "metics"—aliens who could live in a city provided they had a citizen sponsor. Slavery was an accepted institution in the Roman Empire. An estimated 40 percent of the empire was not free during the first century A.D. Redemption from slavery meant buying one's freedom, a price many could not pay.

D. *Political control.* Jesus was born during the reign of Augustus and executed during the reign of Tiberius. (A timeline of major Roman emperors will follow.) Paul preached his message during the reigns of Claudius and Nero. Nero, Domitian, and Trajan all persecuted Christians, but the major attempts to wipe out Christianity were made during the reigns of Decius (249–251) and Diocletian (284–305). Persecutions ended with the first Christian emperor, Constantine (306–337); eventually Christianity became the official religion of the Roman Empire. Leadership of the provinces (areas conquered or annexed by Rome) was determined by imperial appointment. Taxation and armed garrisons were constant reminders of Roman authority, even in the hinterlands. The Pax Romana was expensive. Law and order has its price, as the Romans well knew. Generally, the Roman Empire respected local custom (the case with the Jews being problematic, as we shall see); in practice this respect depended on the political ambitions of the appointed leaders.

E. *Judea as a Roman province.* Judea actually came under Roman domination with Pompey's conquest in 63 B.C. As you might imagine, the end of Jewish leadership (the Hasmonaean dynasty) was a problem theologically and politically (Israel did not become independent again until 1948!). The problem was intensified by the procurators appointed by Rome. Herod the Great (ruled 37–4 B.C.) was named king of the Jews. He married a woman of Hasmonaean stock to legitimize his reign, then proceeded to wipe out every one of her family members. Eventually he had his wife killed, and two sons as well, on conspiracy charges. Benevolent and tolerant he was not. Besides being the ruler at the time of Jesus' birth, he is best known for his urbanization projects (the cities of Caesarea and Samaria) and enlarging the Temple in Jerusalem. At his death, the territory was divided among his three (remaining) sons, but from A.D. 6 on, the rule of Judea, Samaria, and Idumaea (Edom) was by Romans appointed governors by the emperor. These governors had supreme authority—unlimited power over life and death, control of the police, and power to tax at will. However, they often left matters to local courts, as the trial of Jesus shows. The most famous of these governors was Pontius Pilate (26–36). Felix and Festus were governors during the time of Paul's work (between 52 and 62).

F. *The Jewish wars.* Imperial Rome recognized that Jews had to be treated differently from other subjects because of their unique religion. Jews were not compelled to worship the emperor and were permitted to try religious cases in their own courts. Jewish revolutionaries were a constant problem for Rome, however. These revolutionaries represented the basic Jewish desire for independence. By A.D. 66 the whole nation was ready for rebellion. Dissatisfied with corrupt Roman governors and eager to bring in God's kingdom, the Jews revolted. The Jewish wars broke out in A.D. 66, during the reign of Nero, and ended in 74, during Vespasian's reign. The climax came in 70, with the conquest of Jerusalem. The wall around the city was leveled and the Temple was burned. Rebels at Masada, a fortress in the heights near the Dead Sea, held out until 74, when they all (960 of them) committed suicide the night before the Romans stormed the garrison. Before Jerusalem fell in 70, a rabbi named Johanan ben Zakkai established an academy on the coast at Jamnia for the study of Jewish torah. Jamnia became the center for Jewish leadership after the fall of Jerusalem. In A.D. 90, the question of the Hebrew canon was settled at Jamnia with the establishment of a list of authoritative scripture, the "Old Testament" as we have it today.

A second Jewish war broke out in A.D. 132, after the emperor Hadrian banned circumcision and announced plans for rebuilding Jerusalem as a pagan city with a temple to Jupiter on the old Temple site. The leaders, including Bar Kokhba ("Son of a Star"), were captured as the Romans drove all Jews out of Jerusalem. The city was renamed Colonia Aelia Capitolina, with temples built to the Roman Jupiter and the Greek Aphrodite. In the fourth century, Constantine allowed Jews to enter the city once a year, when they went to pray at the "Wailing Wall"—the western wall that remained of the old Temple.

Roman Emperors at the Time of the New Testament Writings

Augustus, 31 B.C.–A.D. 14
Tiberius, A.D. 14–37
Gaius Caligula, 37–41
Claudius, 41–54
Nero, 54–68 (end of Julio-Claudian dynasty)
Vespasian, 69–79
Titus, 79–81
Domitian, 81–96 (end of Flavian dynasty)
Nerva, 96–98
Trajan, 98–117
Hadrian, 117–138

II. Judea

A. *The Temple and the priesthood.* The Temple of Jesus' time was actually the second to be built on the site in Jerusalem. The first Temple was built by King Solomon around 1000 B.C. and destroyed by the Babylonians in 586 B.C., when much of the Jewish population was deported from Judah to Babylon. The exiles returned from Babylon, built the second Temple, and

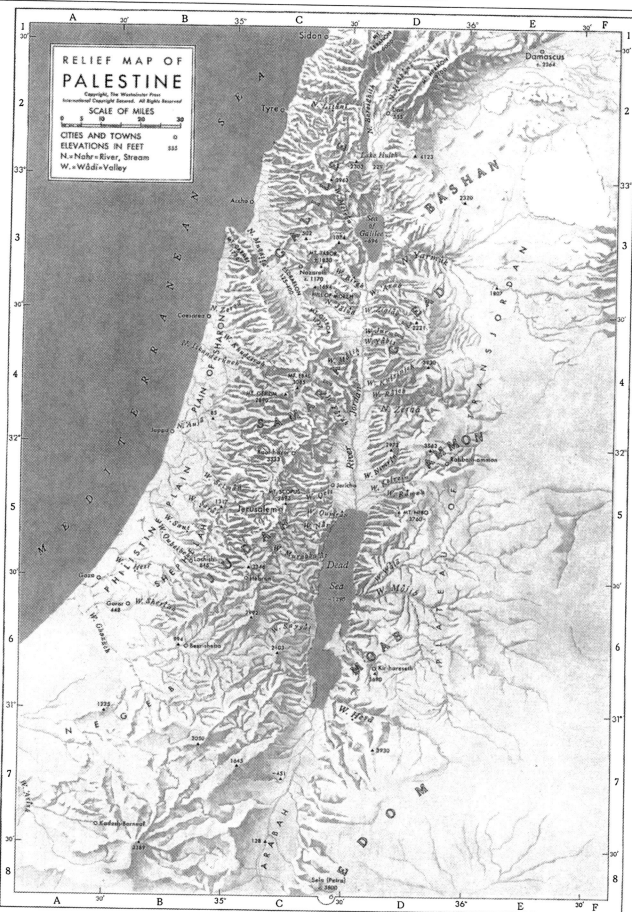

Fig. 1.1

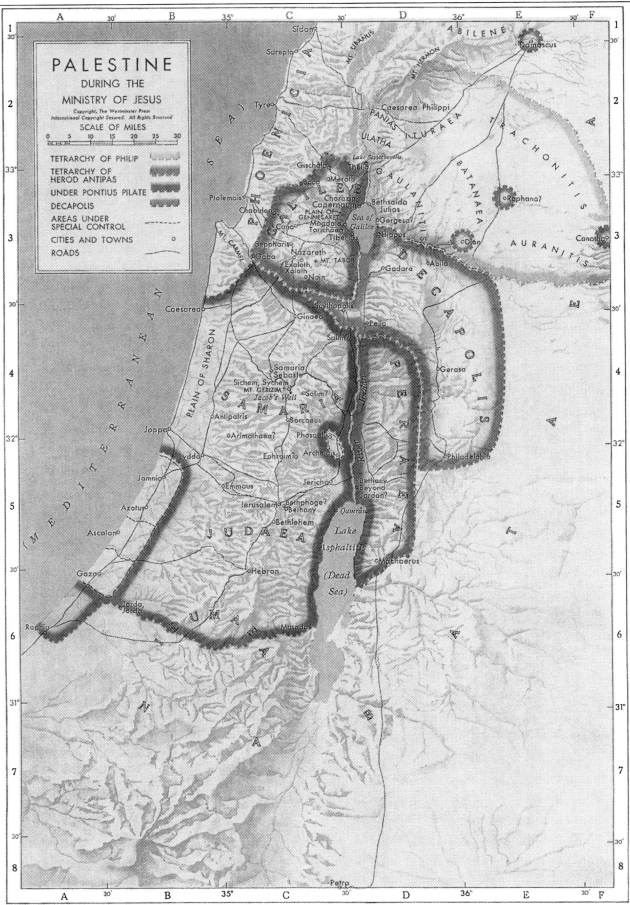

Fig. 1.2

dedicated it in 515 B.C. Herod the Great rebuilt and enlarged the Temple site in 10 B.C. Inside the Temple, following the plan of the ancient tabernacle, were the Holy Place and the Holy of Holies. Priests entered the Holy Place twice daily to offer incense on a golden altar. Male lamb, grain, and drink offerings were made at dawn and at midafternoon. Additional sacrifices were made on Sabbaths and feasts. The high priest entered the Holy of Holies once a year, on the Day of Atonement. Money changers set up shop in the Temple grounds outside, because Roman coins bore the image of the emperor and could not be used to pay the Temple tax (the equivalent of two days' pay for a laborer). The Temple was central to the life of the Jewish people. They went to the Temple to mark special occasions in their own lives and to offer sacrifices. The priests served at the altar, while the Levites were responsible for music and for policing the Temple. The Temple was not only a symbol of Jewish unity; it was a sacred space, where the presence of God abided.

Figure 1.3, "Jerusalem in the Time of Christ," shows the relationship of the Temple to the rest of Jerusalem.

B. *Synagogues.* When the Jews were dispersed throughout the ancient Near East after the Babylonian invasion of 586 B.C., they maintained their faith and identity by meeting in small congregations. Where there had been only one Temple, in Jerusalem, synagogues existed wherever a quorum of ten males gathered together. Unlike the Temple, which was attended by priests and Levites, the synagogue was run by the adult male Jews of the town. Also unlike the Temple, sacrifices were not (indeed, could not be) offered in synagogues. The synagogue substituted things that are *said* (teachings) for things that are *done* (sacrifice). Worship consisted of reading the Shema (Deut. 6:4–9; 11:13–21; Num. 15:37–41), prayer, reading a selection from the Torah (first five books of our Hebrew scriptures), a reading from one of the prophets, a sermon, and a closing benediction. The pattern of synagogue worship greatly influenced the liturgy of early Christian churches.

As we have many Christian denominations today, Judaism had many groups, or parties, in the New Testament era. The following items identify the major groups.

C. *Sadducees.* A priestly and well-to-do party, the Sadducees were not above compromising with Rome to keep their aristocratic status. They held power by their close association with the Temple and by the seats they held in the Sanhedrin, or governing council for the Jews. They considered the Torah (first five Old Testament books) alone to be sacred. They rejected the oral tradition that was associated with the Pharisees. They also rejected belief in angels, spirits, and the resurrection of the dead. With the destruction of the Temple in A.D. 70, this party came to an abrupt end.

D. *Pharisees.* Opposed to the Sadducees on almost every count were the Pharisees, or teachers of the law. They were probably urban middle class, but they had the support of the peasantry. The Pharisees were progressive: they valued the oral interpretation of the Torah, which interpreted and updated written laws. They tried to take general principles and apply them to concrete situations of their time. For instance, they dealt with the commandment "Keep the Sabbath holy" by defining the precise limits of the Sabbath and figuring out exactly what constituted "work" and was forbidden. They believed in angels, spirits, and the resurrection of the just after death. They were the scholars and leaders in synagogue worship. Rabbinic Judaism, that is, the Judaism that survived the destruction of the Temple in A.D. 70, is the work of the Pharisees.

E. *Zealots.* Had it not been for the Roman domination of Judea, Zealots would not have existed. They were fierce in their desire for independence. Convinced that God alone should lead them, they thought nothing of persecution and pain. They no doubt instigated the rebellion against Rome in A.D. 66.

F. *Essenes.* The "monks" of Judaism, this group insisted on strict separation from all that was unclean, including Gentiles, the Temple (which they believed was run improperly), and even other Jews. They accepted converts only after three years of rigid preparation. Essenes were celibate and ascetic. They believed that the end of time was at hand, and in fact their time ended with the Jewish wars. The Romans attacked the large Essene community at Qumran near the Dead Sea, wiping out the monastic settlement and leaving for us their library: the Dead Sea Scrolls.

G. *Samaritans.* Not one of the groups above would include the Samaritans as a group or sect within Judaism. They were instead detested as apostates and halfbreeds. When Assyria conquered the Northern Kingdom of Israel in 722 B.C., many of Israel's citizens were taken into exile, and colonists were brought in from other areas to settle. The colonists brought their gods with them and intermarried with the Israelites. Samaritans at the time of the New Testament had their own temple on Mt. Gerizim and looked forward to a Messiah like Moses. Their scripture consisted of the Torah, with some modifications.

H. *Diaspora Jews.* Any Jew living outside the Holy Land is a Jew of the Diaspora, or the dispersion. The first major wave of diaspora Judaism was due to the Babylonian invasion of 586 B.C. By the first century A.D., more Jews lived outside Judea than lived in it. Jews settled in places such as upper Mesopotamia and Babylonia because of the conquest, while others avoided the

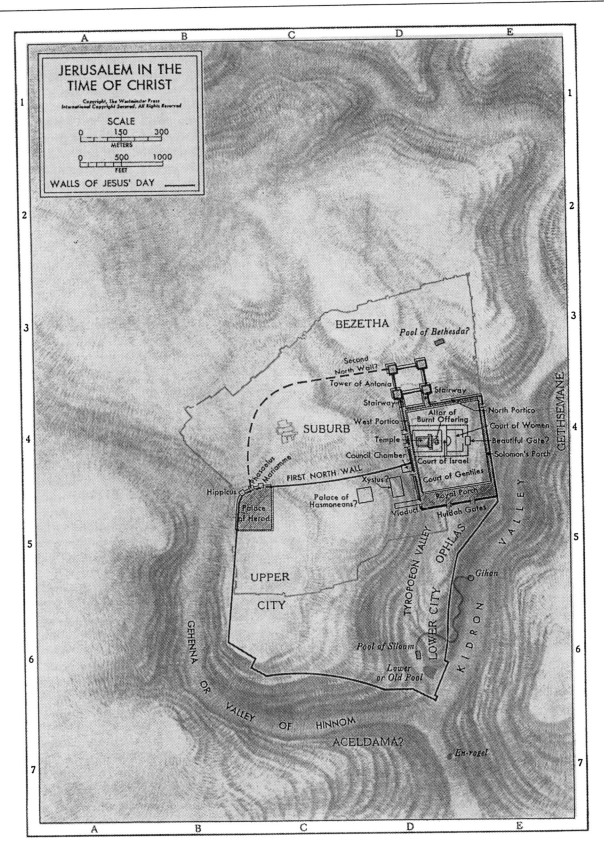

Fig. 1.3

conquest by fleeing to Egypt. Diaspora Jews were influenced by Hellenistic, or Greek, culture. Meanwhile many Gentiles, living in close proximity to diaspora Jews, were attracted to Jewish beliefs. It was among such Gentile people that Paul found fertile mission territory.

NEW TESTAMENT BACKGROUND:GRECO-ROMAN MILIEU

Within the first decades after Jesus' ministry the Christian church bounded out of the synagogues and into the pagan world. The jump from Judaism to Hellenism (the Greek-speaking and Greek-thinking world) was formidable; the contrast between the two terrains cannot be overestimated. Despite all the varieties within Judaism, Jesus spoke to a culture that was consistent and clear in two respects: monotheism (belief in one God) was a given and torah (teaching or law) was the will of God. On the other hand, we can but scratch the surface of the overwhelming multiplicity of gods, beliefs, and practices in the Greco-Roman world. As you read the descriptions that follow, try to imagine the difficulties faced by the New Testament writers as they wrote to churches in this variegated environment. Then, for fun, imagine to which religion or school you might have belonged in the first century A.D. before you converted to Christianity.

I. Mystery Religions

Our sources are slim for the practices in these religions, as secrecy was demanded of the initiates (wherefore, "mysteries"). All were built on myths; most myths involved a dying and rising god or goddess. All promised deification of the initiate through association with the resurrected god. And all promised immortality for the believer. The *Eleusinian mysteries* originated in Eleusis, near Athens. They centered around Demeter, goddess of vegetation, whose daughter Persephone was carried off to the underworld for eight months a year. Every spring she was brought back to this world, every fall she was carried away again. The *mysteries of Cybele* came from Phrygia in Asia Minor. Cybele, the mother of all gods and humans, loved Attis, a hero born from a virgin. Guilty of infidelity to Cybele, Attis castrated himself and died. Cybele restored him to life. A distinctive and unbelievably gruesome ritual in this mystery was the taurobolium, in which the initiate bathed in the blood of a bull and drank its blood. Likewise gory was the yearly festival in which a pine tree (representing the dead Attis) was set up in the temple. Worshipers cut themselves and sprinkled the tree with blood, while an elite few castrated themselves. Through these rituals, the believer partook of the life of the god. The *Dionysian mysteries* got totally out of control and were discouraged by New Testament times. They originated in Thrace (Bulgaria) and centered on Dionysus, god of wine. Early worshipers roamed about intoxicated and in search of wild animals, which they would tear to pieces and eat raw. In this way they gained access to the spirit of the god and became immortal. The *Orphic mysteries* tried to correct these frenzies; they strictly controlled the wildness through diets and ritual purifications. They stressed the sin and guilt of humans and eternal punishment in the afterlife. For the initiates of Orphism, eternal salvation was the reward. The *Isis mysteries* came out of Egypt and became immensely popular in Greece and Rome. The emperor Gaius Caligula erected a temple in Isis's honor in A.D. 38. Isis was a friend to women and the only goddess who offered real sympathy. Her spouse Osiris died, and (of course) rose again. As a wife and mother she had suffered and she understood. Sacrifices were offered to her by black-robed priests, and in the springtime a gorgeous pageant/parade celebrated her glory. The *Mithraic mysteries* originated in Persia and spread rapidly throughout the Roman Empire by means of the army. Soldiers were attracted to Mithraism because of its call to righteousness, law, and order. Mithra was "the unconquerable sun god," born from a rock on December 25, when his birthday was celebrated annually. Only men were allowed into Mithraism, and they had to pass through seven stages of initiation before they obtained virtue and eternal life. At the end of history, Mithraism taught, a great fire would consume all demonic powers and evil persons.

II. The Imperial Cult

While the mysteries satisfied the need for a personal religion, the cult of the emperor did not. Instead the "worship" of the emperor was enforced as a symbol of patriotism and loyalty to the empire. At its most banal, emperor worship entailed nothing more than a pledge of allegiance. It started when Augustus declared his predecessor, Julius Caesar, to be divine. Augustus did not encourage worship of himself, a living emperor, but he also was deified at his death. Sacrifices were offered to the "genius" or spirit of the emperors in gratitude for the peace they brought. The emperor cult also gave the Roman army a feeling of pride and unity. It should be noted that the terms "savior," "lord," and "Son of

God" were applied to the emperors. In their own lifetimes, the emperors Gaius Caligula, Nero, and Domitian insisted on divine status. Only the Jews were exempt from observance of the imperial cult.

III. Hellenistic Philosophy

If the mysteries appealed to the heart, the schools of Hellenistic philosophy appealed to the intellect. Originating in Athens at the time of Alexander the Great, two great philosophers made a huge impact on the Greco-Roman world in their rational approach to the problems of human existence.

A. *Epicureanism.* The two major problems of existence are fear of the gods and fear of death. Thus reasoned Epicurus (c. 340–270 B.C.). The goal of life is well-being and the absence of fear. The life lived well is characterized by virtue, by affection for other human beings, and by the absence of selfishness. The gods exist, but they do not interfere with us in terms of rewards and punishments. When we die, we die. The body and soul are composed of atoms, which merely dissolve with death. A hedonistic reading of "Eat, drink, and be merry, for tomorrow we die," is a misunderstanding of Epicurus's teaching. He felt that true pleasure was found in life well lived and free of death's fears.

B. *Stoicism.* Zeno (c. 335–c. 263 B.C.) opened a school at the Painted Porch (stoa) in Athens around 310 B.C. The success of Zeno and his disciples (most notably Epictetus) was due to their appreciation of the Logos. The Logos is the harmony and reason basic to the universe. It is also basic to who we are: each of us possesses a divine "spark" from the Logos fire. Therefore, (1) all humanity is bound together, (2) all humanity is bound to the Logos, and (3) life should be lived reasonably, in harmony with reason or the Logos. Practically speaking, this meant that the emotions must be restrained. The Stoic ideals were *apatheia*, freedom from the passions, and duty, which followed from a right use of reason. We are obligated to each other as kin who share a common parent, the divine Reason.

IV. Magic and Astrology

Perhaps, many thought, none of the above were true. Life is simply a quirk of fate, ruled (if at all) by blind Tyche, Chance. (Tyche was the patron goddess of many Hellenistic cities, including Antioch in Syria.) Who really knows? And if fate rules our destinies, then the best bet is to determine what fate has in store for us. The quickest way to do so was through study of the stars, or astrology, based on Greek and Babylonian calculations. And then what? Perhaps fate might be manipulated through sorceries, magical words, and seances. Demons were everywhere, but they could be exorcised. Bad omens were everywhere, but they could be countered by superstitious practices. In an insecure and baffling world, the popularity of magic and astrology was immense. These gave a (limited) sense of control and power to folks who had neither. The alternative, succinctly expressed in this epitaph, was cynical despair:

I was not,
I came to be,
I died,
I am not.

CHAPTER 2

The Gospel of Mark

INTRODUCTION TO MARK

There are days when life is rich and full, when time seems to stand still and we are flooded with a sense of well-being: "God's in [God's] heaven: all's right with the world."

Then there are times when life is "nasty, brutish, and short." Suffering and pain numb us. Well-wishers offend us with their breezy optimism. Death and taxes are the only certainties. In the midst of suffering we wonder, What's the use? Is there a point of contact between this vale of tears and God? Like Job, our pain is immense. And like Job we wish to be heard and understood.

Keep this second picture in your mind and add the following details. The time is Rome in the late 60s A.D. The mad Emperor Nero has made a sport of feeding Christians to wild animals and making human torches of them. The apostle Peter, founder of the Roman church and eyewitness to Jesus' life, has been crucified. Insanity and malevolence are all the great empire can offer the church in Rome. Meanwhile war has broken out in Judea, threatening the holy city of Jerusalem and the Temple. The immovable rocks of the early church, Rome and Jerusalem, are no longer stable. Times are changing, and for the worse.

The Gospel of Mark was probably written to the Roman church at this time (c. A.D. 65–70) and under these conditions. It is short, and it was written in a hurry. Mark wrote in rough Greek, stringing together clause after clause with breathless *and*s. Jesus in the Gospel is no less hurried, "immediately" calling the disciples, "immediately" entering the synagogue, "immediately" discerning the hearts of those who encounter him as he rushes by. And to what end is he hurrying? To the cross. Mark's Gospel has been called "the Passion with an extended introduction." The Passion meant suffering, plain and simple. Afterward, his disciples too will suffer. But suffering is not the last word.

"You will be hated by all because of my name" (Mark 13:13). Be aware! Keep awake! Endure! Jesus shouts in the Gospel to those who will be tried and handed over, as he himself was.

"But in those days, after that suffering,

the sun will be darkened,
and the moon will not give its light,

and the stars will be falling from heaven,
and the powers in the heavens will be shaken.

Then they will see 'the Son of Man coming in clouds' with great power and glory. Then he will send out the angels, and gather his elect from the ends of the earth to the ends of heaven."

(Mark 13:24–27)

Just in case his congregation didn't get the point as the gospel was being read to them (and it can be read easily, aloud, in a little over an hour), Mark repeats these words a chapter later (14:62). The point is that Jesus is coming soon, to bring the faithful home to himself. Jesus has established his reign through suffering and death.

For Mark the model, in fact the only model, for living is Jesus. The disciples are not the worthies we might expect, quick to respond and understand and act in an exemplary fashion. Instead, they are slow to come to any understanding whatsoever. They are more interested in bids for power than in servanthood (10:35–44). They are prone to nod off to sleep rather than be with their leader while Jesus grieves at Gethsemane (14:32–42). Even Peter, the great founder of the Roman church, is last seen in the Gospel swearing an oath and denying any connection with Jesus, for fear of losing his skin (14:66–72). In other words, Jesus' own handpicked Twelve are no better than we are. But Jesus stuck with them just the same. Mark reminds his church that Jesus came "not to be served but to serve, and to give his life as a ransom for many" (10:45). That is the point of the Gospel.

The title that Mark gave his book is what we now read as Mark 1:1: "The beginning of the good news [or, *gospel*] of Jesus Christ, the Son of God." This title is crucial to understanding what Mark is saying. First, the book of sixteen chapters we now have (or better, the scroll that Mark first wrote) is *merely* the beginning. The gospel continues to unfold, going beyond the events Mark tells us about and into the future. The "gospel" has not ended because Jesus has been raised; God is still active in the Son. Second, the gospel is "of Jesus"; it is about him, and it is brought by him. Jesus is both the message and the messenger. His words and deeds together are gospel. Mark understands the word *gospel* not as good news of the sure-to-cheer-you-up variety. Instead, discipleship means suffering on behalf of the gospel (8:35). Third, the gospel is about a specific, unique person: the Son of God, the Christ. These words were loaded with meaning for both Jew and Gentile. You will examine these titles as you read Mark.

The ending of the book in the oldest manuscripts is chapter 16:8. The three women have discovered the empty tomb. The angelic messenger tells them not to be afraid, but to tell the disciples that Jesus has been raised. They are to go to Galilee and meet him there. Nevertheless the women flee the tomb and say nothing, for they are afraid. You will see that fear and awe are characteristic responses to the works of Jesus in the Gospel, and in this sense the word "afraid" is a fitting end. Likely, however, is an end in which the resurrected Jesus *does* meet the disciples in Galilee as promised by the angel, and by Jesus in 14:28. Perhaps something happened to Mark that forced him to cut off his writing prematurely. Perhaps the original ending, which would have been located on the outside of the rolled up scroll, was damaged and thereby lost to us forever. Mark's is the earliest Gospel, dated c. 70. Not long after the Gospel was written, a "shorter ending" (two sentences) appeared. The "longer ending" (16:9–20) is found in manuscripts dating from the early second century.

It is intriguing to picture the author as the youngster in 14:51 who was caught in Gethsemane and ran away, minus his loincloth. Irenaeus (c. 185) identified the author with John Mark, a companion of Paul's in Acts. Papias (c. 130) describes Mark as a follower of Peter in Rome who served as Peter's interpreter, writing down all that he remembered, "but not however in order." As is the case with so many New Testament documents, the author is ultimately known to God alone.

Outline of the Gospel of Mark

I. Galilean Ministry: chapters 1—9
   A. Baptism and temptation
   B. Teaching and preaching on the kingdom of God
   C. Healings and miracles, signs of the kingdom of God
   D. Jesus with his disciples
   E. Conflicts with the Pharisees
II. Journey to Jerusalem: chapter 10
III. Judean Ministry: chapters 11—13
   A. Entry into Jerusalem and cleansing the Temple
   B. Teaching in the Temple
   C. Teaching the disciples on the Mount of Olives
IV. The Passion: chapters 14—15
   A. Last Supper
   B. Gethsemane
   C. Arrest and trials
   D. Crucifixion and burial
V. Resurrection: 16:1–8.

THE SYNOPTIC PROBLEM

Why do we have *four* Gospels? Life would be simpler (and this book much shorter) if we had only one. We could simply take *all* the pericopes (literary units) in Matthew, Mark, Luke, and John, edit out the redundancies, and create a harmony of the Gospels. Or we could keep *only* the pericopes shared by all four sources, and create a condensed Gospel that omits material found in *only* one writer. The early church, in its wisdom, chose instead to preserve all four. In spite of redundancies here and unique material there, no successful attempts were made to create either a cumbersome harmony or a condensed version.

As you read each Gospel, you will see different perspectives on the life of Christ. All agree that Jesus was the Son of God, but the writers each paint distinctive word pictures to show us what his Sonship means. Their audiences and circumstances differ. Their reasons for writing differ. And their sources (oral tradition and written notes) differ. To toss one out or to harmonize one view with another is to lose not just a snapshot, but a full-length portrait.

The Gospel of John stands apart from the other three. John's Gospel is full of theological commentary. Jesus does not speak in parables here, and only seven miracles (called "signs") are included. Of these signs, only one—the feeding of the five thousand—is found in all four documents. Over 90 percent of the Gospel is unique to John; about 9 percent of John is found in the other three Gospels. John is like a distant cousin to the closely related writings of Matthew, Mark, and Luke. These three are called "synoptic" Gospels because they may be laid out in parallel columns, side by side, and seen together (syn-opsis) for purposes of comparison and contrast. And here is where the synoptic problem begins.

The synoptic problem is really not a problem, if we mean that it must be solved before we can proceed with biblical studies. The "problem" deals with the relationship between Matthew, Mark, and Luke. It asks questions like, Who wrote first? and, Who copied whom? First let us examine the data.

1. Over half the material in the Synoptic Gospels is common to all three. They agree in outline, events, and sayings. More strikingly, passages often agree in unusual words or harsh grammatical constructions.

2. Mark has 661 verses. Over 600 of these are found in Matthew (with a few differences in wording). Almost half of Matthew's Gospel is substantially paralleled (that is, shared, duplicated, or copied) in Mark.

3. About 40 percent of Luke is substantially paralleled by Mark.

4. Matthew and Luke share some 200 verses that are *not* found in Mark. These verses are mostly teachings of Jesus (not narrative material).

5. Matthew has some 300 verses that are unique (not found in Mark or Luke). This material comprises almost 20 percent of the Gospel. It includes many of Jesus' teachings (some parables and the Sermon on the Mount), the birth stories, and the resurrection appearances. (Mark has neither birth narratives nor resurrection appearances.)

6. Luke has some 520 verses that are unique, 25 percent of the Gospel. This material includes Luke's birth stories, resurrection appearances, and many of Luke's parables.

STOP for a moment. Consider the data before you go any farther. How do *you* solve the problem? Take a guess as to which Gospel writer(s) wrote first and which was (were) then used by the other(s).

Two major hypotheses have been advanced to solve the problem. (A) The first is called the two-document hypothesis. It goes something like this: Mark, the roughest and most primitive writing, came first. Matthew and Luke both had Mark's document before them as they wrote. However, Matthew and Luke also had another document called Q (German for *Quelle*, or Source), which was a record of Jesus' sayings. They both incorporated Q (now lost) into the Markan outline. Finally, out of the abundant *oral* tradition that circulated in the years before the Gospels were written, Matthew chose some materials (unique to Matthew) and Luke used others (unique to Luke). The relationship may be diagramed as shown in figure 2.1.

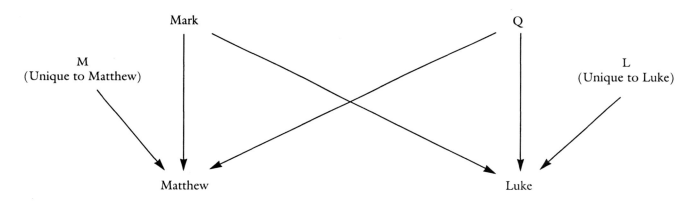

Fig. 2.1 The Two-Document Hypothesis

(B) Another theory, called the Griesbach hypothesis, says that Matthew came first. This idea agrees with tradition: Augustine thought that Mark was an abbreviation of Matthew, and Matthew of course is placed first in the canon. According to this hypothesis, Luke used Matthew, and Mark used both Matthew and Luke. There is no need for a Q source. The relationship may be diagramed as shown in figure 2.2.

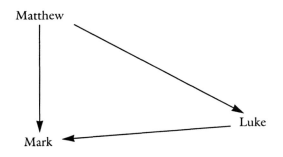

Fig. 2.2 The Griesbach Hypothesis

Whether you answered "A" or "B" or "Neither of the above," you are not alone. The problem is not resolved, and we must live with irresolubility. However, as you read the Gospels you will notice similarities and differences among them. You might wish to account for why this is so, to come up with an explanation. One theory or another might be helpful to you.

STUDY GUIDE FOR THE GOSPEL OF MARK

1. Read Mark 1 through quickly, then close your Bible and jot down your first impressions of how Jesus' ministry was launched.

_____

_____

John the Baptizer is clearly identified here with Elijah, the prophet who will come again to prepare the way of the Lord. He resembles Elijah in dress (v. 6) and in his strange, hermitlike existence (v. 4). John serves as a bridge between the Hebrew scriptures and the Gospel.

"Baptism" at the time of John meant something different than it means in the church today. It was a preparation for bigger things to come. If the water of John's baptism cleanses and prepares the people, what will Jesus' baptism give them? (1:8)

_____

Why was Jesus baptized? Underline the possibility you think best explains his baptism: (a) It was a sign to John. (b) It was a sign to Jesus of his Sonship. (c) It marked the beginning of Jesus' public ministry. (d) It showed Jesus' identification with his people. (e) It was his anointing as Messiah. (f) Other:

_____

What happened to Jesus immediately after his baptism? (See Luke 4:1–13 or Matthew 4:1–11 for details on this episode.)

_____

Write out and memorize Mark 1:15, the summary verse for the entire Gospel:

_____

_____

_____

The first full day of Jesus' public ministry is found in 1:21–38. Identify the day of the week, who is with him, where they go, the miracles he performs, and the reaction he provokes.

_____

_____

_____

2. Binding the strong man. One of the signs of the coming kingdom is Jesus' victory over the spirits and forces of evil. In 3:27, Jesus refers to his mission of binding up the strong man (Satan) and plundering his house. Briefly describe his actions in these passages:

1:23–26 _____

1:32–34 _____

3:11 _____

5:1–20 _____

9:14–29 _____

What titles do the unclean spirits use for Jesus in 1:24; 3:11; 5:7?

_____

Why do you think Jesus commands these spirits to be silent?

_____

3. Healing the sick. Another sign of the inbreaking of the kingdom is Jesus' power over physical illness and death. Briefly describe his actions in the following passages:

1:40–45 _____

5:21–24, 35–43 _____

5:25–34 _____

8:22–26 _____

10:46–52 _____

What is the relationship between faith and health in these miracles? In what ways does 9:24, "I believe; help my unbelief!" apply to each of these miracles?

_____

_____

4. Controversy stories: Mark 2:1—3:6.

How do the paralytic's friends show their persistence, creativity, and faith in 2:1–12?

_____

How did the scribes answer the question of 2:9? How do *you* answer the question?

_____

What was controversial about Jesus' behavior in 2:15–17?

_____

The Pharisees fasted on Mondays and Thursdays. Why does Jesus say that fasting is not appropriate for his disciples (2:18–22)?

_____

Technically speaking, Jesus allowed his disciples to "work" on the Sabbath. They broke the *letter* of the law by picking grain (see 2:23–28). How did Jesus, and David before him, understand the *spirit* of the Sabbath laws?

_____

Read 3:1–6. Again, proper behavior on the Sabbath is the issue. Why didn't Jesus simply wait a day to heal the man? What point is he making to the Pharisees?

_____

In 3:6, what is the result of the growing controversy? Do you think this result was inevitable?

_____

5. A new look at old laws. As new wine bursts old wineskins, Jesus' teaching bursts open traditional treatment of law. Paraphrase the principle he uses in 2:27:

_____

The scribes and Pharisees were concerned with the letter of the law, external appearances, and tradition. In 7:6–8, Jesus contrasts this concern with the spirit of the law, what's inside, and the commandment of God. How is this contrast made evident in these passages?

7:1–5_____

7:9–13_____

7:17–23_____

10:2–9_____

6. Responses to Jesus. First read the parable of the sower and its explanation in 4:1–20. Jesus sows the proclamation of the coming kingdom. The types of soil reflect various responses to his word. List these four possibilities:

_____

_____

_____

This parable, which is central to Mark's Gospel, reflects a rural environment. How might you rewrite it in an urban, big city setting?

_____

7. The responses to Jesus: those dense and cantankerous disciples. Like the seed thrown on rocky ground (4:5–6), the Twelve are quick to follow Jesus (see 1:16–20). They are given the secrets of the kingdom of God (4:11) and Jesus explains everything to them (4:34). But their immediate positive response to Jesus is short-lived.

What does the episode on the boat tell you about the disciples (4:35–41)?

_____

Skim the miracle of 6:30–44 and its repetition in 8:1–9. Then read carefully 8:14–21. Why is Jesus astonished at his disciples' response?

_____

What issue were the disciples arguing about in 9:33–37? How does Jesus react here?

_____

_____

What is the issue in 10:35–45, and Jesus' reaction?

_____

Ironically, those closest to Jesus understood him least. This is true of the disciples, as well as others. Identify them in:

3:21_____

6:1–6_____

8. The responses to Jesus: the often nameless believers who have faith, or the good soil that brings up an abundant crop. Returning to the woman in 5:25–34, what do her thoughts and actions tell you about her faith?

_____

_____

Look at the story of the foreign woman in 7:24–30. She is the only non-Jew to approach Jesus in the Gospel, the only person Jesus is not willing to help, and the only one who wins an argument with him. In what ways is her belief bold, convincing, and clever?

_____

_____

How are little children examples of faith in 10:13–16?

_____

How does a little child help Jesus teach about discipleship in 9:35–37?

_____

9. Teaching on the kingdom and discipleship. Jesus uses two metaphors to describe the kingdom of God.

Read them, then give each a subtitle:

4:26–28 _____

4:30–32 _____
(Some possible subtitles: "From Little to Big," "Automatic Growth," "Don't Judge a Book by Its Cover.")

The mission of the Twelve: read 6:7–13. What directive do you consider most important?

_____

How did the disciples share Jesus' authority as they went out two by two?

_____

Now see 9:38–41. What problem do the disciples have with this unnamed person?

_____

How does Jesus respond to them and why?

_____

Losses and gains: read 8:34–38. What must Jesus' followers lose, and what will they gain?

_____

_____

Then see 9:42–48. What must be lost here and why?

_____

Now see the sad story of the rich man in 10:17–23. What were his gains? What was his loss?

_____

_____

Finally, what does the discussion in 10:23–27 tell you about entering the kingdom?

_____

10. One of the most difficult teaching tasks Jesus had was to redefine the role of Messiah. It is not the warrior-king, as expected by many, but the suffering servant. (See the article on "Messiah" later in this chapter.) Summarize his teaching in these passages:

8:27–31 _____
Why does Peter rebuke Jesus in this passage?

9:30–32 _____

10:32–34 _____

Given the fact that no one expected the Messiah to suffer and die, what difficulties would Jesus have with being called the Messiah? What is the relationship between this teaching and the command to "be silent" in 1:43–44; 3:12; 5:43; 7:36; 8:30?

_____

_____

How then do you account for this "messianic secret"?

_____

_____

If you thought the narrative moved along at a clip in the first ten chapters of Mark, you will need to hold onto your hat for the last six. This is the story of the Passion week (from the Latin word "to suffer"). A chronology of that week looks something like this:

Sunday: Jesus' triumphal entry into Jerusalem
Monday: Jesus clears the Temple; curses fig tree on the way
Tuesday: Teaching in the Temple
Wednesday: Teaching the disciples (the "little apocalypse")
Thursday: Passover and the Last Supper
          Gethsemane and the arrest
          Before the Sanhedrin
Friday: Meeting with Pilate
          Mocking and beating
          Crucifixion
          Burial
Saturday: ?
Sunday: Resurrection

11. Zechariah 9 is an oracle proclaiming the coming of the Prince of Peace. In Zechariah 9:9, the Prince is described as both triumphant and humble, riding on a donkey's colt, while Jerusalem shouts its acclamations. Show how Mark 11:1–10 parallels this oracle ("Hosanna" means "Save, Lord"):

_____

What has happened to the "messianic secret"?

_____

12. Jesus spends the night in Bethany and enters Jerusalem again the next day, a day of intensity and anger. He immediately curses the fig tree, in 11:12–14. The fig tree with leaves is supposed to have fruit as well. Perhaps Jesus cursed it because flashy foliage covered up its fruitlessness. How might this episode relate to the clearing of the Temple in 11:15–17?

_____

_____

Returning to the fig tree (now withered!) the next day, what teaching does Jesus give now about God's power and faith (11:20–24)?

_____

Four test questions are put to Jesus by the Jewish authorities. Summarize the issue at stake, and Jesus' response, for each:

11:27–33 _____

12:13–17_____

_____

12:18–27_____

_____

12:28–34_____

_____

The last question, put to Jesus by a scribe, is the only truly heartfelt question. All the others seek to entrap Jesus or ridicule him. How does Jesus respond to the scribe in 12:34? What is it about their dialogue that puts an end to further questions?

_____

_____

In what ways does the parable of the vineyard in 12:1–11 show Jesus to be the Messiah? In what ways does it show him to be the Suffering Servant?

_____

_____

Contrast the behavior of the scribes and the wealthy in 12:38–41 with the behavior of the widow in 12:42–44:

_____

_____

13. Mark 13 is known as the "little apocalypse." Apocalyptic writings in Jewish literature (e.g., Isaiah 34, Daniel 7—12, and the apocryphal book of 2 Esdras) were concerned with the end times and the coming of God's kingdom. The New Testament contribution to full-blown apocalyptic discourse is the book of Revelation.

In Jesus' day, Jewish hopes were high for the overthrow of Roman rule and the establishment of God's kingdom on earth. Jesus' disciples certainly shared this hope, and the question they ask in 13:4 indicates their eagerness to shore up their expectations with cold, hard facts.

Jesus' discourse differs from all other apocalypses in a few key ways. He does not use images of beasts, symbols from dreams, and cryptic numbers; all these devices invite "guesswork" and interpretation of when the end will come. Instead, what does he say, in 13:32–37, about our ability to predict the end?

_____

Jesus does not dwell on the fire and brimstone that await the wicked. Instead of punishments, what does he look forward to in 13:26–27?

_____

Instead of passively awaiting the last days, what does Jesus say the believers are, rather, to do? See 13:10, 34.

_____

Go back to the transfiguration in Mark 9:2–8 and read. How does this account embody Jesus' words in 13:26?

_____

_____

Mark's church in Rome was threatened with annihilation. What verses in chapter 13 would encourage its people?

_____

challenge them?_____

What impact does this chapter have on you, twenty centuries later?

_____

14. The anointing at Bethany: read 14:3–9. The unnamed woman is scolded for her actions. Why?

_____

In contrast, Jesus says she will always be remembered favorably. Why?

Christ (Greek) and Messiah (Hebrew) both mean "anointed one," a sign of kingship in the Old Testament. In contrast, how does Jesus interpret his anointment in verse 8?

_____

15. Judas's betrayal. We are not given the motive for Judas's betrayal in 14:10–11. Underline the reason you think best explains his action:

A. Judas was destined to betray Jesus. It was part of God's plan, and he had no real freedom of choice.

B. Judas was simply a thief who betrayed Jesus for monetary gain (although his payment was little more than a day's wages).

C. Judas was the only Judean (Iscariot = "of Kerioth") among the Galilean disciples. As an outsider he became alienated from Jesus and the rest.

D. Judas was convinced that Jesus was in fact a false messiah, a pretender, and dangerous.

E. Judas was convinced that Jesus was in fact the King of the Jews, the Messiah, but he was disappointed by Jesus' failure to decisively carry out this role. Jesus' arrest would merely speed up the process and propel Jesus to act.

16. See the account of the Last Supper in the upper room, Mark 14:12–26. If you were one of the disciples, what events here would you find odd? disturbing?

_____

_____

How do you understand Jesus' words about the new covenant in verse 24? (Go to Jeremiah 31:31–34 if you wish to dig deeper.)

_____

_____

17. The agony and the arrest. Isaiah 52:13—53:12 foretells a "Suffering Servant," saying,

> He was despised and rejected by others;
> a man of suffering [sorrows] and acquainted
>   with infirmity [grief].

>   (Isa. 53:3)

You have seen how Jesus tried to teach that, contrary to popular notions, the Messiah would suffer on behalf of others. How does Mark 14:27–50 parallel the Suffering Servant description above? Give verse numbers to show

A. that Jesus was rejected and deserted: _____

B. the sorrow and grief of Jesus: _____

What does his prayer of verse 36 tell you about Jesus?

_____

18. The trials and the trail of tears. Read 14:53–15:24. Beside each name, fill in a brief description of that person's behavior, or give a metaphor that comes to your mind as you read about that person.

Caiaphas (the high priest): _____

Peter in the courtyard:_____

Pilate: _____

the soldiers: _____

What do Jesus' words to the high priest and Pilate tell you about him? What do they tell you about his understanding of his mission?

_____

_____

In 15:6–15, Barabbas is released in exchange for Jesus. How does this substitution show that 10:45 is beginning to take effect?

_____

19. The crucifixion. Jesus' separation from others and from God is complete on the cross. No one is there with him. Even God has forsaken him. His cry of 15:34

is preserved in the original Aramaic. These are the awful words of sheer and utter abandonment.

Two events immediately follow Jesus' death in 15:37. The "curtain" in the Temple separated the Holy Place from the Holy of Holies, where the Ark and the very presence of God dwelled. How do these verses indicate that separation from God has ended?

15:38 _____

15:39 _____

20. Who witness Jesus' death from afar (15:40–41)?

_____

What happens to them in chapter 16?

_____

How do you react to their behavior in chapter 16: with impatience? understanding? compassion? anger?

_____

How do you suppose *you* would have behaved?

_____

The Gospel ends abruptly with verse 8. Perhaps the original, longer ending of Mark was destroyed. Or perhaps Mark intended the Gospel to end at verse 8. In what ways might his readers have been challenged by such an ending?

_____

_____

Discussion Questions

1. Jesus is a controversial figure in Mark's Gospel. What are some of the things he does and says that cause controversy? With respect to his teaching and mission, why was conflict inevitable?

2. Drawing from Mark's Gospel (and using a concordance!), what did Jesus mean when he said, "The *kingdom* is at hand" (emphasis added)?

3. What do you think of Jesus' disciples? Why did they follow him? How well did they know him? Can you identify some distinct personalities as they emerge?

4. Given the inevitable misunderstanding of the term "messiah," why did Jesus use it anyway? In what ways did he give the term new meaning in his teaching? in his death?

"MESSIAH" AS TITLE FOR JESUS

What first comes to your mind when you hear the term "Messiah"? Perhaps you think of a church by that name near you, or Handel's "Hallelujah Chorus." What about the word "Christ"? Most children (and many adults) will tell you that Christ is Jesus' last name.

What did the Jews think "messiah" meant at the time of Jesus' ministry? Did he need to change their understanding of the title? If so, why?

Both Messiah and Christ mean "anointed one." The first is Hebrew (*mashiah*), while the second is Greek (*christos*). In the Old Testament, kings and priests were anointed—smeared with aromatic oils—as a sign of their service to Yahweh. Yahweh could even designate a person to be *mashiah*, anointed, who was unaware of his service to God. Thus Cyrus, the Persian king who issued the Edict of Toleration and freed the Jews from their Babylonian Captivity (538 B.C.), is called "God's anointed"; "I surname you, though you do not know me" (Isa. 45:1, 4). David was anointed by Samuel as a young boy and again by the tribes when he actually became king. Saul was anointed king (by Samuel) before David and Solomon (by Zadok) after him. Priests and the objects in the tabernacle were anointed as well (see Ex. 40).

By the time of Jesus, the term *mashiah* was associated with a godly, powerful figure. This figure had yet to come. However, the messiah would be announced by Elijah, the Old Testament prophet who was carried off to the heavens in a chariot of fire. Because people believed that Elijah never actually died, popular belief arose that he would come again. And according to Malachi, God will send Elijah "before the great and terrible day of the LORD comes" (Mal. 4:5) as fair warning. Look for Elijah, and the Messiah will be along shortly.

What did Jesus' contemporaries expect the Messiah to be? Here are some possible models that circulated in Palestine during the first century A.D.

A. *The prophetic type.* "The LORD your God will raise up for you a prophet like me from among your own people; you shall heed such a prophet" (Deut. 18:15). Perhaps this person will be like Moses, or perhaps Moses himself will come again. He will be known by his signs and wonders, his mighty deeds and terrifying displays of power. And, like Moses, he will be one whom the Lord knows face to face (see Deut. 34:10). It is interesting to note that the deeds (in Egypt) rather than the words (the law) of Moses are stressed here.

B. *The charismatic type.* Here we mean not someone with charm and personal appeal, but one on whom the Spirit of the Lord descends. This is not a hereditary office, but a gift (*charis*). The model is the Old Testament judge, who receives the spirit and is enabled to perform mighty acts on behalf of his people in battle (as in the book of Judges). The spirit equips an otherwise ordinary Israelite to lead the tribes in war.

C. *The dual messiahs.* The Old Testament prophet Haggai (see Hag. 2:1–9, 20–23) anticipated two rulers in the coming kingdom of God: a kingly one (Zerubbabel, who was governor of Judah c. 520 B.C.) and a priestly one (Joshua, the high priest at this same time). Similarly the Essenes at Qumran looked for the messiahs of Aaron and Israel. The Dead Sea Scrolls describe the messiah of Israel as a political ruler who is subordinate to the messiah of Aaron, a priest.

D. *The Davidic type.* King David ruled over a united, powerful, and geographically vast empire. The covenant made with David promised the eternal reign of his house, or dynasty (see 2 Sam. 7). The great prophets Isaiah, Jeremiah, and Ezekiel all spoke of Davidic kings to come. With the Roman occupation of Judea in the first century A.D., hopes were high for this type of messiah. He would be a descendant of David. He would throw off Roman rule, confirm an independent Holy Land, and establish the kingdom forever. This was by far the most popular expectation in Jesus' day.

Every one of these models includes an image of coercion. Most of them are partisan, on the side of the Jews exclusively. And the most popular looks for a restored Israel under a Davidic king. Not one of these models expects the messiah to suffer as Jesus did.

Jesus was unwilling to accept these models based on political power and nationalistic zeal. Instead, he redefined the term Messiah. He upheld the law like Moses and the prophets, emphasizing that what was required was love of the neighbor. He was spirit-filled like the judges, but with a spirit of peace rather than hatred for enemies. He made sacrifices like the high priest: the supreme sacrifice of self. Service to others, not victorious rule, is what God meant for God's anointed one. As Messiah, Jesus showed a new way and gave new meaning to people's hope for human life.

PARABLES: SETTING THE STAGE AND WHAT TO EXPECT

Perhaps you have heard sermons preached on parables or read articles based on them. Often when we hear a parable for the first time, people give us almost immediately an interpretation or a commentary to help us along, much like the news analysts who come on instantly after the President's speech with an explanation of what was said (and with no time for reflection on our part!).

If you come to the parables with a sense of "I've heard this before," try to suspend your assumptions and read each one anew. If you come to the parables for the first time, you are actually better off. You are closer to the position of those who heard these stories from Jesus' lips, fresh and without prior notions about what they are "supposed" to mean for you.

First we will look at what parables *are* as a literary genre or type. Next we will look at what parables *do* as they are heard and understood by their audience (you). Last we will look at a few parables in Mark's Gospel. There is a list of Jesus' parables and where they are found near the end of this chapter.

What are parables? They are the characteristic teaching form for Jesus, and a common form of rabbinic teaching in Jesus' day. The rabbinic parable (Hebrew *mashal*) used imaginative stories of contemporary figures (kings and servants, fathers and children) to show the application of the torah to life. Popular rabbinic parables often had a *nimshal*, or short interpretation, attached to them. The *nimshal* was similar to the "moral" appearing at the end of one of Aesop's fables.

No other teacher had as many parables attributed to him as did Jesus. The Gospel writers selected over two dozen parables out of possibly many more. Some have a *nimshal* attached; many do not. Some are only one verse long (parables of the leaven and the hidden treasure); some are over twenty verses (the prodigal son being a long parable in three "acts"). Some are concerned with torah, as were rabbinic *meshalim*; many strike a new note with their talk about the kingdom, Jesus' characteristic concern.

All Jesus' parables draw from the commonplace events of life. Seeds and weeds, wedding feasts and dinners for guests, servants, sons, judges, and laborers: these subjects of parables are firmly attached to the ordinary stuff of Judean experience. All tell a story. They are narratives of the "once upon a time" variety, not theorems or propositional statements. But they are not bedtime stories intended to soothe or lull us to sleep. Instead, Jesus' parables have hooks, twists, surprises. Who would expect the dignified Jewish father to hike up his skirts and run toward the prodigal son with joy?

What sensible shepherd would leave his flock in search of one lost sheep? Who would imagine the kingdom of God, surely a regal and grand thing when it comes, to be like a tiny mustard seed? There is a strangeness, a conflict between what is expected and what is said, that marks Jesus' parables. Occasionally the oddity is immediately apparent to us in our time, but often we need a bit of background information to help us see it. Ours is not a world of vineyards and shepherds, nor do we feel hatred for Samaritans and tax collectors. Those sermons you heard, commentaries you will read, and this *Guide* will serve you well if they make the Palestinian setting fresh and real and the strangeness of the parables apparent.

Up until the late nineteenth century, parables were treated as allegories by most biblical scholars. In an allegory (like Bunyan's *Pilgrim's Progress* or C. S. Lewis's *Chronicles of Narnia*) the characters and places each stand for something else: there is a one-to-one relationship between each element in the story and a theological reality (Christ, God, sinners, the true church, for example). This allegorical interpretation was jettisoned in favor of the "one point" interpretation in our century. One extreme (a parable has many points) gave way to the other extreme (a parable expresses only one key idea). Interestingly, scholars rarely agree as to what the one point is. Either extreme is harmful if it imposes a flat, obvious formula on the parables themselves. When it comes to reading parables, we are not in control! Some will come to us as allegories, others as a single point of lightning. The key idea we received from a parable today might not be the same one we receive tomorrow or next year.

You might come across attempts to put Jesus' parables in different categories. I have seen one list: parables informing perceptions (learning), parables influencing attitudes (feeling), and parables summoning responsibilities (doing). Another list groups them by subject matter: parables on the nature of God, parables on the nature of the kingdom, parables on our response to the above. You may find these attempts helpful or arbitrary. They usually say more about the person who classifies them than anything else. For this reason, I suggest you try making your own set of categories!

So here we have a parable before us, a picture of homely realism painted with simple words. What does it *do* to us, for us?

The Greek *parabole* means "cast alongside of." Imagine throwing down a simple story next to a Big Idea. Or imagine striking a tuning fork and placing it next to a piece of crystal. The interaction between the two, the vibrations (and perhaps a loud crack!), are what parables are about. So, you think you know what the kingdom is? Hear this story and then see what you think. You have a pretty clear idea of how God's love fits into life? Try this parable on for size. Through his parables Jesus challenges us to think differently, to conceive of old ideas in new ways. "Let anyone with ears to hear listen!" (Mark 4:9, 23). The challenge is not to accept a dogmatic formula, but to enter into the strange world of the parable and allow it to open our stopped ears and blinded eyes.

The parable opens us up to Jesus' message in a variety of ways. A good joke grabs us because of its incongruity: we *expect* one thing to be said or done but the punch line catches us off guard, and we laugh. The Zen koan is a question or riddle that cannot be answered by normal, logical channels. It teases, frustrates, and finally exhausts the mind so that it becomes open to satori, or the flash of insight that changes everything. The icons of the Orthodox Church are simple, flat pictures of saints, yet their eyes can be windows to heaven. Metaphorical language, images in poetry, can forever transfigure the way we look at nature and life. Parables, jokes, koans, icons, metaphors, all share a common, right-brain home. They are intuited and felt. They displace us. They beckon us to another reality.

A word about the *nimshalim*, or interpretive tags, placed at the end of some parables. Sometimes the interpretation seems forced. Interpretations of the same parable may differ (compare the lost sheep of Matthew 18:10–14 with the parable of Luke 15:3–7). Much debate centers on whether a parable's particular interpretation belonged to the parable originally, or whether it was attached by the disciples, or by the early church, or by the Gospel writer. Try covering up the interpretation, reading the parable, and stopping when the story proper ends. In the same way, try bracketing what *you* think is meant by the parable. Be open to a variety of interpretations. Better, allow the parable to interpret you.

Finally, in describing what a parable does, we see that it offers us a glimpse of what is true and real, of what the kingdom is like. It starts with the world around us because this is God's world. Through it, and in it, we come to understand something of who God is. Through God's creation, and in it, we are asked to participate in the kingdom. "Let anyone with ears to hear listen!"

Two of Mark's parables are central to understanding his entire Gospel: the sower in 4:1–9 and the wicked tenants in 12:1–12. The following list of questions will help guide your reading as you study these parables now, and others later:

1. Setting and context: Where is Jesus? To whom is he speaking? What is going on in the verses preceding and following the parable?

2. The meaning of sentences: How are the sentences arranged structurally? What is the progression of the parable?

3. The meaning of words: Are there any key words that strike you as you read? any special terms that need to be defined?

4. Tone: Do you find evidence of irony in the parable? Where is the unexpected twist in the story?

5. Parallels: Does the parable appear in more than one Gospel? Note any differences.

6. Why is Jesus telling the parable? What did it mean at the time? What does it mean to you now?

The sower of Mark 4:1–9 broadcasts the seed in typical Palestinian fashion, strewing it by handfuls far and wide. Plowing will come later; for now his task is to scatter the seed everywhere. The sower would not expect all the seed to bear fruit; in fact, his 75 percent failure rate is common. What is incredible is the astounding success of the seed sown on good soil, with yields of "thirty and sixty and a hundredfold." The parable challenges us with these questions: What sort of soil are we now? What sort might we become in the future, starting right now? Our response (bearing fruit or not) shows us who we are.

The parable (like so many!) is a judgment in that it presents us with the need to make a decision. The Greek word for judgment is *krisis*. A crisis carries with it the opportunity for choosing and deciding, for a turning point to occur. Hearing the parable, we make a judgment on ourselves. Some will choose not to hear (see 4:11–12). Others will choose to truly listen.

The interpretation, or *nimshal*, that follows in verses 13–20 will appeal to the allegorical bent in you. Here Jesus makes an equation between each type of soil and the types of folk he encounters. The ones on the path are the Pharisees and Jewish leaders, who hear the gospel and reject it at once. The ones on rocky ground are like Peter and the rest of the disciples, who respond immediately but fall away when the going gets tough (as at Jesus' arrest and crucifixion). The ones sown among the thorns are like the rich man and possibly Jesus' immediate family. They are basically "good ground," but they are choked by the concerns of wealth or "the cares of the world." Finally, those sown on good soil are the countless, and often nameless, folk who believe.

The parable of the wicked tenants in Mark 12:1–12 is addressed to the chief priests, scribes, and elders in the Temple (see 11:27ff.). They have questioned Jesus as to his authority and they wish to arrest him. Again the situation described in the parable is a common one. The owner plants a vineyard, fences it, builds a watchtower, then leaves. As absentee landlord he leases out the vineyard to tenant farmers, sending servants back to them for reports. Some are mocked and beaten, others killed. Clearly the tenants left in charge hope to take the vineyard by squatters' rights. The owner finally sends his beloved son, his heir, who is killed. The shocking thing about the parable is not the greed and malice of the tenants, nor the punishment they richly deserve. Instead, the shock is found in the interpretation (v. 10): the rejected stone has become the cornerstone, "and it is marvelous." Apparent defeat (even death of the son!) gives way to ultimate victory. This is the Lord's doing.

After King David had taken Bathsheba from Uriah, the prophet Nathan approached him and told him a story. There was a rich man with many flocks of sheep and a poor man with one ewe lamb, a pet whom he dearly loved. The rich man took away the lamb and prepared it for dinner. Upon hearing the story, David shouted in anger, "The man who has done this deserves to die!" "You are the man," was Nathan's reply. The force of this parable lies in its ability to convict the hearer. David at once perceived the injustice ("the man had no pity") and spoke the words of judgment, which turned back on himself. (See 2 Sam. 12:1–7.)

Similarly the elders and priests found themselves convicted by the parable of the wicked tenants. They realized Jesus had spoken about them. While their anger was immense, so was their fear. They left him and went away.

Both these Markan parables are calls for recognition. Who are we? What will we become? Who is Jesus? What is his relationship to God? And both are calls for decision. The *krisis* of the parables is the opportunity to use our judgment, to respond to the word, and to enter into the mystery of the kingdom.

See figure 2.3 for a chart of the parables.

Parable	Matthew	Mark	Luke
Sower	13:1–23	4:1–20	8:4–15
Weeds in the field	13:24–30	—	—
Mustard seed	13:31–32	4:30–32	13:18–19
Leaven	13:33	—	13:20–21
Hidden treasure	13:44	—	—
Pearl of great value	13:45–46	—	—
Dragnet	13:47–50	—	—
Lost sheep	18:10–14	—	15:3–7
Unforgiving servant	18:23–34	—	—
Workers in vineyard	20:1–16	—	—
Two sons	21:28–32	—	—
Wicked tenants	21:33–46	12:1–12	20:9–19
Wedding feast	22:2–14	—	—
Thief in the night	24:43–44	—	—
Faithful servant	24:45–51	—	—
Ten maidens	25:1–13	—	—
Talents	25:14–30	—	—
Great judgment	25:31–46	—	—
Seed growing secretly	—	4:26–29	—
Good Samaritan	—	—	10:25–37
Rich fool	—	—	12:16–21
Great feast	—	—	14:15–24
Lost coin	—	—	15:8–10
Prodigal son	—	—	15:11–32
Unjust steward	—	—	16:1–9
Rich man and Lazarus	—	—	16:19–31
Unjust judge	—	—	18:1–8
Pharisee and tax collector	—	—	18:9–14
Pounds	—	—	19:11–27

Fig. 2.3 Parables of Jesus

ON MIRACLES

While Jesus *preached* the inbreaking of the kingdom, he *demonstrated* its arrival through mighty works, or miracles. Jesus made explicit the relationship between the kingdom and miracles. The two go hand in hand. Jesus also demonstrated the universal character of his ministry through healings. He healed all, regardless of race or nationality, Jew and Gentile alike, throughout Galilee.

Modern medicine is only beginning to discover the intimate relationship between mind and body that the New Testament takes for granted. When Jesus said, "Your faith has made you well," he showed us that the inner orientation (that is, trust) of the person had made the decisive difference in that person's health. Jesus presented the opportunity for the soul to trust and for the body to be cured.

Nowhere is this relationship more dramatically presented than in the story of the paralytic whose friends brought him, bedridden, to Jesus (Mark 2:1–12). When Jesus saw the faith they had, he said, "Son, your sins are forgiven" (2:5). When the scribes called this statement blasphemy, Jesus asked, "Which is easier, to say to the paralytic, 'Your sins are forgiven,' or to say, 'Stand up and take your mat and walk'? But so that you may know that the Son of Man has authority on earth to forgive sins . . ." Then Jesus commanded the man to get up and walk (2:9–11). Faith and the forgiveness of sin were preludes to healing.

Miracles are signs of God's restoration of order in a disorderly, broken world. Miracles do not always produce faith; rather, it is the other way around. Through the eyes of faith we recognize an event, not as strange or circumstantial, but as an act of God.

A dictionary definition for miracle is "an event that appears unexplainable." But is this definition always the case? The birth of a child, the restoration of a broken relationship, the recovery from an illness: these are not rare or unusual events. But again, seen through the eyes of faith, the hand of God is discovered at work. Perhaps it is better to define a miracle not by what the event *is*, but by what it *does*.

Miracles strengthen faith. Once we open ourselves up to belief in the living God, we see signs of God's activity in even the most everyday occurrences in our world. A wise person once noted, "When I pray, coincidences happen. When I don't pray, they don't happen." There are many folks in churches today who persist in understanding miracles, not by what they do for faith, but by how rare or inexplicable the events actually are. Such limitations are not helpful. A rare event is not necessarily a sign of God's activity in the world. And to say that God acts only on rare occasions is indeed a bleak thought. Limiting miracles by describing what they must look like is to severely limit our ability to see God's hand at work in the world.

Whatever strengthens belief, that is a miracle. Signs and wonders do not come from a lazy attitude: Jesus will take care of it all. Our reading of Mark shows us persons who came to Jesus with confidence. We see in the Gospel individuals who knew their needs, asked for help, and expected to receive it. In a mysterious and powerful sense, humans cooperate with the grace of God. We open ourselves up to miracles; we enable them to occur. Miracles proceed from faith.

CHAPTER 3

The Gospel of Matthew

INTRODUCTION TO THE GOSPEL OF MATTHEW

Matthew is the great systematizer. His Gospel was appreciated very early in the life of the church because it served so well the need for instruction. Following the five books of the Torah (Genesis through Deuteronomy) we have Matthew's five discourses of Jesus. Heeding the timeless truths of Hebrew torah (teaching), we find in Matthew the invitation to a higher righteousness. Observing the prophetic hopes found in scripture (the Old Testament), we see in Matthew their fulfillment in Christ. Matthew stands first in the New Testament canon as the premier handbook for the *ecclesia*, the church.

Matthew wrote not only for all time, but for a particular community. More than any other Gospel, Matthew's reflects the struggles of the early church to define itself in relation to its Jewish past. Matthew addresses the question asked by Jewish Christians: What is our relation to our Jewish heritage in light of our Easter faith?

Matthew quotes from the Hebrew scriptures at length (fifty-seven times). He presupposes a thorough familiarity with Old Testament prophecies, imagery, and titles. For Matthew, Jesus acted "in order that scripture might be fulfilled." Jesus is the legitimate, intentional fulfillment of the Law and the Prophets. Matthew's infancy narrative shows that God was doing a new thing with a brand-new baby, yet this unique act is consistent with God's activity down through the ages. As God promised Abraham, the first patriarch, "By your offspring shall all the nations of the earth gain blessing for themselves" (Gen. 22:18).

A bridge is an apt metaphor for this Gospel. It marks continuity: between the history of Israel and the history of the church, between the covenant with God's chosen people and the covenant available to all people, between the spirit of the law as understood by the Jews and its spirit as understood by Jesus. "Do not think that I have come to abolish the law or the prophets; I have come not to abolish but to fulfill," Jesus says in Matthew 5:17–18.

But a bridge also spans the space between two separated masses of land. The Gospel marks discontinuity as well as continuity. In Matthew's Gospel more than any other, Jesus' public ministry is devoted to the Jews; the commission to the whole world is not given until after the resurrection. But the Jewish leadership—the scribes and Pharisees—consistently fail to perceive, listen, or understand, fulfilling the prophecy of Isaiah 6:9–10 (Matt. 13:13–15). Their hostility toward Jesus is immense and sustained, culminating in the crucifixion.

Remember that Jesus, the disciples, and the crowds who followed him were Jews. Their spiritual base was the Temple, their places of prayer the synagogues. They were, properly speaking, Jews whose messianic hopes were fulfilled. With the destruction of the Temple in A.D. 70 came the consolidation of Judaism under the Pharisaic rabbis. By the time of Matthew's Gospel, c. 85, Jewish Christians were driven from the synagogues and cursed as heretics by their fellow Jews (see also Matt. 10:17 and 23:34). The Gospel reflects this schism, this discontinuity.

Matthew knows the church must define itself, often in terms of opposition to the synagogue that rejected it. Believers are no longer simply Jews who follow Jesus. The church is a new entity. The church's understanding of the Law and Prophets is continuous with Israel's, yet it has broken with that tradition. "Fulfill" may also be translated "reveal"; while Jesus came to fulfill torah he simultaneously revealed and uncovered a whole new reality. Many Jews were blinded to this revelation. And this is the great problem for Matthew. How will the Gospel show the truth of this revelation and take the blinders off?

One way to demonstrate truth is by proofs and persuasion, another is through force and use of power. The latter way is completely absent from Jesus' life and Matthew's Gospel (see 26:51–52); the former is implied by Matthew's repeated use of Old Testament citations. Matthew (more than any other Gospel) shows the truth of Jesus as Messiah by connecting the circumstances of Jesus' life with Hebrew scriptures. Jesus the Messiah was born in Bethlehem, as the prophet Micah foretold. Hosea predicted the flight into Egypt when Jesus was a baby; Zechariah said he would come riding into Jerusalem on a donkey; Jeremiah said he would be betrayed by a companion for money. You will find plenty of citations that link Jesus explicitly to Isaiah's prophecies.

But, for Matthew, Jesus' foremost demonstration of truth is not by power, proofs, or persuasion. It is by proclamation. "The kingdom of heaven" is the heart of the gospel, and Jesus proclaims that the kingdom of heaven is here, right now: "The kingdom of heaven is at hand!" (Matt. 3:2; 4:17; 10:7). It has begun, already, with his proclamation. The Messiah inaugurates the kingdom of heaven, which is the passion and the focus of Jesus' preaching. The kingdom is not simply a matter of life after death, although it includes that too. It is not limited by time or space. That is because the kingdom is characterized by service.

Unique to Matthew is the wonderful parable of the great judgment (25:31–46), in which we learn that kingdom people are those who do the will of God. Those who have served—who fed the hungry, welcomed the stranger, cared for the sick—discover to their surprise that "just as you did it to one of the least of these who are members of my family, you did it to me." Their service of the "least of these" is identical to their service of the Son of Man, and to their participation in the kingdom of heaven. Hear this proclamation, Matthew says, act on it, and you will find that you have become kingdom people.

Outline of the Gospel of Matthew

I. Introduction: Birth narratives: chapters 1; 2

II. Book One: Narrative of baptism and temptation: chapters 3; 4
Discourse: Sermon on the Mount: chapters 5—7

III. Book Two: Narrative of nine miracles: chapters 8; 9
Discourse: Instructions on discipleship: chapter 10

IV. Book Three: Narrative on controversies: chapters 11; 12
Discourse: Parables of the kingdom: chapter 13

V. Book Four: Narrative on miracles and teachings: chapters 14—17
Discourse: On humility and forgiveness: chapter 18

VI. Book Five: Narrative on the Judean ministry: chapters 19—22
Discourse: The eschaton (the end times): chapters 23—25

VII. Conclusion: Passion, Death, and Resurrection: chapters 26—28

The Gospel was nameless until the second century, when the name Matthew was attached to it. Like Mark's, the Gospel was written anonymously. The word "Matthew" is found twice in the Gospel, where he is called to be an apostle and identified as a tax collector (9:9; 10:3). Mark and Luke give him a different name—Levi. The Gospel possibly contains some recollections of Matthew (Levi) the apostle.

If we follow the two-document hypothesis discussed in chapter 2, the evangelist's sources include Hebrew scriptures, Mark's Gospel, a collection of Jesus' sayings ("Q") also used by Luke, and additional material unique to this Gospel. His is by far the longest Gospel. The outline above shows his tendency to systematize his material. Both the length and the orderly treatment made the gospel well suited to instruction for new Christians in the early church. The writer was well aware of church needs and concerns. In fact, he is the only evangelist to use the term *ecclesia*, or church (16:18; 18:17).

The Gospel is dated somewhere between A.D. 80 and 90, after Mark, the fall of the Temple, and the expulsion of Jewish Christians from the synagogues. The original community from which it arose cannot be determined: Syrian Antioch and Palestine are both possibilities. The writer addresses a Jewish Christian congregation that must define itself in terms both of its continuity with the past and its new relationship with the Messiah.

THE KINGDOM OF HEAVEN IN MATTHEW'S GOSPEL

The phrase "kingdom of heaven" appears over thirty times in Matthew's Gospel. It is the heart of Jesus' preaching and the focus of his public ministry. What is this kingdom? Is it a time, a place, a state of being? What is its scope and significance? Why did Jesus say the kingdom of heaven is at hand?

The kingdom of heaven is the kingdom of God, or simply "God ruling." The covenant Yahweh made with Israel was patterned on ancient Near Eastern treaties that kings made with vassal states. Unique to Hebrew scriptures is the understanding that Yahweh is king, that no matter what practical form of political leadership Israel had (be it judge, king, or governor) the nation existed as a theocracy.

Clap your hands, all you peoples;
shout to God with loud songs of joy.

For the LORD, the Most High, is awesome,
    a great king over all the earth.
He subdued peoples under us,
    and nations under our feet.
He chose our heritage for us,
    the pride of Jacob whom he loves.
                         (Ps. 47:1–4)

The theocracy ("God ruling") of Israel began with Moses c. 1290 B.C.: "If you obey my voice . . . you shall be to me a priestly kingdom and a holy nation" (Ex. 19:5–6). Centuries later, around 1000 B.C., another covenant was made, with King David. Whereas the Mosaic covenant is conditional and depends on Israel's obedience, the Davidic covenant is unconditional and depends solely on Yahweh's promise. The prophet Nathan delivered it to David with these words: "Thus says the Lord: . . . Your house and your kingdom shall be made sure forever before me; your throne shall be established forever" (2 Sam. 7:5, 16; see all of chap. 7). Is the "house" David's palace or his dynasty? Does "forever" denote an eternal reign in heaven or on earth? How does the Davidic covenant square with theocracy? The Davidic covenant may be interpreted in a number of ways.

By Jesus' time, hopes for a Davidic king (*mashiah*, or anointed one) ran high. It had been six centuries since the last heir of David sat on a throne in Jerusalem. Judah was ruled by puppets who answered to Rome rather than to Yahweh. The kingdom was dormant; where was the Davidide who would stir and wake it?

Jesus addressed the issue squarely. He proclaimed that the kingdom of heaven was at hand. As a son of David (Matt. 1:1) he fulfills the promises of the Davidic covenant. As the Christ (Greek for "Messiah") he fulfills the messianic hopes that abounded in the first century A.D. But the kingdom he described was quantum leaps removed from what his audience expected. That is because it is characterized by service rather than by domination, by mercy rather than by justice, by growth rather than by rigidity. He calls for *metanoia*, translated "repentance" and carrying the sense of reformation and complete change.

"The kingdom of heaven is like . . ." With these words Jesus introduces ten parables in Matthew. The wonderful thing about parables is the way they suggest truths through commonplace, simple stories. In reading these parables, bracket what you think is meant. Look at the characters: who they are, what they say. Notice the dramatic unfolding of the narrative, and expect some sort of surprise. Jesus' hearers were certainly surprised by the twists and turns in his parables. What's going on here? Parables tease the mind and promote a different way of viewing reality.

Parable of the weeds: Matthew 13:24–30; see also 13:36–43.

Using Jesus' interpretation of the parable in verses 36–43, identify each of these elements:

the sower _____

the wheat _____

the weeds _____

the enemy _____

the harvest _____

This odd way of growing wheat tells us what the kingdom of heaven is like, Jesus says. What does it tell you about the presence of evil in the world?

_____

What does this parable say about patience and tolerance?

_____

At what point in time does the kingdom begin: with the sowing? the sprouting? the harvesting?

_____

Parables of the mustard seed and the leaven: Matthew 13:31–33.

Both are parables of contrast. Contrary to popular belief Jesus tells the Jews that the kingdom has come (already) in his person. But its beginnings are humble: the kingdom was not the glorious "big bang" they expected. What aspects of Jesus' ministry seem small and insignificant?

_____

The parable is also about growth. The tiniest of seeds grows into the greatest of trees; a bit of leaven makes bread out of a huge heap bushel of flour. What is the relationship between this growth and the power of God? Who or what is responsible for the growth?

_____

His audience held to the "big bang" theory of the messianic age and awaited it impatiently. In contrast, what does Jesus say about the coming of the kingdom (and patience) here?

_____

Parables of the hidden treasure and the pearl: Matthew 13:44–46.

Hidden treasure was a favorite theme in Jewish

literature. There was much danger from foreign attack and brigandry in Palestine. Householders would bury treasure for safekeeping in a field, hoping one day to return and claim it.

What do these parables say about the value of the kingdom?

_____

What sort of emotion and energy did the men display in these parables?

_____

Did they know for what they were looking? Did they know what it would take to make the treasures their own?

_____

From the outside, the peasant looks like a fool (he does not remove the treasure, but buries it again), while the merchant appears rash and imprudent. Neither displayed caution, reflection, or "play it safe" behavior. What is Jesus saying about taking risks? How do these parables relate to Jesus' call, "Follow me!"?

_____

_____

_____

Parable of the net: Matthew 13:47–50.
How does this teaching compare with the parable of the weeds in 13:24–30?

_____

To whom do you think this parable is addressed: The good fish? The bad fish? The fisherman? Why?

_____

_____

Parable of the unmerciful servant: Matthew 18:23–34.
Note the division of the parable into three acts and mark your Bible accordingly: vv. 23–27, vv. 28–31, vv. 32–34.

In act one, the point is made that the servant's debt is enormous. A talent equaled fifteen years' wages for a laborer. Do the math here to see how many years he would work to pay the debt: _____
The servant asks the king for time (!) to pay the debt. What does he get instead?

_____

In act two, what do you think is the servant's tragic fault: Revenge? Brutality? A businesslike attitude? Rigidity? Forgetfulness? Other:

_____

What point is the king making in act three?

_____

The irony of the servant's action is that he is finally judged by his own criteria. What criteria does he use on his fellow slave?

_____

What does the king mean by "having mercy"?

_____

What is the point of the tag to the parable (v. 35) and the opening (vv. 21–22)?

_____

_____

What (if any) distinction do you make between "having mercy" and "forgiving"?

_____

Remember that this is a parable about the kingdom of heaven. Do the tag and opening verses strengthen the force of the parable for you or weaken it?

_____

_____

Parable of the laborers in the vineyard: Matthew 20:1–16.
Warning: This parable makes many good Christians exceedingly angry, especially if they link it to deathbed conversions. The landowner proceeds in the customary way up to verse 8, when we get a hint of the strange. What is this hint, and how is the strangeness of his behavior substantiated in verses 9–10?

_____

Why do the first laborers grumble? Would you? (Be honest!)

_____

From the laborers' perspective, what is wrong with the landowner's actions?

_____

Why did the landowner choose to act as he did? (Note that the order of justice is not violated; he paid the first laborers as they had agreed.)

_____

The landowner's reply in verse 15b literally reads, "Is your eye evil because I am good?" What happens when justice is confronted with mercy and generosity?

_____

The tag of verse 16 is a formula found throughout the Gospel. However, it is not the point of this particular parable. What would be a fitting tag for this kingdom parable instead?

_____

_____

Parable of the marriage feast: Matthew 22:2–14.

This parable has two parts, with two different points. The first (vv. 2–10) is paralleled in Luke 14:16–24; the second (vv. 11–14) is unique to Matthew.

Who finally comes to the wedding banquet?

_____

Why did those who were originally invited refuse to come? What is surprising about their response?

_____

_____

What do verses 2–10 tell you about the kingdom?

_____

What is the problem with the guest in verses 11–12?

_____

What do you think it means to be in the king's presence without wedding clothes?

_____

See verse 15. What impact did this parable have?

_____

Parable of the wise and foolish bridesmaids: Matthew 25:1–13.

The young women may be either wedding guests or servants awaiting the groom. From verse 5, what is strange or unexpected about this particular wedding?

_____

How do the women differ? What characteristics do the wise women display?

_____

_____

From the tag of verse 13 and also 24:42, what is the point made here about the kingdom?

_____

_____

Who are you most like in this parable? Why?

_____

_____

Discussion Questions: The Kingdom of Heaven

1. There is a tension in Jesus' preaching on the kingdom. At times, he speaks of the kingdom that has already begun (see Matt. 5:3; 12:28; 19:14); at other times, he speaks of the kingdom that has yet to come (see Matt. 7:21; 25:34–36; 26:29). The paradox of Jesus' teachings on the kingdom is this: the kingdom is both present now in our hearts and waiting to be fulfilled in the future. The kingdom is already, but not yet. Which of these parables speak of the kingdom as a future event (not yet)? Which speak of it as a present reality (already)?

2. There is another tension in the parables between justice and mercy. In what parables is justice preserved? In what parables is justice transcended by mercy?

3. Of these ten parables on the kingdom, which one is your favorite? Why? Which do you find least helpful, and why?

4. After you finish your reading of Matthew's Gospel, write a poem or a paragraph that shows your understanding of the kingdom of heaven. Artistic types might create a piece of artwork instead.

TORAH AND THE PHARISEES

Torah is a Hebrew word translated "law" in your English Bible. Capitalized and with the definite article, "the Torah" is the term used for the first five books of the Hebrew scriptures: Genesis through Deuteronomy. Without the definite article and in lower case, "torah" refers to all God's teaching and instruction beginning with Moses, elaborated and handed down through the priesthood, and preserved in its final form during the exile. In later Judaism, all Jewish tradition (both written and oral law) is referred to as torah. We are heedless to the force of torah if we think of it as simply the Ten Commandments of Exodus, or even the large body of laws found in Exodus, Leviticus, and Deuteronomy. Simply put, torah includes law but is not limited to it. Torah is God's instruction.

A common misconception held by many Christians in the Western world is that torah was a burden to those who received it. Nothing could be farther from the truth. Torah was the basis of the special covenant given to the Jews by God: "If you obey my voice and keep my covenant, you shall be my own possession among all the peoples; for all the earth is mine" (Ex. 19:5). How were the Jews to know God's voice? It was known by torah. Torah demanded obedience ("All that the Lord has spoken we will do"—Ex. 24:3,7), but the character of this obedience was not the response of a slave to a taskmaster, or even of a citizen to a judicial system. It was the response of a loved one to the beloved who had chosen and freely made this choice known. Torah, then, was the way God made the chosen people God's own. To keep torah was to be made constantly aware of God's choice of Israel. Therefore, to follow it was a joy. "I delight to do your will, O my God; your *torah* is within my heart" (Ps. 40:8). From Psalm 19:7–9, we see the fruits of torah: it revives the soul, rejoices the heart, enlightens the eyes.

Yet another misreading of torah is the idea that it pertains to religious life alone. We think in terms of a separation between church and state, between sacred statutes and secular decrees. No such distinction existed in Judaism. All torah (in the sense of law) was God's law, and torah governed every dimension of human existence, every area of human activity. There are laws, for instance, dealing with planting fields, with building fences on rooftops, with leashing oxen, with eating foods, with shaving beards. Of course much torah is devoted to religious practices. But Yahweh is God of all life, and all matters fall under Yahweh's gracious torah. Again, this is cause for celebration.

While torah defined the covenant people, serving as a hedge around the community, it was part of God's plan for all nations. It was first given to the Hebrews, but torah will finally not be limited to one people. See what the scriptures say about the breadth and scope of torah in Isaiah 2:2–3:

> In days to come . . .
>   Many peoples shall come and say,
> "Come, let us go up to the mountain of the LORD,
>   to the house of the God of Jacob;
> that he may teach us his ways
>   and that we may walk in his paths."
> For out of Zion shall go forth *torah*,
>   and the word of the LORD from Jerusalem.

The *mitzvoth*, or commandments, of torah were many. The rabbis noted that six hundred and thirteen precepts were communicated to Moses. However, the spirit of torah, as the prophets reminded the Jews, was uncomplicated; the mitzvoth could be distilled to simple, pure essence. "For I desire steadfast love and not sacrifice, the knowledge of God rather than burnt offerings" (Hos. 6:6); "Let justice roll down like waters, and righteousness like an everflowing stream" (Amos 5:24).

> He has told you, O mortal, what is good;
>   and what does the LORD require of you
> but to do justice, and to love kindness,
>   and to walk humbly with your God?
>   (Micah 6:8)

In Leviticus we read that you shall love your neighbor as yourself (19:18), and in Habakkuk that the righteous shall live by faith (2:4). The essence of torah is found in the intersection of ethics and religion, of the horizontal vector between persons and the vertical vector with Yahweh. The intersection of these two lines is the starting point of torah. The connection of these two lines is also the goal of torah, as shown in figure 3.1.

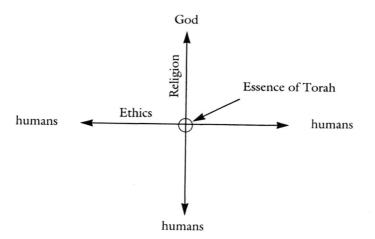

Fig. 3.1 The Essence of Torah

On the other hand, the many mitzvoth found in scripture were often not explicit enough in detail to suit the needs of the Jews. The great example is the mitzvah "Remember the sabbath day, and keep it holy" (Ex. 20:8). As God rested on the seventh day, so shall the entire community refrain from any work on the Sabbath. But what is work? The oral tradition of the Pharisees, and later the rabbis, addressed issues like this. The oral tradition built on the foundation of written scripture, explicating hundreds of rules and regulations that were believed to be implicit in scripture. Reading torah was not work; writing notes (even two letters of the alphabet) as you read was. Spending time with one's family was not work; traveling with them was. Taking a walk was not work; carrying a burden (equal to the weight of a dried fig) on that walk was. Work was not understood as physical exertion, but as purposeful activity that interferes with the created order. The Sabbath is a day to leave God's world alone. The oral tradition listed thirty-nine activities that interfered with the created order, including planting, sowing, lighting a fire, and tearing a thread. The prohibitions were practical and clear. That is because the mitzvoth required real-life application. And real life is not simple.

Imagine you are sitting in on a class lecture. You would take notes, but you would also have the important experience of hearing the words. One key word in your notebook might imply many others; you come away from the lecture having heard nuances and inferences that are vital, but which are not part of your written record.

With this example in mind, the Pharisees understood written torah (found in scripture) to be the class notes. But they also upheld the oral tradition—the unwritten residue of the lecture experience—as the authoritative interpretation and complement to written torah. Where torah drew the outlines of righteous living, the oral tradition filled in the colors and textures of daily life. Oral tradition, then, was a bit like the sermons in our church services today. Because every generation seeks meaning anew, it provided amplification of and insight into the meaning of the written text. It started around 200 B.C. as midrash, commentary and discussion, and ended as the Talmud, a text of thirty volumes and 2.5 million words finally codified c. A.D. 500. This vast undertaking began with the work of the Pharisees.

When we read about the Pharisees in the New Testament, the tendency is to make a distinction between "us" (today's readers, who know better) and "them" (those hypocritical and ineffectual Pharisees). We imagine that the Pharisees are a breed of humanity with whom we share little or nothing. We are not they. But if the Pharisees were concerned with making distinctions and judgments, and we do the same . . . the parallels are clear.

Dietrich Bonhoeffer wrote provocatively about the Pharisee in his *Ethics*.[1] His point is that the Pharisee is really the person for whom every moment of life is a situation in which choices must be made. In each situation the choice is not trivial; it calls for nothing less than choosing between good and evil. The Pharisee is extremely admirable in this strenuous devotion to doing what is right. Life is a matter of conflicts and decisions, to which torah must be brought to bear. And the Pharisee uses this knowledge with thankfulness toward God, who judges all beings (including the Pharisee!) by the standards of God's righteous torah.

The conflict between Jesus and the Pharisees becomes clearer when we understand this tension. The tension is not between one who seeks to serve God and those who do not care about obedience. Nor is it between sincerity and duplicity, for the Pharisees are earnest in their zeal for torah and forthright in their desire for righteousness. As Bonhoeffer says, the conflict is really between union and disunion. Torah in its Pharisaic practice became the means of separating the righteous from the sinners. Doing good, observing the mitzvoth, worked not to heal disunion, but to deepen it further. The Pharisees are baffled by Jesus' call for reconciliation—"Do not judge, so that you may not be judged" (Matt. 7:1). They are puzzled by the freedom and simplicity Jesus demonstrates in his life and teaching. They are finally enraged by the way Jesus disrupts their world and challenges them, who know righteousness in all its detail, to a higher righteousness. Their reaction toward Jesus is nothing less than the reaction of a person who has tried every minute of life to be very good, and is told that is not the point. It is the reaction of those who work hard and know how hard they work. Those who seek to fulfill torah themselves are understandably shocked and defensive when Jesus says he is doing this job for them: "I have come not to abolish [torah and the prophets] but to fulfill" (Matt. 5:17).

Discussion Questions: Torah and the Pharisees

1. A friend remarks to you, "Torah was nothing more than a set of laws the Jews had to obey." What is your reaction to this statement? In what ways does the remark limit and belittle the proper understanding of torah?

2. How do you account for the many mitzvoth (commandments) upheld by the Pharisees in Jesus' time?

3. The Pharisee is not limited to a particular place and time. Instead, pharisaism is a part of human nature. In what sense do you see pharisaism operating today? In what ways do you see the pharisee within yourself?

[1] New York: Macmillan Publishing Co., 1978, 26–37.

STUDY GUIDE FOR THE GOSPEL OF MATTHEW

1. Introduction: Birth narratives

The genealogy of chapter 1 is unique to Matthew. How is Jesus' royal descent established by this list of forefathers?

_____

_____

Who are his foremothers? List the five women, noting how each stood "outside" proper Jewish tradition.

_____

_____

_____

If the line descends through Joseph and not Mary, in what sense is Jesus treated as Joseph's legally adopted son in 1:18–25? Read chapter 2. This material is also unique to Matthew. Note the fulfillment of at least three scripture references in this chapter.

_____

_____

How does the visit of the Magi (Gentile wise men) in 2:1–12 contrast with the reaction of Herod (a powerful Jewish ruler) in 2:13–23?

_____

What resemblances do you see between the material in chapter 2 and the story of Moses in Exodus?

_____

_____

2. Book One: Narrative of baptism and temptation (chaps. 3; 4)

How does John the Baptizer prepare the way of the Lord?

_____

_____

Who or what declares Jesus to be the "beloved Son" at his baptism (3:17)?

_____

In what ways does the tempter (in 4:1–11) appeal to human concerns for practical needs? for safety? to human desire for power?

_____

_____

In 4:18–22, what is the effect of the word "immediately"?

_____

Discourse: Sermon on the Mount (chaps. 5—7)

To whom is this discourse addressed? (5:1–2)

_____

Read the Beatitudes of 5:3–12. "Blessed" may also be translated "fortunate" or "happy." This happiness is independent of earthly changes and fortunes; it is the kind of joy that cannot be taken away. This joy shines even through tears and is characteristic of the kingdom of God.

How does Matthew's version of the Beatitudes differ from Luke's in Luke 6:20–26?

_____

_____

Are these words of exhortation and instruction, or are they statements about reality?

_____

In 5:13–14, Jesus says the disciples are _____ and _____. What exhortation follows this proclamation in 5:16? _____

What does Jesus say about a "higher righteousness" in 5:17–20?

_____

_____

How is this higher righteousness applied to the Sixth Commandment (on murder) in 5:21–22?

_____

How is it applied to the Seventh Commandment (on adultery) in 5:27–28?

_____

What does Jesus say about easily obtained divorces in 5:31–32?

What about swearing and oaths in 5:33–37?

The principle of "eye for eye, tooth for tooth" in the Torah was progressive in ancient times, when two eyes might be taken in retaliation for one, or many lives in revenge for one life. This *lex talionis* of Exodus 21:23–24 put an end to blood feuds common in the ancient Near East. How is the principle carried a step farther by Jesus in 5:38–42?

In light of what Jesus says about loving your enemies in 5:43–47, to what characteristic of God's perfection or wholeness is he referring in verse 48?

In 6:1–16 on almsgiving, prayer, and fasting, we find the Greek word *hypokritai*. It is translated "hypocrites." We usually think of hypocrites as people who say one thing but do another. These *hypokritai* say one thing, and do it! What, then, is the meaning of "hypocrites" in this passage?

In what ways is the Lord's Prayer of 6:9–13 the heart of the Sermon on the Mount?

After reading 6:19–34, what new understandings do you have about your priorities?

What distinction is made between "judging" (condemning another's faults) and using good judgment (discerning and making choices) in 7:1–6? (See also 10:16.)

In the teaching on prayer in 7:7–11, what point do you find most meaningful?

"You will know them by their fruits" (7:16). Based on the entire sermon, what are the good fruits by which kingdom people are known?

3. Book Two: Narrative of nine miracles (chaps. 8; 9).

On a separate sheet of paper, list each of the nine miracles: who is involved, the nature of the problem, Jesus' response (both words and actions), and the result.

Fill in the blanks of the summary statement of Jesus' actions in 9:35. Jesus went about _____, _____ and _____.

Discourse: Instructions on discipleship (chap. 10).

Note that during Jesus' earthly ministry, the mission is confined to the Jews in Matthew 10:5. How are the disciples to prepare for their mission?

What physical and emotional adversity should they anticipate?

Looking at 10:40–42, what reward is implied for those who give "even a cup of cold water"?

4. Book Three: Narrative on controversies (chaps. 11; 12).

John the Baptist is the Elijah figure who prepares the way of the Lord. Yet he is not recognized, because he has not fulfilled the people's presuppositions. From 11:7–10, what did they expect?

From 11:16–19, what presuppositions kept the people from recognizing both John and Jesus?

What does 11:25–30 say about wisdom? How does this passage relate to 9:36?

Reading about Jesus' treatment of the Sabbath laws in 12:1–14, what points is he making through his behavior? through his words?

Again we read that a tree is known by its fruit (12:33). How does this saying apply to the controversy in 12:22–28?

How does Jesus define "family" in 12:46–50?

Turn to 13:54–58. How does the customary definition of family obstruct Jesus' mission?

Discourse: Parables of the kingdom (chap. 13)

You have already examined much of this material in the section on the kingdom of heaven.

What happens to the various seeds in the parable of the sower (13:1–9)? According to the interpretation in 13:18–23, *why* do these things happen?

seeds on the path:

seeds on rocky ground:

seeds among the thorns:

seeds on good soil:

From 13:10–17, what is the difference between seeing and perceiving, and between listening and understanding?

From 13:16–17, do the disciples perceive Jesus' meaning or not?

Do you think Jesus' parables obscure his message or help proclaim it? Why?

5. Book Four: Narrative on miracles and teachings (chaps. 14—17).

Why do you think Jesus withdrew from the crowds in 14:13?

See 14:13–21 and 15:32–39. Given these miracles, what do you think is the tone of the conversation in 16:5–12?

At what point in each episode is Jesus recognized as God's Son?

14:22–33

15:21–28

16:13–20

17:1–18

What does Jesus say about his future in these passages?

16:21–23

17:9–12

17:22–23

How do the disciples react to these foretellings?

Discourse: On humility and forgiveness (chap. 18)

The dominant image in this teaching passage is the child. What is the difference between being "childish" and being "childlike"?

How are disputes between church members to be resolved (18:15–17)?

How does 18:18–20 echo Jesus' words to Peter in 16:19?

6. Book Five: Narrative on the Judean ministry (chaps. 19—22).

Again Jesus refers to children in 19:13–15. Children know that they are not self-sufficient and that they depend on caregivers. They are aware that they are limited in knowledge and power, and that they cannot possess everything. Children are also quick to forgive and "move on" with living. How does the rich young man of 19:16–26 differ from a child?

Jesus predicts his death a third time in 20:17–19. What details are added here to his predictions in 16:21 and 17:22?

What does 20:20–28 tell you about true greatness?

What happened on Palm Sunday (21:1–17)?

The controversy with the Jewish establishment continues in chapter 21. Keeping this audience in mind, what key point is Jesus making in the parable of the two sons (21:28–32)?

in the parable of the vineyard (21:33–44)?

What does Jesus say concerning speculation about the afterlife in 22:23–32?

What is the basis and summary of all torah, according to 22:34–40?

Discourse: The eschaton (the end times) (chaps. 23—25)

In chapter 23, Matthew has gathered together a long list of critical remarks about the Jewish establishment. Imagine that you are a church leader, and that chapter 23 is addressed not simply to "scribes and Pharisees" (others), but to Christian leadership (you). List the particular condemnations that grab your attention, and tell why they grabbed you.

Chapter 24 is teaching material on the end of the age, or the eschaton. It closely parallels Mark 13, one of Matthew's probable sources. However, Matthew has added some material to the Markan material, notably the emphasis on the "whole world" in 24:14 and 24:30. What do these verses say about the universal scope of the eschaton?

Matthew has also added five parables on the last days. In what ways does each parable make points about judgment and/or "being ready"?
the thief in the night (24:43–44):

the faithful and wise servant: (24:45–51)

the ten maidens (25:1–13):

the talents (25:14–29) (Note what happens when one is terrified by the prospect of judgment; he does nothing!):

the sheep and the goats (25:31–46):

This last parable is really a vision. It marks the last teaching in Jesus' public ministry. What is the key verse in this teaching for you, and why did you choose this verse?

7. Conclusion: Passion, Death, and Resurrection.

Matthew shows that rejection of Jesus comes from every quarter. Who rejects him in these verses?
26:14–16

26:69–75

27:20, 41

27:20–23

27:24

The title "Son of God" is confirmed in the Passion narrative. How does Jesus establish this relationship with God in the following verses?
26:27–29

26:39

26:62–64

Note how the crowds establish this relationship in:
27:42–43

27:54

Finally, see Jesus' Great Commission and self-description in 28:18–20:

_____

_____

Discussion Questions

1. Of all the disciples, we know Peter best. Matthew shows him to be, at various times, perplexed, impulsive, bold, timid, devoted, cowardly. Like all of us, Peter is a complex critter. He is a fine example of humanity at its best and at its worst.

Review the Petrine material in Matthew, especially 4:18–20; 14:22–33; 16:13–23; 17:1–8; 26:31–75. Also note his questions in 18:21 and 19:27.

Then put yourself in Peter's place. What are you thinking and feeling in these episodes? What moves and motivates you? What discourages you? How would you like to be remembered? Write (in the first person) or tell your group what it's like to be Peter.

2. Matthew connects Jesus with Hebrew scripture using the formula, "This was to fulfill what was spoken." Look up these formulas and note the scripture references that follow (if you wish to dig deeper, read the Old Testament references as well): 1:22; 2:5; 2:15; 2:17; 2:23; 4:14; 8:17; 12:17; 13:14; 13:35; 21:4; 27:9. What key points can you make about the relationship between Jesus and Hebrew scripture?

3. The Sermon on the Mount shows that the old standards of piety, self-interest, and retaliation are replaced by compassion, love, and reconciliation. The things Jesus taught are not rules and regulations to be taken literally and legalistically. They are illustrations and sketches, not an ethical system.

A good sermon has three key points. If you were to preach a sermon on the Sermon, what three points would you make? How would you illustrate these points in contemporary terms?

GROUP WORK ON THE BEATITUDES

Below are some suggested ways of looking at Jesus' teaching in Matthew 5:3–10. Read the notes for each verse, then put the initials of someone in your group (or, if you are working this project independently, someone you know pretty well) beside the verse that describes this person. If you wish to share your insights, decide how you will do so: group discussion, letter, phone call.

1. The spiritually poor (v. 3) are those who recognize in their hearts that they can do no good thing without God's help. They feel God's acceptance, knowing they cannot earn love by wealth, status, or spiritual refinements. Because they are able to accept themselves (with their imperfections), they enable others to be more self-accepting.

2. The mourners (v. 4) are those who are sorrowful for their own sins and for the suffering and misery in the world. They have the ability to feel what others feel; they have empathy. They feel the empty places in life and share the grief of others without embarrassment. They can weep as Jesus did.

3. The humble (v. 5) are those who bear no grudges and who are gentle in their dealings with others. They do not have to "win" or be the strong one all the time. They can be tender because they are inwardly strong; they can lead without overpowering others.

4. The spiritually hungry (v. 6) want the kingdom of God in their lives. They want to know God and share God's perspective. They are more excited about God's work in the world than their own financial gain, success, or social acceptance. They motivate others to seek a deeper spiritual life.

5. The merciful (v. 7) are those who try to reflect in their dealings with others the mercy God has shown to them. They too have a sensitivity for the suffering of others. They are not interested in keeping score of wrongs; they are able to forgive.

6. The pure in heart (v. 8) are those who do not try to serve God and other interests at the same time. They are sincere. They are able to be themselves without pretense and to be completely open with God and with others. They do not have to pretend to be what they are not. They are transparent in that they have nothing to hide.

7. The peacemakers (v. 9) are not passively docile; instead they are actively seeking or making peace in this world. They have the ability to harmonize differences between others so that neither party hurts the other. They deal with anger and disagreements immediately, not allowing them to fester. They work at keeping the lines of communication open between themselves and those around them.

8. The persecuted (v. 8) are those who suffer because they believe and because they refuse to compromise their belief. They know what they are living for, and they are not afraid to stand alone for what is right. They have the ability to endure. They maintain their position without getting defensive, without feeling self-pity or self-righteousness.

CHAPTER 4

The Gospel of Luke and Acts of the Apostles

INTRODUCTION TO LUKE-ACTS

If Mark is a rugged chunk of granite and Matthew is a cut diamond, then Luke is a polished, precious stone. Stylistically smooth, carefully written in good Greek, the two volumes of history known as Luke-Acts shimmer with beauty and elegance. If we assume that the author is the same physician who accompanied Paul in his travels (Col. 4:14), his medical training taught him to be attentive to structure and detail, that is, to write well. Addressing Theophilus in Luke 1:1–4 and Acts 1:1,

Luke tells this Roman official that "an orderly account" is his aim. And so Luke is the first church historian. Over one fourth of the New Testament canon belongs to this writer, this lover of history. What did Luke have in mind as he penned his two-volume piece?

Structurally, Luke works to bring Jesus to Jerusalem in the Gospel, and the church to Rome in Acts. Indeed, Acts is structured in waves of movement from Jerusalem out, in ever-widening circles, as the chart in figure 4.1 illustrates.

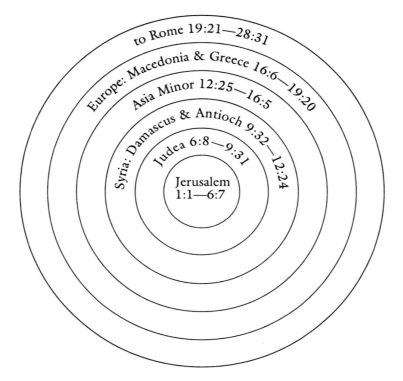

Fig. 4.1 The Movement of the Church in Acts

The movement from the holy city of Jerusalem to the glittering capital of the Mediterranean world cannot be stopped. Simply put, the church is a huge success. As a non-Jew, indeed the only Gentile writer in the New Testament canon, Luke wants Theophilus and the entire Gentile world to know why this fabulous success is occurring.

The success is due to the power of Jesus and, after his ascension in Acts 1, to the power of the Holy Spirit. This power is universal in scope, extending to the Samaritans, women, and the poor—the marginal folk of Jewish society—and then to the entire Roman world. Should his readers be troubled by this gospel, with its power to "turn the world upside down" (Acts 17:6),

Luke wishes to show that Christianity does not threaten the political order. And, in return, Christianity should be tolerated by the state.

In Acts, he describes Roman officials in a positive manner and shows a high regard for Roman justice in its protection of Paul. Luke carefully shifts the blame for Jesus' crucifixion away from Pilate, the Roman governor of Judea. Pilate is willing to release Jesus in Luke's Gospel, finding "no crime" in him (Luke 23:13–16). It is a Roman soldier who sees Jesus on the cross and then declares, "Certainly this man was innocent!" (Luke 23:47). While Jesus is rejected by the Jewish establishment, he is sought out by the Roman centurion in Luke 7:1–10. The church was reviled by Jewish officials; in contrast, the Gentiles "were glad and glorified the word of God" preached by Paul in Acts (Acts 13:44–48; see also 18:5–8). Finally, Luke concludes his two volumes with Paul telling the Jewish leaders in Rome: "Let it be known to you then that this salvation of God has been sent to the Gentiles; they will listen" (Acts 28:29). The history he writes is inexorable, unstoppable good news.

The Gospels of Luke, Matthew, and Mark are called "Synoptics" because they share much of the same material; these three books may be laid out in columns (as in *Gospel Parallels*[1]) and "seen together" (the meaning of syn-opsis) for purposes of comparison and contrast. You will see how Luke modifies some of this common material as you read. In addition, Luke has drawn from a source or sources known simply as "L" (sixty-one pericopes, or small literary units), "L" being unique to his Gospel. While Matthew traces Jesus' lineage back to Abraham, the patriarch of the Jews, Luke goes all the way back to Adam, the father of the human race (Luke 3:38). As the "whole world" and "the ends of the earth" are Luke's concern (Acts 1:8), it is fitting that Jesus'

genealogy is traced back to the biblical progenitor of all peoples. Other "L" passages show Luke's concern for the poor (as in Luke 6:20) and the fact that, with the coming of Christ, things are not as they appear. The lot of the poor appears wretched, yet they are blessed. The sumptuous banquet is set for the high and mighty, yet it is actually served to the poor, maimed, blind, and lame (Luke 14:15–24). The tax collector (who despised himself at least as much as his fellow citizens did) is exalted, while those who think themselves spiritually rich—as did the Pharisee—are laid low (18:9–14). The unjust judge, who has regard for neither God nor humanity, actually vindicates the persistent widow (18:1–8). No, things are not as they appear. The half-breed, contemptible Samaritan becomes the model for what it means to do good (10:29–37). The prodigal son's pragmatic decision to go home becomes the occasion for an extravagant thanksgiving celebration (15:11–24). Indeed, beginning with the gospel, the world is turned upside down.

The last emphasis we will mention here is Luke's attention to prayer. The Gospel pictures Jesus praying at his baptism (3:21), after healing the leper (5:16), before choosing the disciples (6:12) and before questioning them (9:18), at the transfiguration (9:29), on the Mount of Olives before his arrest (22:41–42), and finally on the cross (23:46). Except for the last words on the cross, "Father, into thy hands I commit my spirit!" we do not know the content of Jesus' prayers. But we do have a vivid picture of Jesus withdrawing from crowds, going away by himself, seeking out time for prayer. Similarly in Acts, Luke paints the early church as given continually to prayer. The power of the good news is rooted in prayer, in both the example of Jesus and the history of the church.

Luke's two-volume history is dated somewhere between A.D. 80 and 90.

THE INFANCY NARRATIVES AND PARABLES UNIQUE TO LUKE

If the Gospel of Luke were to be lost and gone forever, what would we lack in our understanding of Jesus' life and teachings? We have mentioned in the introduction the body of material—over sixty pericopes or short literary units—which is conveniently known as the "L" source. Whether "L" was at one time a separate group of writings that Luke incorporated as he wrote, or whether our historian drew from numerous interviews as a journalist might do today, we will never know. But "L," or the material found in Luke's Gospel and nowhere

else, is some of the most profound and best-loved material in the New Testament canon. Without Luke, we would have no record of the great events accompanying Jesus' birth: the annunciation to Mary, the birth of John the Baptist, the prophecies of Zechariah and Simeon, the visitation of the shepherds. It is Luke who preserves the parables of the good Samaritan, the prodigal son, and the rich man and Lazarus, to mention a few.

When you have finished this section, formulate a response to the questions: What important *pictures* of Jesus would be lost if Luke's Gospel had not been written? What important *teachings* of Jesus would be lost?

[1] See pages 15–17 of this *Guide*, under "Doing an Exegesis."

I. The Infancy Narratives: Read Luke 1; 2.
  1. The prologue: 1:1–4.
  In the prologue Luke gives reasons for writing his "orderly account." What are they?

_____

  2. The promise of the birth of the Baptizer: Luke 1:5–25.
  In addition to being husband and wife, who are Zechariah and Elizabeth ?

_____

  Where was Zechariah when he was struck dumb?

_____

  The angel Gabriel's prophecy in 1:17 links John with that colorful Old Testament prophet Elijah (1 Kings 17—21). In 2 Kings 2:9–11, Elijah left this world via a chariot of fire. Because he did not actually die, but was "translated" into the heavens, Jewish tradition arose that Elijah would return to usher in the messianic age (see the last two verses of the Old Testament canon: Malachi 4:5–6). In the Passover seder, for the Jews, Elijah's cup of wine still awaits his return. What will be John's task, according to Gabriel?

_____

  3. The annunciation to Mary: Luke 1:26–38.
  Where does Gabriel's announcement take place?

_____

  Read 2 Samuel 7, Nathan's prophecy to King David. The word "house" here has multiple meanings: palace, temple, dynasty, kingdom. What echoes of this Davidic covenant do you find in Gabriel's prophecy to Mary?

_____

  What portrait or picture of Mary do you have after reading Luke 1:26–38?

_____

  4. Mary's visit to Elizabeth: Luke 1:39–56.
  How did Elizabeth react when her kinswoman arrived?

_____

  Mary's Magnificat (Latin for "[my soul] magnifies") is a powerful poem of praise and thanksgiving. According to Mary, in what ways does God reverse the roles of society?

_____

  What promises did God make to Abraham? (See Genesis 17:2–7; 18:17; 22:17–18 *before* you write your answer.)

_____

  Finally, read Hannah's song in 1 Samuel 2:1–10. In what ways is this Old Testament song a model for Mary's Magnificat?

_____

  5. The birth of the Baptizer: Luke 1:57–80.
  What signs do we have so far that this child, John, will not be an ordinary child?

_____

  You have already read Old Testament references to Elijah, the promises to David, and the covenant with Abraham. How are these themes echoed in Zechariah's canticle?

_____

  John lived "in the wilderness" until he was thirty years old. Look up Isaiah 40:3–5. Write out Isaiah 40:3 here:

_____

  6. The birth of Jesus: Luke 2:1–20.
  Mark makes no mention of Jesus' birth, while Matthew simply says he was born in Bethlehem, giving no other details (Matt. 2:1). Matthew places the visit of the Wise Men immediately after this statement. For Matthew, the birth is marked by a star and adored by the Magi. For Luke, the birth is marked by humble origins and the witness of simple shepherds. Give details from Luke 2:1–20 that show the rustic, humble beginnings of Jesus' life.

_____

_____

  On the other hand, in what way does Luke indicate the magnificence, the heavenly significance, of this birth?

_____

  7. The presentation in the Temple: Luke 2:21–38.
  Read Leviticus 12:2–8. What does the sacrifice of two pigeons indicate about Mary and Joseph's economic status?

_____

  What do we know about Simeon from this passage?

_____

about Anna?

_____

  In what ways are these two characters similar?

_____

_____

Simeon's prophecy in verses 30–32 echoes Isaiah 42:6 and 49:6. The message here, and in Isaiah, is a key theme for Luke. Summarize this message:

_____

_____

8. The boy Jesus in the Temple: Luke 2:41–52.

From the way he behaves and speaks, what is this twelve-year-old boy's understanding of himself and of God?

_____

_____

Imagine Mary retelling this episode to her kinswoman Elizabeth. What thoughts and feelings might she include?

_____

_____

II. The Parables of Jesus Found Only in Luke.
(The historical narrative of the Gospel resumes in our next section.) There are ten parables unique to Luke.[2] We will take a close look at only a few of them here.

1. The good Samaritan: Luke 10:25–37.

Who is Jesus' audience here? What motive do you think this person has in questioning Jesus?

_____

The priest and the Levite both "saw" and "passed by." As good religious leaders, they might have quoted the law given to Moses and Aaron (both Levites!) in Numbers 19:11–13, which says:

_____

_____

Note, however, that the traveler is "half dead" (v. 30) rather than completely dead.

The Samaritan "saw" and "had compassion," an important formula for Luke. In Greek, compassion literally means "moved in the guts." Note what happens in three other passages where this word is used in the Gospel:

1:77–78 (here "tender mercy"= compassion)

_____

7:11–15

_____

15:20ff.

_____

Samaritans were bitterly hated by the Jews. In A.D. 27, a few years before Jesus told this parable, Samaritans

[2] For a fuller listing, see the chart (Fig. 2.3) on page 36 of this *Guide*.

threw the bones of a corpse in the Temple on the eve of Passover, thus defiling the Temple and preventing the Passover celebration that year. The shock of the parable is the identification of "good" with the word "Samaritan." Note too that Jesus does not talk about who the neighbor is, but what it means to be a neighbor.

Follow-up: The example of Mary. Read Luke 10:38–42.

What does Mary do when Jesus comes to her house?

_____

In Ecclesiastes 3:1, the preacher writes, "For everything there is a season, and a time for every matter under heaven." There is a rhythm of action and contemplation, of binding up wounds and of sitting down to reflect. Look closely at Luke 10:27. How does the example of Mary balance the example of the Samaritan? How do both together fulfill the law Jesus gave in Luke 10:27?

_____

_____

2. Banquets and more banquets: Read Luke 14:1–24.
Note the audience and settings for these parables:

_____

The dining table was shaped like a U, with the host sitting at the base of the U and the guests placed out from the host toward the end of the table, in decreasing order of importance.

What point is made in 14:7–11?

_____

What point is made in 14:12–14?

_____

What about 14:15–24?

_____

Jesus talks about "my banquet" in verse 24. What do you think it would be like to partake of this feast? What reversal of roles (in contemporary terms) might you expect at Jesus' banquet?

_____

_____

3. Lost and found. Read Luke 15:1–32.
Who is the audience?

_____

The parable of the lost sheep is also found in Matthew, with the wording, " . . . if he finds the sheep, he rejoices" (Matt. 18:13). Reading Luke 15:3–7, what happens to the word "if"? What difference does this make to the sense of the parable?

_____

What phrase or action do you find most significant in the "lost coin" parable of Luke 15:8–10?

_____

Luke 15:11–32 gives us the story of the prodigal (wasteful) and lost son. What circumstances brought about the younger son's plan to go home?

_____

What did he plan to say to his father?

_____

What did he actually say?

_____

How did the father cut short his son's planned/canned speech?

_____

In many ways this is the father's story. As in the two other parables of Luke 15, the focus here is on the joy of the one who finds. The Jewish father commands respect because of his dignity. What is shocking, then, about this particular father's behavior in verse 20?

_____

How did the father respond to the elder son's anger?

_____

Read Galatians 4:1–7. In what ways did both sons think of themselves as *servants*? In what ways does the father show his acceptance of them as *sons*?

_____

STUDY GUIDE FOR THE GOSPEL OF LUKE

Having read the infancy narratives and some parables unique to Luke, we are now ready to look at the Gospel in its entirety. After the birth and youth narratives, Luke organizes his Gospel thus (paying careful attention to geography):

Outline of the Gospel of Luke

   I. Preparation for Ministry at the Jordan River and in the Wilderness: Luke 3:1—4:13
  II. Ministry in Galilee: 4:14—9:50
 III. Journey to Jerusalem: 9:51—19:27
 IV. Ministry in Jerusalem: 19:28—21:38
  V. Passion, Death, and Resurrection: chapters 22—24

Luke's symbol in Christian art is the ox: the animal of sacrifice. For Luke, Jesus is the sacrifice given for all humanity. A strong note of universal love pervades the book.

1. Jesus prepares for ministry at the Jordan River and in the wilderness.

As John the Baptizer swings into action along the Jordan River, he delivers a message of exhortation *and* good news (see 3:18). What is the good news Luke identifies with John in 3:4–6?

_____

What is the exhortation, or judgment, that John preaches in 3:7–9?

_____

Compare the accounts of Jesus' baptism in Matthew 3:13–17 and Luke 3:21–22. Note how the two accounts agree with respect to
the heavens:

_____

the dove:

_____

the voice from heaven:

_____

Where is John the Baptist in Luke's account? (see 3:19–20):

_____

Read 4:1–13 on Jesus' temptations in the wilderness. How long was he in the wilderness?

_____

What Old Testament narrative(s) use this same number?

_____

List the devil's temptations, and Jesus' responses:
(1) temptation:

_____

   response:

_____

(2) temptation:

_____

   response:

_____

(3) temptation:

_____

response:

_____

_____

2. Jesus begins his ministry in Galilee.

In the synagogue in Nazareth (4:16–30), Jesus makes it clear that his message will be carried to the underdogs. Who are they in the following verses?

4:18 _____

4:24–27 _____

See 4:28–30. What was the crowd's reaction to his preaching?

_____

In what ways does Jesus show his power and authority in the following passages?

4:31–37_____

4:38–39_____

5:17–26_____

In what ways does Jesus overturn traditional teaching and practice in the following passages?
5:27–32 (Levi here is also called Matthew, one of the Twelve)

_____

5:33–39

_____

6:1–5

_____

6:6–11

_____

Compare where Jesus preached his sermon in Luke 6:17 and in Matthew 5:1. What's different?

_____

Find four comparisons between Luke 6:20–26 and Matthew 5:2–12:

(1)

_____

_____

(2)

_____

_____

(3)

_____

_____

(4)

_____

_____

Give a brief "theme" or "title" for each of these sections:
6:27–36

_____

6:37–42

_____

6:43–45

_____

6:46–49

_____

See the two healing miracles in Luke 7:1–10 and 7:11–17. In which healing was Jesus' help sought out by a stranger? _____

In which healing did Jesus act without being asked?

_____

What are the aftereffects of the first healing, in verse 9?

_____

the aftereffects of the second healing, in verse 16?

_____

How do these miracles compare with the two healings in 8:40–56?

_____

_____

On forgiveness: What does the episode with the unnamed woman in Luke 7:36–50 say about forgiveness and love?

_____

_____

Who are the Twelve and what is their mission? (See 6:12–16 and 9:1–6.)

_____

_____

Who accompanies Jesus and the Twelve (8:1–3)?

_____

See 10:1–20. Who is sent?

_____

For what purpose?

_____

What questions are asked in the stilling of the storm episode of Luke 8:22–25?

_____

_____

How are these questions answered in the transfiguration of Luke 9:28–36?

_____

_____

3. Jesus journeys to Jerusalem.
How does Jesus show his relationship to God in Luke 10:16?

_____

in 10:21–22?

_____

What points does Jesus make about prayer in 11:1–13?

_____

_____

_____

Jesus teaches on material needs and anxiety in 12:22–34. What verse(s) in this passage stand out for you?

_____

What is the problem with wealth, according to the following?
(1) The parable of the rich fool (12:13–21)

_____

(2) The parable of the rich man and Lazarus (16:19–31)

_____

(3) The episode with the rich young ruler (18:18–27)

_____

What then is the proper use of wealth, according to the following verses?
14:12–14

_____

16:3

_____

21:1–4

_____

The topsy-turvy world of the kingdom: Things are not as they appear. How are roles reversed in the following teachings?
13:22–30

_____

17:33

_____

18:9–14

_____

18:15–17

_____

22:24–27

_____

What strange teaching does Jesus give the disciples in these verses?
9:22

_____

17:25

_____

18:31–34

_____

Unique to Luke's Gospel is the character Zacchaeus. Read Luke 19:1–10, then note the ways Zacchaeus behaved before, during, and after his meeting with Jesus:

_____

_____

_____

4. Jesus enters Jerusalem.
What happened on Palm Sunday (Luke 19:28–40)?

_____

Read Luke 19:45—21:38, accounts of Jesus' teaching in the Temple. What key points do you find Jesus making in these teachings?

_____

_____

_____

5. Luke recounts Jesus' passion, death, and resurrection.
What eight-letter word do all four accounts of the Last Supper have in common? Read Luke 22:14–23; Matthew 26:26–29; Mark 14:22–25; 1 Corinthians 11:23–26, and find out:_____

What does this word mean?_____
The Last Supper fell on the night of the Jewish celebration called Passover. Skim Exodus 12, the account of the first Passover. What was celebrated on this night?

_____

Read Luke 22:31—23:25, then use a few phrases to describe the role played by each of the following characters:
Peter:

_____

Judas:

_____

Pilate:

_____

Herod:

_____

The account in 23:39–43 is unique to Luke. For what does the criminal ask?

_____

What does Jesus promise him?

_____

Draw lines to match the Old Testament verses on the right with the verses in Luke:

Luke 23:34   Psalm 69:21
Luke 23:46   Psalm 31:5
Luke 23:36   Psalm 22:18
Luke 23:49   Psalm 38:11

How do you account for these similarities?

_____

Read Luke 24:1–11, the first Easter. Who discovered the tomb empty?_____
What did the two angels remind them?

_____

How did the (male!) apostles react to the news?

_____

See Luke 24:13–35. To whom does Jesus appear on the road to Emmaus?

_____

How many days have passed since the crucifixion?

_____

By what experiences and events did Jesus make himself known?

_____

When Jesus appeared to his followers in Luke 24:36–43, they thought he was a spirit of the dead (v. 37). In what ways does Jesus show them his realness?

_____

Where are Jesus' followers to stay and what will they receive (24:49)?

_____

Discussion Questions: The Gospel of Luke

1. What key themes do you find in the Gospel after looking at (1) Jesus' life and the way he lived it? (2) Jesus' teaching?
2. Why are the poor blessed? Why are the wealthy hindered by their wealth? Do the teachings in Luke comfort or convict you? Why?

STUDY GUIDE FOR ACTS OF THE APOSTLES

For Luke, history is divided into three great epochs: the epoch of Israel, covered in the Hebrew scriptures, the epoch of Christ, covered in Luke's Gospel, and the epoch of the church, of which Acts is the introductory volume. All history converges on the time of Christ, the center of the history of salvation, then fans out again after his ascension to reach the ends of the earth (geographically) and last until the end of time (chronologically).

Acts explodes with a host of personalities. Besides the original apostles in Jerusalem, a new cast of characters is swept up in this epoch of the church as it makes its way toward Rome. The variety of sects and groups represented in Acts is staggering. The chart in figure 4.2 briefly identifies some of these groups.

Outline of Acts

I. The Acts of the Jerusalem Church: Acts 1—7
II. The Church Extends Through Judea and Samaria: chapters 8; 9
III. The Church Reaches Syria: chapters 10—12
IV. The Church Extends Through Asia Minor: chapters 13—15
V. The Church Reaches Europe: 16:1—19:20
VI. Conclusion: The Church Reaches Rome: 19:21—28:31

1. Read Acts 1, on the ascension and the twelve apostles. If you are working through this reading as a group, turn to the end of this chapter in the *Guide* for the activity "Sculpting Acts 1:6–11." The Acts of the

Biblical Name	Ethnic Origin	Social/Cultural Status	Religious Beliefs	Example of Christian Convert
Hebrews	Semitic, Jewish	Aramaic-speaking, born in Palestine, unsophisticated & provincial	Adhere to Jewish practices: circumcision, Temple & synagogue worship, respect for Torah	James, Peter, most of the original twelve apostles
Hellenists	Semitic, Jewish	Greek-speaking, born outside of Palestine, worldly, sophisticated	Jewish with Greek philosophical background, synagogue worshipers	Stephen Barnabas Apollos
Pharisees	Semitic, Jewish	scholars, lawyers of Torah, leaders	1. Legalism—scrupulous adherence to law & tradition 2. Apartheid—separation from what is unclean 3. Belief in afterlife, resurrection, angels	Paul—unique combination of 1. Pharisee 2. Hellenist 3. Roman lawyer & citizen 4. Spoke Greek, Latin & Aramaic
Sadducees	Semitic, Jewish	leaders: priestly & aristocratic party found only in Jerusalem. Disappeared with destruction of Temple in A.D. 70	1. Tied to Temple worship 2. No afterlife, resurrection, angels 3. Tended to compromise with Roman establishment	—
Samaritans	mixed: remnants of Northern tribes intermarried with invaders	half-breeds	Worshiped Yahweh, but had their own "temple" in North. Despised by Jews as mongrels, apostates.	Simon the Magician
"God-fearers"	Gentile (non-Jew)	wide variation	Felt pagan Empire to be philosophically barren, accepted theological and ethical teachings of Judaism, but remained uncircumcised	Cornelius
Proselytes	Gentile (non-Jew)	wide variation; often women	"Devout converts" to Judaism: observed dietary laws, paid Temple tax, made pilgrimages to Jerusalem, circumcised	Key issue for early church lies here: Must a Gentile become a proselyte first, before becoming Christian?
"Gentile" used in NT as broad term for non-Jew; also called "pagan" & "uncircumcised"	I. Greek—from Aegean area, including Macedonia & islands in Mediterranean	traders, farmers, educated slaves, under Roman domination	Philosophical schools: Cynics; Stoics; Epicureans Polytheistic mystery cults of Artemis, Dionysus	Luke, Lydia
	II. Roman—specifically those on Italian peninsula, Latin-speaking. But citizenship extended throughout the Empire	patricians, equestrians, plebians, slaves, libertini (freed)	Emperor worship, also Mithraism (mystery cult) Polytheism	Philippian jailer? Cornelius

Fig. 4.2 Sects and Groups in First-Century Palestine

Apostles is actually a record of the acts of the Holy Spirit. What, according to the risen Christ, is the role of the Holy Spirit? (See especially 1:5 and 1:8.)

_____

_____

What criteria do the eleven use for choosing another apostle? See 1:3; 1:21–26.

_____

_____

2. Read Acts 2. Pentecost was the Jewish feast commemorating the day torah, or the law, was given to Moses. What was given to the church on this Pentecost?

_____

What unusual signs accompanied this gift?

_____

_____

How is Acts 2:5–12 a reversal of Genesis 11:1–9 (the Tower of Babel story)?

_____

_____

Read Peter's sermon in 2:14–36. According to verses 17–18, 21, and 39, what is the extent of the gift the people have received?

_____

What do you find most interesting about the description of the early church in 2:41–47?

_____

The Greek word for this fellowship is *koinonia*.

3. Read chapters 3 and 4: Peter heals, preaches, and gets arrested.

What adjectives would you use to describe Peter in these episodes?

_____

How do you account for the change in Peter since Luke's Gospel?

_____

What do the verses in 4:13–20 indicate about the power of the Holy Spirit?

_____

_____

4. Read 4:32—5:11 on the communal church. What do you consider to be the strengths of this arrangement? the weaknesses?

_____

How do you react to the deaths of Ananias and Sapphira?

_____

5. What is the central message of the apostles' preaching, and why does it enrage the Sanhedrin (council of priests, elders, and scribes in Jerusalem)? See 3:13–15; 3:25–26; 4:8–12; 5:30–32.

_____

_____

Given the heated atmosphere in the Sanhedrin, how does the wise Gamaliel cool things off for a while? See 5:33–42.

_____

_____

6. The first Christian martyr: Skim Acts 6 and 7, on Stephen. Who was Stephen (6:1–6)?

_____

Given his very Jewish, very learned audience, why do you think Stephen gives the long Old Testament history lesson in chapter 7?

_____

In what ways was Stephen like Jesus? See 6:8, 13 and 7:59–60.

_____

7. Read Acts 8: The gospel spreads through Samaria. What happens on the day of Stephen's death?

_____

Who is the ringleader? See 8:1–3. _____

Philip, one of the seven deacons mentioned in 6:5, has great success in Samaria. Give some proofs of this success.

_____

How would you characterize Simon the magician in 8:9–24? Gullible? Ignorant? Greedy? Trying too hard? Wicked? Other?

_____

How would you characterize the Ethiopian eunuch in 8:26–40?

_____

In what sense does the Spirit lead Philip (v. 29)?

_____

In what sense does Philip take the initiative (v. 30)?

_____

In what ways does the eunuch take the initiative (vv. 28, 31, 34, 37)?

_____

8. Read 9:1–31: The conversion of Saul.
Why was Saul heading to Damascus?

_____

What was the early church called at this time?

_____

If you were one of the persons with Saul on the road, what would your travel diary say?

_____

_____

In Damascus, how is Ananias persuaded to go see Saul?

_____

Note: According to Galatians 1:15–20, three years pass between Acts 9:25 and 9:26.
How does Barnabas show great courage in 9:26–30?

_____

9. Read chapter 10: The conversion of Cornelius.
What in 10:1–8 indicates that Cornelius is both an important and a devout person?

_____

in 10:24–27?

_____

What is the meaning of Peter's vision in 10:9–16? (See also 10:34–35.)

_____

Why do you think the vision is repeated *three* times?

_____

See 10:44—11:18, then tell why the story of Cornelius is a turning point in the history of the church:

_____

_____

What term do you find first used in 11:26?

_____

10. Read chapter 12: The last days of Herod Agrippa.
How does Herod show his thirst for blood in 12:1–4 and 12:18–19?

_____

What touches of humor do you find in 12:6–17?

_____

Peter goes to Caesarea in 12:19. The event recorded in 12:20–23 occurred in the spring of A.D. 44. Other than a speech he gives in 15:6–11, this is the last appearance of this key figure in the Jerusalem church. The focus of the missionary movement now passes from Peter to Saul of Tarsus, or Paul.

11. Let the journeys begin! Check the back of your Bible for a map of Paul's missionary journeys. How many did he make? _____
Into what modern-day countries did his journeys take him?

_____

_____

12. Skim chapters 13; 14: Paul's first work in Asia Minor (A.D. 46–48).
What evidence do you find showing Paul's success in Pisidian Antioch?

_____

_____

What trouble do Paul and Barnabas have there, which is repeated in 14:1–2?

_____

In Lystra (14:8–20), Paul and Barnabas are mistaken for the Greek gods _____ and _____. Why?
How did Paul and Barnabas react to the crowd's enthusiasm?

_____

13. Read chapter 15, on the first Jerusalem council.
What do certain unnamed individuals insist happen in 15:1, 5?

_____

What compromise does James propose in 15:19–21, 28–29?

_____

_____

Why do you think the Jerusalem church insisted on any restrictions whatsoever?

_____

14. The second journey (A.D. 49–52).
Who parts company with Paul, and who joins him instead (15:36—16:5)?

_____

How does Paul know he is to go to Europe (16:6–10)?

_____

What does the word "we" indicate in 16:11?

_____

Read 16:11–40, the account of Paul in Philippi, then describe the following characters using a few good adjectives for each:

Lydia _____

the slave girl _____

her owners _____

the jailer _____

15. Paul and Silas in Greece.
Read 17:1–9. What charges are brought against Paul and Silas in Thessalonica?

_____
_____

What arouses the curiosity of the Athenians in 17:16–32?

_____

How does Paul's argument "fit" his audience there?

_____

Nevertheless, Paul is singularly unsuccessful in Athens. Why do you think he could not reach the Athenians?

_____

What church is founded in 18:1–11? _____
16. The third journey (A.D. 53–57).
Read 18:24—19:7. Who is Apollos?

_____

In what sense did a "second Pentecost" occur at Ephesus?

_____

What evidence do you find that the Ephesians were fascinated with magic in 19:11–20?

_____

Read 19:23–41. Why did a riot break out in Ephesus? Were the reasons religious, political, or economic ones?

_____
_____

Where does Paul resolve to go in 19:21? _____
17. Paul returns to Jerusalem.
What does 20:7–12 tell you about Paul?

_____
_____

In his last speech to the Ephesian elders (20:17–35), what key autobiographical points does Paul make?

_____
_____
_____

What does 20:22–25 indicate about Paul's future?

_____

How is his premonition confirmed in 21:7–14?

_____

Compare Paul and Jesus by jotting down what happens to them in the following passages:
Luke 9:22, 44 and Acts 20:23

_____

Luke 18:31–33 and Acts 21:4, 11

_____

Luke 22:42 and Acts 21:14

_____

Luke 23:5 and Acts 21:28

_____

Luke 23:18 and Acts 21:36

_____

Luke 23:22 and Acts 22:24

_____

Luke 22:66 and Acts 22:30

_____

Show the ways in which Paul used his birthright(s) and training at these critical points:
21:37–40

_____
21:40—22:2

_____
22:25–29

_____
23:6–9

_____

18. Paul imprisoned in Caesarea.
Why does Claudius Lysias send Paul to Felix? See 23:26–27.

_____

Why does Felix keep Paul in prison (24:24–27)?

_____

Paul's long defense before Festus and Agrippa ends with 26:24–32. What ironies do you find in this passage?

_____

19. The voyage to Rome (A.D. 59–60).
Read 27:9—28:10. If you were with Paul on this trip, what episode would have frightened you most?

_____

What episode would have encouraged you most?

_____

20. Conclusion of Acts: Paul in Rome.
Why does Paul tell the Roman Jews that he is bound with a chain (28:20)?

_____

What is the "hope of Israel," according to Acts 23:6, 24:15, and 26:6–8?

_____

What is Paul's situation at the close of Acts, according to 28:16 and 28:30–31?

_____

Given the fact that Paul was martyred in Rome, why do you think Luke ends this history on an upbeat note?

Discussion Questions: Acts

1. Discuss the ways in which Paul was uniquely qualified to be the premier missionary apostle of the early church.

2. What have you learned about conversion experiences from reading Acts? What are some incentives to conversion? some obstacles?

3. Luke's purpose in writing Acts is to narrate the history of the early church. What key factors facilitated the phenomenal growth of Christianity?

4. You are a Hollywood producer preparing for a film based on the book of Acts. You need to send out a memorandum describing your new project. What sort of movie will it be? What are some of the more powerful issues the film will reflect? What feelings will it evoke? What are the central scenes for you? Briefly describe some of these issues, feelings, and scenes as you try to give your people an idea of what your picture wants to do. Also, for the actors and actresses, describe the personalities and roles of some of your major characters. Lastly, give the film a tentative title and wait for the phone to ring.

SCULPTING ACTS 1:6–11

SCENE: So when they had come together, they asked him, "Lord, is this the time when you will restore the kingdom to Israel?" He replied, "It is not for you to know the times or periods that the Father has set by his own authority. But you will receive power when the Holy Spirit has come upon you; and you will be my witnesses in Jerusalem, in all Judea and Samaria, and to the ends of the earth." When he had said this, as they were watching, he was lifted up, and a cloud took him out of their sight. While he was going and they were gazing up toward heaven, suddenly two men in white robes stood by them. They said, "Men of Galilee, why do you stand looking up toward heaven? This Jesus, who has been taken up from you into heaven, will come in the same way as you saw him go into heaven."

CHARACTERS: Two (or more) disciples who are looking at each other in amazement
Two (or more) disciples who are filled with joy at what they are witnessing
Two (or more) disciples who are sad to see Jesus go; they would like to keep him from going
Two angels announcing that Jesus will return

FREEZE SCENE: "Men of Galilee, why do you stand looking up toward heaven?"

INSTRUCTIONS:
1. Group members each pick a character. As a narrator reads the passage above, members act out their roles. At the freeze scene, all the characters stop.
2. Stay frozen for one minute.
3. At a signal, everyone speaks a sentence that he or she has decided on, three times, all at once.
4. Each character says his or her sentence, one at a time, so all can hear.
5. Refreeze to reflect.
6. Debrief: What happened? What thoughts and feelings came up? Each person speaks.

CHAPTER 5

The Gospel of John and the Letters of John

INTRODUCTION TO THE GOSPEL OF JOHN

Entering the world of John's Gospel is disconcerting at first. The exuberant, hurried pace of the Synoptic Gospels (Matthew, Mark, Luke) slows to a stately promenade. Jesus the teacher/rabbi becomes Christ the philosopher-king. The pithy language of parable is replaced by the symbolic and often convoluted language of theological discourse. There is no messianic secret for John; from the very beginning Jesus is the Man from heaven who knows exactly what his business is, and makes it known to all who will hear.

The author of the Gospel assumes the readers' knowledge of the historical facts. While chronology (the life of Jesus) is a framework for the Gospel, history is not the focus. Instead we see the amplification of themes and ideas that are merely hinted at in the Synoptic Gospels. The author gives us the innermost thoughts of Jesus, the interpretation and meaning of who he is. For these reasons, the Gospel is dated late, c. 100, a generation after the Gospel of Mark. The author has reflected on the revelation found in Christ, and he writes (20:11) "that you might believe." Theology (talk about God) and Christology (talk about Christ) are his most prominent concerns. So masterfully are these concerns addressed (indeed, it is difficult to know where Jesus' words about himself end and John's words begin), it appears that the author was a hellenized Jew, well educated and cosmopolitan in outlook.

This brings us to the issue of authorship. One would not expect John Bar-Zebedee, a Galilean fisherman and one of the original twelve apostles, to pen the most abstract and theological of gospels. Acts 4:13 calls John illiterate and ignorant. Yet we have seen tremendous changes in character occur in the early church: Peter moves from weakly denying Jesus to forcefully proclaiming him, Paul changes from the hater of Christians to the premier missionary of the early church. It is possible that the unschooled Galilean fisherman, called the "beloved disciple" in this Gospel, became a literary master late in life. As early as A.D. 185, Irenaeus identified the "beloved disciple" as John Bar-Zebedee and attributed this Gospel to him.

Our concern with authorship appears misplaced, or at least irrelevant to our study of the Gospel, when we reflect on the conception of ownership and authorship in the ancient world. The readers of Hebrew scriptures, for instance, would understand that the author (whose ideas are expressed in the work) is not the same as the writer—the one who actually pens the words. Perhaps John son of Zebedee is the "author," supplemented by a later writer or writers. As the Gospel concludes, "*We* know that his testimony is true" (21:24, emphasis added).

Whatever its origin, the Johannine world is Hellenic (Ephesus in Asia Minor, perhaps), rather than Hebraic. The Greek titles for Jesus vibrate with meaning and with an openness to a variety of interpretations. John asks to be read on many levels, as we can see by looking at a sample of Greek terms found in this Gospel.

"In the beginning was the word" (John 1:1). Greek readers would agree. This word, or *logos*, was a philosophical term as old as Heraclitus (sixth century B.C.), who said "all things happen through this *logos*." It was the rational principle of the universe, according to the Stoics. Stoics used Logos to account for the order, wisdom, and harmony by which all things are steered. The Logos was not, could not be, personal for the Greek; it was Reason itself. The mystery religions of the Hellenistic world understood the Logos in a slightly different sense: it was the power that enabled the believer to know God and themselves. Not simply knowledge, the Logos was the bearer and bringer of knowledge. By the time of Philo in Alexandria (around the time of Jesus' ministry in Palestine), the *logos* was identified with the creative word of God (Genesis 1: "And God said, 'Let there be . . . '"). God's word brings about the created order. For hellenized Jews, the Greek *logos* was associated with the Hebrew word "wisdom." The Wisdom figure in Proverbs 8:22–30 rejoices with God in the creation of the world, working alongside God in marking out the foundations of the earth. To summarize, we have these possibilities for *logos*:

1. For Stoics, the rational principle ordering the universe
2. For mystery religions, the power that helps us know ourselves
3. For Jews, the creative word of God

All would agree that in the beginning was the *logos*, and the *logos* was with God, and the *logos* was God.

However, none of these would allow for what John goes on to say in 1:14: "The [*Logos*] became flesh [*sarx*] and dwelt among us." For the Logos to be divine and transcendent was acceptable. Unacceptable (to the Greek mind) was the intermingling of the divine and the earthly, fleshly, evil existence, which the Greek mind wished to be rid of!

What John's prologue does, then, is take a *principle* and embody it in flesh and blood. Better, what John does is take an axiom and give it a name: Jesus Christ. Put in chronological terms, the Logos extends backward in time ("In the beginning," of 1:1; "Before Abraham was, I am," of 8:58) and forward into the future, when the Man from heaven returns to the Father. The time of the fleshly, human Jesus is but a tiny part of the entire time of Christ, the Word of God. What we must understand is the newness of this teaching for the Greek mind, which would be shocked to think that God could or would become human. Whether the prologue was read through the eyes of a Greek or a Jew, Logos as a title for Christ was rich in connotations.

The prologue affirms that all who believe in his name are given power to become children of God (1:10). Here a second word study is in order: *pisteuo*, to believe. The Gospel is littered with this very active verb, while its counterpart *pistis*, or the noun "belief," "faith," is absent. John does not write about *having* faith but about the *act* of faith. One may show faith by simply accepting a set of doctrines or theories. But "to believe" is more active in its connotations. It implies a relationship, entering into a system of trust and reliance. It is not merely spoken assent to propositional statements. Faith is a verb.

For John's Gospel, more than any other, word studies and thematic studies are a must. Use a good concordance to see how words such as *judgment, life, light, truth,* and *love* are used in the Gospel. Resist flat or obvious interpretations as you try instead to expand the range of possible meanings for John's vocabulary. Use schemes and diagrams to show the relationships between love, knowing, and obeying in John (after looking these words up in your concordance). Use another chart to show the antonym pairs found in John, for example, death/life, darkness/light, truth/lies, above/below. Finally, look for the relationships between the Father, the Son, and the Holy Spirit as they are developed by John. You will see that by reading this "spiritual gospel" (as Clement of Alexandria called it), you will find yourself actually thinking in a new and more spiritual way.

The study-guide questions will ask you to look at theological themes rather than chronological flow, so be prepared to skip back and forth through the Gospel!

STUDY GUIDE FOR THE GOSPEL OF JOHN

Outline of the Gospel of John

I. The Book of Mighty Works: chapters 1—12
   A. Prologue (1:1–18)
   B. Preparation (1:19–51)
   C. Early ministry (chaps. 2—6)
   D. Growing conflict with unbelievers (chaps. 7—12)
II. The Book of Glory: chapters 13—21
   A. Teaching believers (chaps.13—17)
   B. Passion and death (chaps. 18; 19)
   C. Resurrection (chap. 20)
   D. Appendix (chap. 21)

1. "Signs" in the Gospel. John chose to record seven of the many signs Jesus did because he saw a link between these signs and belief in Jesus as the Son of God (John 20:30–31). Like miracles, signs show Jesus' power over natural laws, sickness, even death. But John, lover of symbolism, treats these signs as symbols of Jesus' teaching, fusing synoptic "parables" and "miracles" into richly loaded events. A sign points beyond itself to a heavenly truth about Jesus. Read each of the sign stories carefully, filling in the chart "Signs in John's Gospel," figure 5.1, as you go.

Passage in John's Gospel	Title	Setting; Audience	What the Sign Says About Jesus	Area of Power	Result
2:1–11	Changing Water Into Wine			Quality	
4:46–54	Healing Noble-man's Son			Space	
5:1–15	Healing Lame Man			Time	
6:1–14	Feeding Five Thousand			Quantity	
6:16–21	Walking on Water			Natural Law	
chap. 9	Healing Blind Man			Misfortune	
11:1–46	Raising Lazarus			Death	

Fig. 5.1 Signs in John's Gospel

2. The "I ams" of the Gospel. The seven signs are complemented by seven discourses, conveniently called the "I ams," through which Jesus develops teaching on his identity. These seven images are Christological in nature, that is, they are keys to understanding the nature of Christ and his work in the world. Again, fill in the chart "'I Am' Discourses in John's Gospel," figure 5.2, as you read.

Passage	"I Am"	Setting & Audience	Your Understanding of the Teaching
6:25–59	(6:35, 48, 51)	(6:25–34, 59)	
chap. 9	(8:12; 9:5)	(9:1–5, 35–39)	
10:7–10	(10:7)	(10:19–31)	
10:1–6, 11–30	(10:11, 14)	(10:19–31)	
11:1–44	(11:25)	(11:1–6, 45–46)	
14:1–7	(14:6)	Farewell discourse; disciples	
15:1–11	(15:1)	Farewell discourse: disciples	

Fig. 5.2 "I Am" Discourses in John's Gospel

3. Judgment in the Gospel. As you might expect by now, John uses key words on a variety of levels. The term "judgment" and Jesus' role as judge carry two different sets of meanings. Read John 3:17 and 12:47, then summarize the verses here:

_____

_____

Now read John 9:39 and 5:22, summarizing here:

_____

_____

How do you reconcile these teachings? The Greek word *krisis* means both "judgment" and "decision" (reflecting the fact that a moment of crisis almost always involves a decision). The *judgment* is the fact that Jesus has come and we must make a *decision* concerning him. It is Jesus' audience who must make a judgment, or a decision. Jesus is the opportunity for us to make a determination; the judgment is the fact that Jesus has come. In him the decision rests; because of him a decision must be made. And what does Jesus say about our judgment of others? Go to John 8:1–11 and write what you find here:

_____

_____

4. Eternal life in the Gospel. Eternal life is promised to those who believe. Again we look at two groups of teachings, this time with regard to "eternal life." Read 6:40, 44, 54; 12:25, 48; and 5:28–29. What do these verses say about eternal life?

_____

_____

On the time line that follows, mark where you would place the judgment regarding eternal life after reading these verses.

PAST   PRESENT   FUTURE

←———————————————————————————→

Now see 3:36; 5:21–24; 11:25–26; 17:1–3. What tense is used for the verbs in these verses: present or future?

_____

What do the verses say about eternal life?

_____

_____

When does eternal life actually begin? Mark it on this timeline.

PAST   PRESENT   FUTURE

←———————————————————————————→

Finally, is eternal life a matter of *quantity* (of time) or *quality* (of life)? Explain your answer.

_____

_____

5. The Holy Spirit in the Gospel. John uses the word *paraklete* to refer to the Holy Spirit. The roots are *para* (Greek for "alongside of") and *kaleo* ("I call forth, bid"). The Paraclete is thus the Spirit, which is called forth to stand alongside of us. English Bibles use a variety of translations for *paraklete*: Comforter, Advocate, Helper. See 15:26. What is the Paraclete's origin?

_____

See 20:22, after noting the context of this verse in chapter 20. Also remember that "Spirit" (*pneuma* in Greek, *ruach* in Hebrew) may also be translated "breath," as in Genesis 2:7. At what point did the believers first receive the Paraclete?

_____

Read the verses that appear in the chart "The Work of the Paraclete," figure 5.3, and fill in the chart as you go. Make note (*) of the verses on the chart that describe the Paraclete in the same terms as Jesus. Note that the Paraclete functions exactly as Jesus did. Why then does Jesus say it is best that he go away (16:7)?

Passage	Function/Characteristic of the Paraclete
14:15–17	
14:25–26	
15:26–27	
16:7–11	
16:12–15	

Fig. 5.3 The Work of the Paraclete

THE VINE METAPHOR IN JOHN'S GOSPEL*

In John 15:1–11 Jesus paints a picture of the Christian community with his metaphor of the vine and the branches. The metaphor is quite vivid: Jesus is the vine, those who love Jesus are the branches, and God is the vine grower who tends the vine, pruning and trimming branches so that they bear fruit.

Two aspects of this metaphor are striking. First, the vine metaphor characterizes the Christian community as a community of inter-relationship, mutuality, and indwelling. This mutuality is conveyed by the use of the verb "abide," which occurs ten times in 15:1–11. To "abide" means to remain and suggests constancy of presence. The term "abide" describes Jesus' relationship to God (15:10), Jesus' relationship to the community (15:4, 9), and the community's relationship to Jesus (15:1, 7). In their mutuality, Jesus and God anticipate the possibilities of life for the community.

Individuals in the community will prosper only insofar as they recognize themselves as members of an organic unit. No individual is a free agent, but is one branch of an encircling and intertwining vine whose fruitfulness depends on abiding with Jesus: "Just as the branch cannot bear fruit by itself unless it abides in the vine, neither can you unless you abide in me. I am the vine, you are the branches. Those who abide in me and I in them bear much fruit, because apart from me you can do nothing" (15:4–5).

The life envisioned in this metaphor stands in striking contrast to contemporary Western models of individualism, privatism, and success based on individual accomplishment. This metaphor assumes social interrelationship and accountability. In the vine metaphor, an individual is fruitful only as he or she abides with others in Jesus' love. The mutuality envisioned by the vine metaphor is a sign of the presence and work of God: "As the Father has loved me, so I have loved you; abide in my love" (15:9).

Second, the metaphor of the vine provides a radical nonhierarchical, perhaps even antihierarchical image for the composition and constitution of the church. One branch is indistinguishable from another; no branch has pride of place. All branches are rooted together in the one vine, and only as a result of their common root can they bear fruit. The task of assessing fruitfulness falls to God alone (15:2), not to any of the branches. As the vine grower, God works to prune and shape the vine so that it produces the maximum fruit. God decides what is dead wood and determines where and when to prune back a dead stick to find green wood and the promise of new life. Since God and God alone is the vine grower, all branches are equal before God. The future of the vine, of the church, is entrusted to God, not to any of the branches. There is no bishop branch, elder branch, or church bureaucrat branch with special status in this vine. One cannot distinguish between clergy and laity in this vine.

Jesus is the vine of the church, out of, into, and around which all the branches grow. The vine metaphor is a powerful image of the church: the center vine out of which the branches grow is identifiable, but the mass of intertwining branches is indistinguishable. One cannot tell which branch sprouted first, which branch is longest, where one branch stops and another branch begins. Hierarchy among members is impossible in the vine of the church, because all members grow out of the same vine and are tended equally by the one vine grower.

STUDY GUIDE FOR COMPARING JOHN AND THE SYNOPTIC GOSPELS

You might already be familiar with this analogy. The Synoptic Gospels are to John as the front page of the newspaper is to the editorial page. Matthew, Mark, and Luke tell us what happened; John tells us what it all means.

Put differently, the Synoptics read like a detective story that abounds with problem situations, clues, and deftly drawn supporting characters. The identity of the hero—the whodunit—the solution to the mystery—is saved for last. The Fourth Gospel reads, instead, like an autobiography. The subject knows who he is and meditates—through long discourses—on the meaning of his life. There are no secrets or mysteries; instead we have the hero's journal entries woven into the framework of life events.

In comparing John to the Synoptic Gospels, we will look for John's special emphases in handling common material, and also examine material that is unique to

*This excerpt is reprinted from "John," by Gail R. O'Day, in *The Women's Bible Commentary*, ed. Carol A. Newsom and Sharon H. Ringe (Westminster/John Knox Press, 1992), 303.

John. Finally we ask: If John were dropped from the New Testament canon, what would we lose? What perspectives does John provide us on the ministry of Jesus, on the life of Christ?

1. Cleansing the Temple. See John 2:14–22. This event takes place at the *end* of Jesus' public ministry in the Synoptics (see Mark 11:15–17). Why do you think John places it at the *beginning* of Jesus' public ministry?

_____

_____

What does Jesus call God in 2:16?_____

2. Nicodemus. See John 3:1–21. This episode is unique to John. Who is Nicodemus?

_____

What teachings of Jesus does he find difficult to understand?

_____

_____

What terms with double meanings does Jesus use?

_____

Martin Luther called John 3:16 "the Gospel in miniature." Write out this verse and memorize it:

_____

_____

3. The woman at the well. Read John 4:4–42, another episode unique to John. In what ways is this conversation similar to the one with Nicodemus?

_____

_____

How is it different?

_____

What is the result of their conversation?

_____

4. The temptations in the wilderness, dramatized in Matthew 4:1–11 and Luke 4:1–13, are presented as part of Jesus' public ministry in John. Compare the wilderness drama with these verses:

Synoptics	*John's Gospel*
Satan offers the kingdoms of the world	6:15
Satan says turn stones to bread	6:30–31
Satan says display your power	7:3–4

5. The Synoptics record the first Eucharist, or Communion, at the time of the Last Supper in Jerusalem. John does not mention the sharing of bread and wine with the disciples. Instead, Jesus teaches on the *significance* of bread and wine (the body and blood) in John 6:51–58. What is the significance?

_____

6. The Last Supper in John's Gospel is unique in that it shows Jesus performing a simple, dramatic act. Read John 13:1–20. What does Jesus do here, and why does he do it?

_____

7. In the Fourth Gospel, Jesus' last words on the cross are again unique. Read John 19:25–30. What are these words?

_____

_____

_____

Compare Mark 15:33–37 with the last moments on the cross in John. The suffering and graphic details of the crucifixion found in the Synoptics are replaced by a triumphant death in John. The way to the cross is no *via dolorosa* (trail of tears), but a triumphant processional. To be put on the cross is to be exalted, lifted up. What is the effect of this exaltation (see John 12:32–33)?

_____

8. John's chronology places the crucifixion on the Day of Preparation, the evening before Passover. Read Exodus 12:1–7, 12–13, 46. What steps were taken in preparing the lamb for Passover?

_____

John includes an account of the soldier piercing Jesus' side with his spear. Read John 19:31–37. How does John show Jesus to be the Passover lamb?

_____

How does this account relate to what Jesus said earlier in John 4:10 and 7:37–38?

_____

9. Resurrection appearances. Again, John includes material not found in the Synoptic traditions. Read John 20:11–18, the great recognition scene. To whom does Mary Magdalene suppose she is talking in v. 15?

_____

What causes her to recognize Jesus?

_____

How does her declaration in 20:18 compare to her first report in 20:2?

Read John 20:19–29. In what sense is Jesus like a ghostly apparition in verses 19 and 26?

In what ways did he show his realness in verses 20, 22, 27?

Although John does not record the Sermon on the Mount, he does give us the "last beatitude" of the Gospels in 20:29. What is it?

10. The appendix to John. Read chapter 21. Mark's Gospel ends abruptly with the women fleeing the empty tomb in fear. Luke's Easter appearances all occur in or near Jerusalem. Matthew, after telling of Jesus' appearance to the women, records the revelation of Jesus to the disciples in Galilee. John completes the resurrection stories with this account at the Sea of Galilee.

How does this account in John compare with Luke 5:1–11 in terms of:
the catch of fish?

Peter's response?

Jesus' teaching?

How does Jesus' breakfast preparation relate to what he did for the disciples at the Last Supper (John 13:3–16)?

Jesus asks Peter three times, "Do you love me?" Remember that Peter had denied his discipleship three times in John 18:17, 25–27. Peter could not appeal to his faithfulness as evidence of his love. To what does Peter appeal instead (21:17)?

According to tradition, Peter was crucified upside down in Rome under Nero (c. A.D. 64–68). What allusion do you find to Peter's martyrdom in 21:18–19?

Discussion Questions: The Gospel of John

1. If John were dropped from your New Testament, what pictures of Jesus would you miss? What teachings?
2. Does John succeed in his intent, to write these things "that you might believe" (20:31)? What do you believe? What captured your attention in reading this Gospel?

INTRODUCTION TO THE JOHANNINE LETTERS

What happens when a good thing is taken too far? when certain features of a rich teaching are emphasized at the expense of others? The letters of John address problems that arose in the churches due to radical, extreme emphasis on certain doctrines implicit in the Gospel of John. Here is the origin of this problem:

1. The Gospel portrait of Jesus is one of unique, solitary grandeur. Jesus is the man who was more than human, the stranger par excellence. The intentional answer to the question, Who is Jesus? is always the Son *of God*, the Man *from heaven.*

2. In Jesus' prayer of John 17 and elsewhere in the Gospel, he stresses the importance of the disciples' *knowledge.* "They *know* that everything you have given me is from you . . . and *know* in truth that I came from you" (17:7–8, emphasis added); "Righteous Father, the

world does not *know* you, but I *know* you, and these *know* that you have sent me. I made your name *known* to them" (17:25–26, emphasis added). Although John goes on to establish the link between knowledge and belief, at first glance it appears that *knowing* (using the intellect) is the key to salvation. "You will know the truth, and the truth will set you free" (8:32).

"Docetism," from the Greek *dokeo,* "to seem," was (and still is!) a radicalized, faulty teaching on the nature of Christ. Docetism said that Jesus only *seemed* to be human; he appeared to be like one of us, but in reality he was not. This teaching comes from an extreme rendering of the portrait of Jesus outlined in point 1 above. Docetic Christians believed Jesus to be the Son of God, but he did not really become flesh (but see John 1:14), did not really suffer a human death, did not really experience the human condition (but see John 11:35: "Jesus wept"). Docetic tendencies had arisen in the church as early as A.D. 100. The Johannine letters tackle this tendency head-on.

"Gnosticism," from the Greek *gnosis*, or knowledge, encompasses a variety of philosophical teachings prevalent in the Greco-Roman world at the time of Christ. Put simply, Gnosticism insisted that a special, secret knowledge was necessary to salvation. For the "Christian Gnostics" addressed in the letters, the line was firmly drawn between those "in the know" and those ignorant of the true (and secret) intellectual system. Again, an extreme rendering of John's Gospel, sketched in point 2 above, supports the Gnostic claim to intellectual, and spiritual, superiority. For Gnostics, *knowledge about* Jesus took the place of *believing in* Jesus (but see John 1:12: "To all who received him, who *believed* in his name, he gave power to become children of God," emphasis added). Furthermore, Gnostic doctrine was inherently elitist and cliquish. Gnostic tendencies are separatist (thus they are as timeless as humanity and will exist as long as human beings live and breathe). Those in the know felt they should separate themselves from the ignorant and unsaved. Those in the know were without sin, whereas those outside their group were sinners. Again, the Johannine letters tackle this problem head-on. The church is not defined by intellectual superiority, but by love. This ethical attitude, while certainly found in John's Gospel, is emphatic in the letters.

The letters of 1, 2, and 3 John were probably grouped together in a packet. First John is addressed to a group of churches who already knew John's Gospel, and it is the most important theologically. Second John is addressed to one church: "the elect lady," and warns against false (Docetic) teachers. Third John is written to an individual, "the beloved Gaius," and includes a recommendation of one "Demetrius," perhaps the bearer of the letters. The letters are dated c. 100, and after the Gospel. The study guide that follows will deal only with First John.

STUDY GUIDE FOR THE FIRST LETTER OF JOHN

1. A shift occurred between the time of John's Gospel and the letters of John. Although the Gospel and the letters came from the same pen or school, they reflect different circumstances. What problems are the churches encountering now?
2:18–20

_____

2:26

_____

4:1–5

_____

_____

2. The shift was caused by theological and ethical differences. What do the false teachers say about Jesus?
2:22

_____

4:2–3

_____

_____

What do these false teachers do contrary to Christian ethics?
2:4 _____

2:9 _____

4:20 _____

3. The response to false teaching: the great commandment.

What is the commandment that the writer insists be obeyed? (See 3:11, 23; 4:21.)

_____

_____

Why does the writer insist on obedience to this commandment? (See 2:3–6.)

_____

Then see 4:11–12 and summarize here:

_____

_____

4. The response to false teaching: the realness of Jesus' death on the cross. Read 1 John 3:16; 4:2; 4:10; 5:6. What does the writer say to counter Docetic teachings about Christ?

_____

_____

5. The response to false teaching: creedal confession. Read 1 John 1:1–10. Give verse numbers that correspond to the key elements of this creed.

A. Faith is rooted in history; these roots are visible, tangible, real. Verses _____

B. Jesus is the Son of God. Verses _____

C. Not one of us is without sin. Verses _____

D. But Jesus provides us with forgiveness and the means of atonement. Verses_____

E. Finally, this creed is confirmed by the *community*. Verses _____

6. Gnostics claimed a special salvation through knowledge, either of secret lore, or by intellectual mastery of a philosophical system. In contrast, 1 John speaks of what we (the Christian community) know and how we know it. Summarize this knowledge and its verification in

3:14

_____

3:24

_____

4:13

_____

Discussion Questions: The First Letter of John

The letters show us a refinement of teaching necessary when certain features of John's Gospel are taken too far. The result is a creative one. What beliefs needed correction? What strong points in the letter do you think would touch the hearts of its original audience? What strong points touched you?

CHAPTER 6

Paul

INTRODUCTION TO PAUL: PROJECTS

There is no substitute for interactive, "hands on" learning as a way of introducing Paul to the modern reader. Each of the following projects may be worked by a small group (four to six participants) or as an individual assignment.

I. Introduction to Paul: Worksheet on His Career as an Apostle

Using your Bible, read and summarize the verses in the spaces provided. Keep in mind that the citations from Acts are written by Luke; all other citations come from Paul's letters.

A. *Saul Before His Conversion to Christianity*
1. Galatians 1:13–14, 22–23

_____

2. Philippians 3:5–6

_____

3. 1 Corinthians 15:9

_____

4. Acts 7:59—8:3

_____

5. Acts 21:39; 22:3–5

_____

B. *Paul's Conversion*
1. 1 Corinthians 9:1; 15:3–8

_____

2. Galatians 1:15–17

_____

3. Acts 9:1–26

_____

_____

4. Acts 26:12–18

_____

C. *Paul's Mission as Apostle to the Gentiles*
1. Galatians 1:18—2:21

_____

2. Romans 1:14–15

_____

3. Romans 15:14–21

_____

4. Acts 13:46–47; 14:27

_____

D. *Persecution of Paul*
While Luke records many accounts of Paul's hardships in Acts, Paul gives his own description in 2 Corinthians 11:22–33. List here his "catalog" of hardships after reading this passage.

_____

_____

_____

II. Missionary Journeys
You will find plenty of maps, both in this chapter and in the back of your Bible, to help you see the extent of Paul's missionary work in the Mediterranean world. (See Fig. 6.1, "The World of Paul," and Figs. 6.2 and 6.3, showing the church before and after Paul's missionary activities.) However, making your own map is the best way to assimilate place names and geography. Using a poster board and markers, sketch a schematic outline of the Mediterranean basin. Your sketch may be

angular and geometric, or it might be curved and rounded. In either case, forget about the details of coastlines and political boundaries. Next, use a "proper," detailed map and locate the following place names. Label them on your schematic map:

Tarsus. Paul's hometown and capital of the Roman province of Cilicia in Asia Minor. Tarsus was a university town and trading center, attracting scholarship and commerce from all over the East. Ships sailed up the Cydnus River to the city, bearing wheat, wine, and oil. Tarsus was a seat of Stoic philosophy.

Syrian Antioch. The Roman capital of Syria, this great city sprawled along the Orontes River near the Mediterranean Sea. Commerce came upstream from the port of Seleucia. Alexander the Great erected an altar to Zeus on this site. Antioch included a large Jewish community, and it served as Paul's home base. It was the first place where Jesus' followers were called Christians.

Jerusalem. Capital of Judea and the heart of Judaism. Jerusalem's gleaming Temple (destroyed by Rome in A.D. 70) stood in stark contrast to the harsh brown Judean hills on which Jerusalem was perched.

Damascus. It was on the road to Damascus, through the desert that separated this city from Jerusalem, that Paul met Christ and became an apostle. Travelers entered the city through an arched gate; the street ran straight to the other end of the city. On each side were merchant stalls selling a variety of goods. It possessed a large Jewish colony with several synagogues.

Cyprus. A large, rectangular island in the Mediterranean, forty miles south of Asia Minor, with two mountain ranges, in the north and south. Paul and Barnabas walked the valley in between from east to west, about 140 miles, starting from the port city of Salamis. The island was famous for copper mines and lumber mills. Paphos at the western end of the island was the capital city.

Perga. From Cyprus, Paul sailed to Pamphylia, a coastal plain in Asia Minor. His boat came upriver from the port of Attalia to Perga, chief town of the region. The town was known for its shrine to the goddess Artemis.

Galatia. This Roman province stretched north and south across the heart of Asia Minor, from Pontus to the Mediterranean. The chief city in the southern section was Pisidian Antioch, a bustling commercial town with a beautiful temple to the local fertility god.

Iconium. This simple mountain town was a garden spot of apricot and plum orchards, flax fields, and sheep pastures. It was located in the high plateau country of Lyconia.

Lystra and *Derbe.* Smaller towns in Lyconia visited by Paul and Barnabas. From Derbe they retraced their steps back to Attalia where they took a ship to their base in Syrian Antioch.

Phrygia. On his second journey, Paul traveled northwest of Pisidia to this rugged hill country, where sheep and horses pastured and where copper, iron, and cinnabar were mined.

Troas. On the northwest tip of Asia Minor, Troas was the major port for commerce with Macedonia across the Aegean Sea, and the logical point of departure for Paul to Europe. Troas had Roman baths, a Greek theater, great temples, and an aqueduct.

Macedonia. This Roman province stretched across the Balkan peninsula north of Greece. Neapolis was the port for ships coming from Troas; it was located on the great Roman highway known as the Egnatian Way that led to the Adriatic Sea.

Philippi. Located on the Egnatian Way, Philippi was colonized with Roman veterans who raised grain crops outside the city. The city prided itself as a "little Rome," with a forum and Roman temples. Here Paul and Silas were thrown into prison. Paul maintained a close relationship with the Philippian church.

Thessalonica. This "free" Roman city, also on the Egnatian Way, was built on steep mountain slopes along the Aegean shore. Wharves received trade from many countries. Here among eager harbor workers Paul founded a church.

Athens. Classical city in the Roman province of Achaia (Greece) and intellectual center of the empire. What Rome was to administration and justice, Athens was to philosophy and the arts. The beautiful city was noted for its superb architecture and statuary. The Areopagus where Paul preached is a hill by the city's shimmering Acropolis, yet another sacred shrine.

Corinth. Commercial center and capital of the province, noted for its temple to Aphrodite. A four-mile-wide isthmus made Corinth accessible to two ports—Cenchreae on the east and Lechaeum on the west. Shops sold textiles and foodstuffs, including meats that had been offered to idols. Streets leading to temples were lined with booths for sacred prostitutes. Corinth was a spectacular city of pleasure.

Ephesus. The large Roman province called "Asia" was the western end of what we now call Asia Minor (Turkey). Its capital and chief seaport was Ephesus. Ships from Corinth arrived daily, and from it great highways branched eastward. The city was dominated by a hillside temple, a shrine to the goddess Artemis. The tourist trade included making and selling images of Artemis in silver, gold, copper, and terra cotta.

Caesarea. After his arrest in Jerusalem, Paul was taken to this city built as the seat of government for Roman officials on the coast of Judea. Paul was imprisoned there for two years. Paul was sent to Rome on a ship that stopped at *Fair Havens,* a small bay on the southern coast of Crete. He was shipwrecked on *Malta,* a rocky island sixty miles south of Sicily. Malta was sparsely settled at the time by a simple, non-Greek-speaking people. *Syracuse* was the most prosperous city on the island of Sicily. *Rhegium* was opposite Sicily in the boot of Italy. The *Appian Way* was the well-paved road to Rome from southern Italy. There were rest stops south of Rome on the Way: the Forum of Appius and Three Taverns.

Rome. All roads led to Rome, the center of imperial government and commerce. Shops, apartments, temples, government buildings, and close quarters characterized this great city. Rome was the last place Paul visited.

III. Letters of Paul: Epistolary Structure

We must keep in mind that, with the exception of the little letter to Philemon, Paul's writings are not private letters written to friends. Paul is not interested in promoting personal or social relations in his letters. Nor are the letters official church announcements for the purpose of conveying information. Furthermore, we read them incorrectly if we suppose the letters to be sermon outlines or theological treatises. Paul's letters are the expression of his unique mission as an apostle. They show us a new way of communicating to new churches, communities that were the first fruits of what Paul hoped would eventually be the spread of the gospel throughout the empire.

Paul is the author of his letters in the sense that they were composed under his direction. But it is likely that the letters were group efforts, in that he did not write in his name alone. Either Timothy, Silas, or Sosthenes is mentioned as a coauthor in seven letters. Furthermore, Paul used scribes to whom he dictated his words, as writing on papyrus was awkward and tedious. We might imagine Paul working out the content of the letters in a room with a secretary (amanuensis) and his coworkers in a communal effort. The wide variety of styles found in the letters supports this picture.

The letters have a simple structure that follows the format of Hellenistic epistles. Read the following blueprint. Then use the epistolary structure to compose your own letter. Decide who your audience is, what problems its members are experiencing, and what advice you wish to give. Be specific!

1. The *greeting*. Here is where we learn who the author is and who the audience is. Included are some of the characteristics of the audience—how the author sees them, what kind of people they are. For examples of Pauline greetings, see Romans 1:1–6; Galatians 1:1–2.

2. The *prayer*. Here Paul expresses thanks to God for the things God has done on behalf of the audience and introduces themes found later in the body of the letter. For examples, see 1 Corinthians 1:4–9; 2 Corinthians 1:3–7.

3. The *body* of the letter. Here is the real heart of the matter. The author gives the reasons for writing, the problems reported to the author about the audience, the things the author wants them to know, and the things they should be doing. Paul addresses specific situations in the community and develops his arguments.

4. The *final greetings*. Here the author names certain individuals in the audience, gives final exhortations and advice, and makes plans for the future, including visits. For an example, see Romans 16:1–23.

5. The *farewell*. Here the author gives a final prayer on their behalf, wishing grace from God on the readers, and says goodbye. For examples, see the closing verses of any of the letters.

NEW TESTAMENT ETHICS ACCORDING TO PAUL*

Much of what the average person knows about the New Testament is related to ethics and morality. When he or she thinks about Jesus, it is often in terms of what Jesus taught about "loving your enemies" or "turning the other cheek." Persons may remember Jesus' words about divorce or about committing adultery "in one's heart." Often, the ethics of the apostle Paul come to mind: Paul's views on the "place" of women, his description of love in 1 Corinthians 13, his teachings on immorality. Because of the important place Paul's writings hold in the New Testament and the influence of his views on Christians today, we need to examine the broad outlines of Pauline ethics.

Citizenship in Two Worlds

In order to appreciate what Paul has to say about ethics, one must understand the way he described the experience of faith in Jesus.

We think of our lives as having a past, a present, and a future. Paul did too, but each of these time periods was affected by the way in which God had intervened and was intervening in the life of the Christian. The past

*The author wishes to thank the Rev. Dr. Leslie Weber, chaplain of the Lovett School in Atlanta, Georgia, for permission to use his discussion of New Testament ethics according to Paul, which follows.

was not simply yesterday or the day before; it was when those now Christian were "weak" or "sinners" or God's "enemies." It was in this past that God's grace had broken through and replaced sin with faith, replaced being an enemy of God with being at peace with God.

Paul uses the language of the Jewish Pharisees to talk about what God has done. He calls this being "justified." God, the almighty Judge, acquits those who are sinners. The basis on which God justifies sinners is their faith in the grace of God shown in Christ. It is not the person's deeds or efforts that make that person "righteous" (another important word for Paul) or "okay" in God's sight. It is what Christ did—and people's trust in what Christ did—that makes them righteous before God.

Christ's death and resurrection, therefore, was the hinge on which the life of the individual rested and opened. A marvelous thing had occurred in the life of the believer: "We know that our old self was crucified with him so that the body of sin might be destroyed, and we might no longer be enslaved to sin" (Rom. 6:6). Christ's death and resurrection had changed the life of the believer so that the past was passed. The present life is very different from the past life. How so?

Living in faith is different from living without faith. Living in faith is a sign of the "new creation" brought into being by God alone. The relationship God intended at the beginning of the world is being restored. When Christ returns, this newness will be shared with the rest of creation (Rom. 8:21).

On the one hand, Paul thought that sin continues to annoy the believer and seeks to gain a hold on the believer's life. It searches for a "base of operations" from which to regain control. On the other hand, however, what the future holds has already begun to happen in the present.

What does the future hold? In the future, believers will arrive at "maturity" or "perfection." Sometimes they may seem like babies in terms of their faith and life, as were some of the first Christians (1 Cor. 3:1–2). Another way of describing what the future holds is to use the word "salvation." Believers are being saved. Salvation is the goal toward which believers live out their lives (Phil. 2:12–13).

For Paul, the Holy Spirit connects believers between the present and the future. God gives the Holy Spirit to people, and this Spirit works faith in their hearts and works other signs of God's presence in their lives (Rom. 12:6–8). This is God's assurance that God has more to give in the future—the Holy Spirit is the down payment on more to come (2 Cor. 1:22).

Christians, then, live in two worlds at the same time. They no longer live in the past, the time of opposition to God. They live in the present, where sin still annoys them but where they are "made righteous" in God's sight because they live "in Christ" by faith. In their present relationship with God they begin to taste what God's future will be like. The fullness of the future awaits Christ's return.

Human Nature

To appreciate the change that Jesus' death and resurrection had brought about, let's look for a moment at the matter of human nature. What were believers like in the past? What are they like in the present? What are all human beings like? We may speak of humans as "sinners," but what exactly does this mean?

In the first century, slavery was a common practice. It was not necessarily a result of racism; victory in war assured that your enemies would become your slaves. However, if a slave's owner was a person of importance, that slave might have a fair amount of power that many free persons might not have.

For Paul, all humans are slaves to a power that is outside themselves but that is at work in them. Their thoughts, words, and deeds serve an alien master. They depend on this false "master." They trust in this "master" for deliverance. Who or what is this "master"? It is their own will, their own desires. This is what it means to be sinful.

Such a state of being places one at odds with God; it makes a person God's enemy. Actions, words, or thoughts that are hurtful, selfish, or destructive—whether to others or to one's self—are only "symptoms" of the deeper problem that affects people's lives. Such symptoms point to a deadly sickness incurable by people, but curable by God.

The "cure" for Paul has to be more radical than simply dealing with the symptoms. It is not a matter of thinking good thoughts, saying nice things, doing good deeds. The "cure" must get to the heart of the problem—it must deal with the power that makes slaves of people. This cure has occurred in Christ's death and resurrection. In the Christ event, the stranglehold of sin has been broken and people are set free from their slavery to sin.

But true freedom does not mean doing whatever one pleases, willing whatever one desires. That kind of "freedom" is sin. Instead, real freedom for Paul is being a "slave" of Christ. What this means is depending on Christ, trusting Christ, and serving Christ with one's life. Because of who Christ is, the servant of Christ has powers and freedom that the servant of sin only thinks he or she has. The slave of the power of sin has a false sense of his or her power. The choice is, then, between being a slave to sin or a slave to Christ.

Faith Active in Love

Paul speaks about faith in two ways. First, faith is a *right relationship* with God. This kind of faith is true for all believers in Christ.

Second, Paul speaks about faith as a *gift in a certain measure* (Rom. 12:3). Faith may vary in degree. Faith may be weak or strong; it is capable of growing to maturity. Thus, some believers are more advanced than others in their growth in faith, since people are at different stages in their faith journeys. Faith should become stronger as time goes by (Phil. 1:25; 2 Cor. 13:9).

Faith expresses itself in love (Gal. 5:6). There is no list of loving actions. The ultimate test of any act is whether it shows love or builds up others (1 Cor. 8:1). Love involves carefully considering the well-being of others. As such, love set limits on a person's "rights" because, as Paul says, "the love of Christ urges us on" (2 Cor. 5:14).

Doing God's Will

An alternative way of describing the moral responsibility of the Christian is "doing God's will." Paul speaks of this in the same way that he speaks about love. He doesn't give a list of things one must do. Instead, with a mind renewed in Christ, believers understand God's will as they respond to the challenges of their everyday lives: "Do not be conformed to this world, but be transformed by the renewing of your minds, so that you may discern what is the will of God—what is good and acceptable and perfect" (Rom. 12:2).

Though Paul doesn't set forth a list of things believers must do, he does give the boundaries of accepted behavior. There are certain vices. In 1 Cor. 6:9–10, the vices listed are as follows: "Do you not know that wrongdoers will not inherit the kingdom of God? Do not be deceived! Fornicators, idolaters, adulterers, male prostitutes, sodomites, thieves, the greedy, drunkards, revilers, robbers—none of these will inherit the kingdom of God."

Within these farthest boundaries, the individual Christian has some additional help in knowing what *not* to do. One's conscience and one's doubts and misgivings set forth "fences" for the individual, which he or she should not go beyond. When one receives a warning signal from one's conscience or from one's misgivings, one should refrain from a certain action. As one's faith grows, one's doubts about right and wrong decrease and the range of possible action increases.

Motivation

What motivates a Christian to do what is to be done? Doing nothing is not an option for Paul. One is not to be motivated by guilt or a desire to make up to God. One does not do right as a way of winning future reward. Nor does one do right to win respect, honor, or admiration from others.

There are two reasons for doing what is to be done. First, there is gratitude for God's deliverance in Christ from the power of sin. Second, as God's stewards, persons will be granted the fullness of glory on the day of judgment. Judgment is not something they fear; it is feared only by those who are slaves to sin. In either case, believers do what is to be done because first and foremost God is at work in them (1 Cor. 15:10).

THE WORLD OF PAUL*

As we begin the study of the letters of Paul, it is helpful to consider the world in which Paul lived. This world, however, was not a simple one; for Paul moved in several circles that defined various worlds. First of all, he was a Jew—as he declared, "a Pharisee of Pharisees"—and therefore his was a Jewish world. But his letters were written in Greek, to a Greek-speaking church, indicating that his was also a Greek world. In addition, Paul was a Roman citizen, and therefore his world was also a Roman world. But above all he was a Christian, and as such all his worlds—Jewish, Greek, and Roman—

*The material in the section "The World of Paul" is excerpted from "The World of Paul," by Justo L. González and Catherine G. González, in *Adult Bible Studies Teaching Helps*, September–November 1984. Copyright 1984, Graded Press. Scripture quotations have been changed to New Revised Standard Version.

were seen and reinterpreted under the overarching Christian vision.

Paul's Jewish World

The earliest church, in Jerusalem, was clearly all Jewish. The original leadership was from the rural provinces, not from Jerusalem. Even within this all-Jewish church we find evidence of conflict between Aramaic-speaking Jewish Christians who were from the provinces and Greek-speaking Jewish Christians who were most likely Jews living only temporarily in Jerusalem who became Christians. These two groups of Christians are often referred to as "the Hebrews" and "the Hellenists" (Acts 6:1).

Many Pharisees in Palestine, including Paul, were quite concerned about this new Jewish sect of the

Christians, most especially about the Hellenist Jewish Christians. Exactly what their concern was is not clear, though it may have been that they feared Rome would be upset at the claims of this group and make life more difficult for all Jews. Perhaps some of these Hellenist Jewish Christians were less concerned about the Law because of their Christianity. For whatever reason, the first persecution of the church was really from within Judaism. Jews who were not Christians were persecuting Jews who were Christians. The first attack was against the leadership of the Hellenist Jewish Christians, in the person of Stephen. Paul was present at the stoning of this first Christian martyr.

Although currently living in Jerusalem, Paul was a part of what is called "Diaspora Judaism." That is to say, he was one of a group of Jews who did not normally live in Palestine. Diaspora Judaism was strong and well-established in the eastern and western cities of the Roman Empire. Jewish families had roots in these cities, and though they felt great attachment to Jerusalem and the land of Palestine and would visit the Temple for some of the great festivals, they did not live there and did not intend to move there. Paul had been sent to study in Jerusalem with the great rabbi Gamaliel, but his home city was Tarsus in Asia Minor.

As was the case with most of Diaspora Judaism, Paul was a Pharisee, accustomed to the study and worship of the synagogues and the teaching and community leadership of the rabbis. The issue of the relationship of Jews and Gentiles was critical for those Jews who spent most of their lives in constant contact with Gentiles. Pharisaic Judaism had grown strong in the Diaspora as a way of strengthening one's identity as a Jew in the midst of a non-Jewish culture. The laws that made a clear separation between Jews and Gentiles were particularly important: circumcision, food laws, sabbath laws—all were ways of maintaining such identity and communicating it to the next generation.

Paul's conversion to Christ demanded from him a great rethinking of the relationship of Jew and Gentile. The result was that he viewed himself as specifically sent of God for the purpose of carrying the gospel to the Gentiles. In no way was he saying that Jews had been wrong to make a drastic separation between themselves and others. That was God's will and God's law. The cross and the resurrection of Jesus, however, altered that situation. The cross made peace between the two groups, and the resurrection was the beginning of a new reality in which Jew and Gentile were brought together as the body of Christ. The division between Jew and Gentile was the single greatest division for Paul. All other divisions of humanity paled in comparison. Yet God had brought about a reconciliation in Christ. Outside of Christ there was indeed such a division, but to

make such a division still within the Christian community was to deny the new reality that Jesus had created and therefore to deny the power of the cross.

The Law remained God's law. What God did in Judaism must not be denied. Paul was proud of his Jewish heritage and never denied it. But now God has done a new thing. The Law had a specific purpose of making God's will known in Israel, of training in righteousness and therefore the meaning of sin. But the Law itself could not overcome sin. That is what Christ has done. In Christ hearts and minds are changed, lives are transformed. Through the activity of the Spirit, love is active in the community. Where such love reigns, no law is needed. To return to the Law as central is to deny the power of the cross and resurrection.

Yet Paul understood Christianity as the fulfillment of Jewish expectation, not as a new religion. One of the characteristics of Judaism in Paul's time was the expectation of the Messiah, who would come at the end of history. Among Christians, Jesus was seen as the Messiah; and therefore Christians held that in Jesus the messianic time—the end of history—had begun. Because he was a devout Jew, Paul realized the radical importance of Jesus. But also because he was a devout Jew, he initially had great hostility toward the church. His conversion marked a drastic change in Paul's life and brought to the church a vision of its place in history more cosmic than other early Christians. For all these reasons, Paul's missionary work in the infant church is central to the New Testament.

Paul's Greek World

Paul wrote his letters in Greek. When he quoted the Hebrew Scriptures, he did not quote them from their original Hebrew text but rather from a Greek translation that by then had become quite common among Diaspora Jews—a version known as the Septuagint. The reason for the use of Greek was that more than three hundred years earlier Alexander the Great, king of Macedonia, had set out to conquer the world and to take Greek culture to all of it. Although Alexander's empire did not last long, his project of Hellenizing the world—that is, of making it like Greece—succeeded to an amazing degree. By Paul's time, Greek was the common language of trade, travel, and literature for all the eastern portion of the Mediterranean basin.

Many of the Diaspora Jews who lived in the eastern Mediterranean—Egypt, Syria, and Asia Minor—no longer knew Hebrew, or at least were not at ease in speaking it. For that reason, the Scriptures had been translated into Greek. Christians found this translation ready-made in their efforts to take their message, not only to Diaspora Jews, but also to Gentiles who would not have been able to read the Scriptures in Hebrew. One of the first Christians to use the Septuagint in this fashion was probably Paul.

Hellenistic culture had other characteristics that also affected Paul and early Christianity. One of these was its syncretism—that is, its tendency to mix and match religion, taking whatever seemed useful from various sources. As we shall see, the Roman Empire facilitated this practice by making travel safer and more frequent. But in any case, the cities that Paul visited had heard of many gods, and people were often willing to hear of a new god or religious doctrine to be added to what they already believed. In Athens, Paul found an altar inscribed "To an unknown god" (Acts 17:23), and this was typical of the religious tenor of the times. Some people collected religions like people today collect stamps. In that situation Paul found it necessary to make very clear how his message differed from the common religiosity of the time.

Another characteristic of the Hellenistic world was a deep quest for a personally satisfying religion. Syncretism was an easy answer to that quest. But what had happened was that the ancient national and city deities had lost a great deal of their appeal. At an earlier time, when almost all the inhabitants of a city or country were born there and spent most of their lives there, the national gods gave people a sense of identity and belonging. But now, with people of all nationalities mixing in every city, the old religions had lost their power. People were seeking a religion that gave meaning to life, not because one was born into it, like one was born an Athenian or a Syrian, but rather because one had joined it by a personal decision. Christianity was such a religion, and that was part of its appeal.

A society such as Paul's Greek world, in which people of different origins and traditions are constantly forced to come in contact with one another, is both cosmopolitan in its outlook and deeply divided within itself. In today's large cities people from all parts of the world mix, but the same people resent that mixing and try to keep their distance from those whose background is different. The same was true in the Hellenistic cities of Paul's time. There is no place where people can be as alienated from one another, nor as lonely, as in a city. Paul insisted that his message was one that brought unity to people from all different sorts of origins. As he declared, "There is no longer Greek and Jew, circumcised and uncircumcised, barbarian, Scythian, slave and free; but Christ is all and in all!" (Col. 3:11).

There was always the danger that this unity [would] be understood in purely "spiritual" terms, as if it had nothing to do with the physical realities of daily existence. Actually, this tendency to spiritualize matters and to consider that the physical was not as important was one of the common characteristics of most Hellenistic religions and philosophies. Christian leaders—Paul among them—had to struggle constantly against it. Christianity, with its basis in Judaism, knew God as creator of the physical world, Christ as incarnate in a physical human being, and eternal life as the resurrection that had begun in Jesus and would be fulfilled in the end of history. Therefore, Paul insisted that the gospel must take shape in the totality of the lives of the believers—physical as well as spiritual. For this reason, for instance, he repeatedly stressed the importance of the virtue of hospitality. For us this practice might seem a trite matter. But at that time it meant taking into your home brothers and sisters from distant places, unknown except that they shared your faith.

Paul was a Jew, and his world was Jewish. But he also lived and worked in a Hellenistic world, and his faith and preaching took that into account as well.

Paul's Roman World

The culture in the eastern portion of the Mediterranean was Greek, but the Empire was Roman. By the time of Jesus, Rome, the major city of the western part of the Mediterranean, had become the seat of an empire that included the eastern, Greek part of the Mediterranean as well. Though the language and culture remained generally Hellenistic in the East, Rome brought to that area a form of administration and law that was western and Roman in origin. To make sure that the East was clearly subservient to Rome, colonies were established in the form of Roman-populated new cities in the eastern areas, changing the culture there to some degree.

Paul was proud of his Roman citizenship, and well he might have been. Citizenship was not the common lot but rather had to be purchased or received as a gift for service to the Empire. It was hereditary, and in Acts we read that Paul was born a citizen (Acts 22:18). Roman law established a system of justice for citizens that was highly esteemed. The expectation was that justice would be done, that taxes would be fair, that public officials would not be corrupt. This might not always be the case, but the system allowed for complaints to higher officials. In Paul's time, generally, the system worked well. For that reason, he could urge Christians to be supportive of the government and its officials. There was at this point no persecution from the Empire, nor were Christians viewed as dangerous. That would come later. In fact, tradition has it that Paul was put to death by the Empire.

Rome also brought to the whole Mediterranean basin a new unity. This unity was not based on culture or even language, since the West was Roman and spoke Latin whereas the East was Hellenistic and spoke Greek.

But it was unified physically by a good system of roads that allowed rapid movement from one city to another. Arrangements were made by law for the constant maintenance of these roads. The Empire needed them for the rapid deployment of information and troops so that the peace of the Empire could be controlled. But it also made commercial and private travel relatively easy.

Beyond the physical fact of roads, Rome had made travel safe. Imperial forces had ended much of the highway robbery that had plagued travel before this time. The sea routes also had been freed of pirates so that the much more rapid travel of the Mediterranean was available for both East and West. Paul's travels were made possible by these policies put into practice by the Roman Empire. The safe and efficient conditions that Rome created also gave rise to a growth in commerce between various parts of the Empire.

Until he was taken to Rome under imperial guard, Paul does not appear to have been in the western portion of the Empire. He obviously had not founded the church at Rome. He wrote his letter to the Romans as an introduction to them, saying specifically that he had never seen them and was looking forward to going to Rome. At that point, Paul's expectation was to make a private journey to Rome, evidently as a prelude to carrying the gospel as far as Spain. Instead, Paul was taken there by Roman authorities because he appealed to Caesar, a right he had as a citizen.

Roman influence was obviously stronger in the West where it was the native culture. That means that the western portion of the Empire had a longer tradition of that legal system. Especially in terms of family legislation, having to do with the rights of women in general and wives in particular, Rome was much more egalitarian than the East. Reforms had been made in the laws in order to encourage women to marry and have children, and these reforms gave greater rights to women. In the East local custom was much more conservative, and the legal code often did not challenge such local customs. For that reason, the Hellenistic portion of the Empire had fewer legal rights for women than did Rome; and this is reflected in some of the Christian household legislation. . . .

Common to both East and West, however, was the enormous power of the male head of the extended family over the children and over slaves. All these were considered members of one household, including many generations. Therefore, when we read phrases such as "those of Caesar's household" or "Chloe's people," it refers to these extended households and can refer to slaves or relatives of the person named. When one member of a household became a Christian, the faith could spread fairly rapidly to other members.

Rome had contributed a great deal to the whole area

of the Mediterranean. Though it continued many practices we would consider unjust, it was, for the time, a great unifying force, allowing law and order to structure a peace under which the area flourished. No wonder that for many early Christian writers part of the "fullness of time" that marked the birth of Jesus was the Roman Empire with the new possibilities for rapid communication that made possible the surprising spread of the gospel in the time of Paul.

Paul's Christian World

All the various worlds in which Paul had to live—the Jewish, the Greek, and the Roman—were seen in the light of the cross and the resurrection of Jesus. Paul's world was one to which Jesus had come. It was one to which Jesus would come again. Paul's world was one in which the church had been placed as God's vanguard to witness to the victory of Jesus. Therefore, while taking his Jewish heritage, his Roman citizenship, and his Hellenistic culture seriously, Paul did not let any of these have the final word. Perhaps the greatest lesson that we must learn from Paul is that in Christ "all things in heaven and on earth were created, things visible and invisible, whether thrones or dominions or rulers or powers—all things have been created through him and for him" (Col. 1:16).

Timeline: The Life of Paul

(All dates are A.D.; all dates are approximate.)

10 Saul is born in Tarsus. As a young man, he goes to Jerusalem to study as a Pharisee under Gamaliel.

29–30 Crucifixion of Jesus

30–31 Stoning of Stephen; Paul's conversion on the Damascus road. He spends some time in the (Syrian) desert, preaches three years in Damascus, makes a brief visit to Jerusalem to meet Peter, sets up a base of operations in Antioch.

46–48 Paul's First Missionary Journey, with Barnabas, to Cyprus and Galatia

48–49 The Jerusalem Council

49–52 Paul's Second Missionary Journey, with Silas and Timothy, through Asia Minor to Greece. Returns to Antioch.

53–57 Paul's Third Missionary Journey, again through Asia Minor and Greece. Returns to Jerusalem.

57–59 Arrest in Jerusalem; imprisonment in Caesarea by Roman authorities

59–60 Paul's voyage to Rome, followed by two years under house arrest in Rome

62–65 Paul is martyred (beheaded) in Rome during Nero's persecution.

70 Destruction of Jerusalem and the Temple

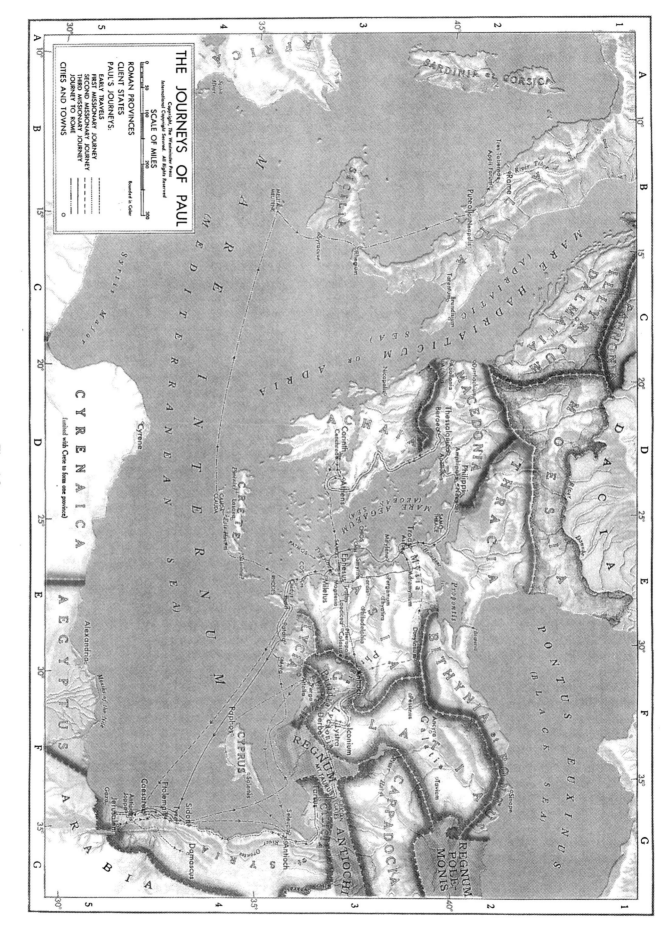

Fig. 6.1

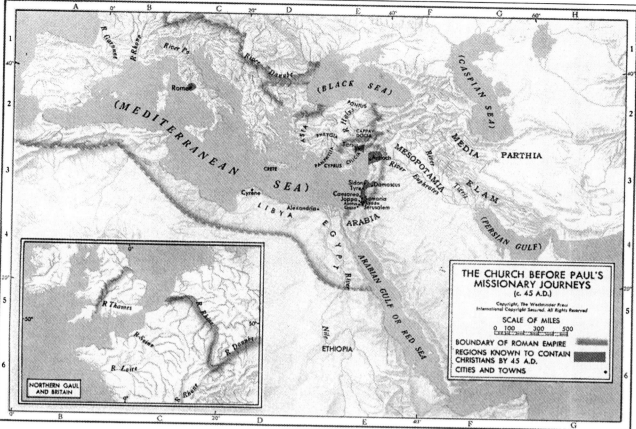

Fig. 6.2

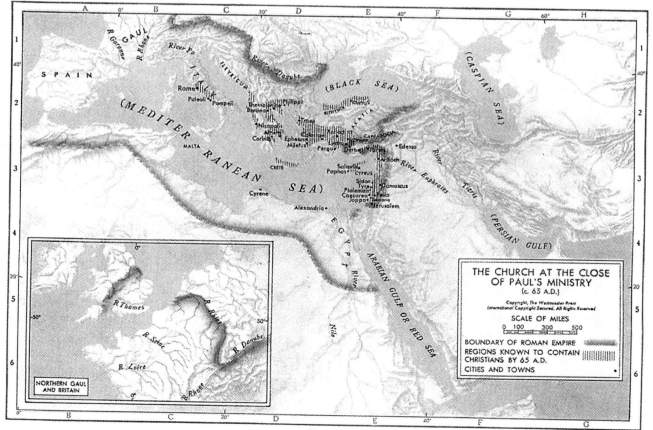

Fig. 6.3

CHAPTER 7

Letters to the Thessalonians and the Corinthians

INTRODUCTION TO THE LETTERS TO THE THESSALONIANS

These letters, written c. A.D. 50, stand as the earliest documents of Christian literature. In them many of the major motifs of Paul's teaching are introduced. While the letters do not mark the high point of Paul's work, they do mark its inauguration.

Acts 17:1–9 tells of Paul's successful establishment of a church in the town of Thessalonica in Macedonia (northeastern Greece). He preached there for three Sabbaths. The converts received the gospel with much enthusiasm, but their understanding of the gospel was skimpy. Paul was driven out of town before he could lay a good foundation for the church, and the turmoil and persecution he experienced there continued as the infant church tried to establish itself. From Athens, Paul sent Timothy to visit, and Timothy's report was reassuring. In spite of the opposition (from Jews? Gentiles? or simply fellow Macedonians?) the young church at Thessalonica showed promise of stability and growth. For this Paul is thankful, and the correspondence begins. Paul, Silas, and Timothy write to the church from Corinth.

In the first letter, we find that the Thessalonians are troubled by deaths of those in their congregation. Was not the Lord to come before any of them experienced death? Where was he, then? What could Paul have meant when he preached to them of the "resurrection of the dead" and of "the day of the Lord"? In the second letter, dispatched a few weeks after the first, we see that the church is even more preoccupied with the coming of the Lord. The people have come close to quitting this life altogether as they drop everything (even their work) to wait. The fledgling church wishes to fly off into the future, ignoring the first steps the members need to take as Christians.

Eschatology literally means "discourse about the last things." It has its rightful place in the kerygma, or the proclamation of the gospel: Christians "look for the world to come." But that is not all they do!

If the present world is threatening and precarious, the human tendency is to focus on a way out. Such was the case with the Thessalonians, and their way out was the future. Paul wishes to affirm the kerygma (announcement of the good news) but strike a balance. Yes, Christ will come again. Those who have died will not miss out! But in the meantime, they need to know that *already* they are participating in the life of the saints, of all who belong to God. "We will be with the Lord forever" (4:17). As you read, look at the ways Paul makes these points, and decide for yourself how successful he is in doing so. If you were young in the faith and anxious about the end times, what in these letters would comfort you? hit you right between the eyes? turn you around?

STUDY GUIDE FOR 1 THESSALONIANS

1. Thessalonica was the capital of Macedonia, the chief seaport of that region, and strategically important for the Roman Empire. The church was a composite of Jews and Greeks; it also included many women. The Gentile element of the church probably predominated, as Paul makes no mention of the synagogue nor does he give any quotations from the Hebrew scriptures. Read Paul's thanksgiving in 1:2–10. What does he say here to support and encourage the young church?

_____

_____

2. Paul defends his authority. After reading 2:3–6, reconstruct the accusations made against Paul in Thessalonica.

_____

_____

What images does Paul use to describe his care for the believers in Thessalonica in 2:7 and 2:11? Which image is more meaningful to you?

_____

_____

What examples does he wish them to follow? See 2:9–10 and 2:14.

_____

_____

Paul's authority is rooted in the bond he has with the church. In what striking ways does he express this alliance in 2:17—3:10?

_____

_____

3. The key themes of the letter are eschatology and work. The first refers to the "end times." The church understood that none would "fall asleep" (RSV) before Christ came again. No doubt this expectation was based on Paul's own teaching. The kerygma he preached is found early on in the letter: They must turn to God from idols and "wait for his Son from heaven, whom he raised from the dead" (1:9–10). This they are doing. But while they wait, believers die. What is to become of them? See Paul's answer in 4:16–18:

_____

_____

On what principle is his teaching based? See 4:14.

_____

Paul warns that the coming of the Lord is not a matter of timetables and predictions ("the times and the seasons"). Instead, how will "the day of the Lord" come (5:1–3)?

_____

_____

Why do you think it is important to put away timetables and predictions?

_____

_____

4. As "saints"—persons who belong to God—they are being sanctified. Describe what sanctification means, using these verses:

2:12 _____

3:12 _____

4:3 _____

5:23 _____

Paul wants the Thessalonians to live appropriately. With one eye awaiting the future, they must keep the other on the here and now. They must be watchful and alert. In two parallel columns, show the contrasts Paul makes in 5:4–10 between these groups:

children of darkness	children of light
_____	_____
_____	_____
_____	_____
_____	_____

5. What are the value and benefits of work? See 4:11–12 and 5:12–13.

_____

_____

Paul implies in 4:11–12 that the church is to avoid political activity. Are these words specific to this particular situation, or do you think they should be universally applied? What reasons can you give for your answer?

_____

_____

6. Elsewhere in his letters, Paul will write about building up the body of Christ. How is this dynamic expressed in these exhortations?

4:18 _____

5:11 _____

5:14 _____

7. Finally, note that Paul tells the church not to quench the Spirit or despise prophecy, but to test everything and hold fast to what is good (5:19–22). Keep these remarks in mind as you turn to the Second Letter of Paul to the Thessalonians.

Discussion Question

Having read the first letter, what is the relationship between eschatology and work?

STUDY GUIDE FOR 2 THESSALONIANS

1. "Wait on the Lord . . . thief in the night . . . prophecy . . ." Put these ingredients from 1 Thessalonians together in a container of persecution, add a bit of misunderstanding and a heap of feverish anxiety, and you've got the situation Paul addresses in 2 Thessalonians. The church has quit everyday living and devoted itself to the second coming of Christ.

Compared to the first letter, the crisis is heightened

and Paul's tone is sharper. See what he says about these matters:

their persecution, in 1:3–5

_____

the judgment awaiting their persecutors, in 1:6–9

_____

the consequences of not working, in 3:10

_____

the consequences of ignoring what Paul says in the letter, in 3:14–15

_____

2. What the church needs to realize is this: its people are experiencing, already, God's glorification. They are not simply marking days in an "in-between" time. This life is theirs from God. Even their persecution works for them to strengthen their identity. See how Paul makes these points in 1:3–5, 11–12.

_____

_____

3. The distinctive part of the letter is found in 2:1–12. Paul needs to be more explicit with them about the coming of the Lord, because his first letter (or perhaps a false letter from someone else—see 2:2) left them thinking the day of the Lord has come. What must happen *before* this day comes? Trace his points, in:

2:3 _____

2:4 _____

2:9 _____

2:10–12 _____

2:8 _____

4. In 2:1–11, what or who do you think is meant by the one who restrains it: The Roman Empire? God?

Paul? Other? Is the fact that we no longer know and scholars cannot agree important to you or not?

_____

5. In the meantime, what is the proper focus of the Christian life? See the two prayers in:

1:11 _____

2:16–17 _____

Finally, see the example of Paul himself in 3:7–9.

_____

_____

6. Write out these verses:

1 Thess. 5:24

_____

_____

2 Thess. 3:13

_____

_____

How do the concluding verses of each letter together make a simple and complete design for the Thessalonian church?

_____

_____

Discussion Questions

1. When you think of work, what comes to mind: Drudgery? Toil? Chores? Getting by? Achievement? Accomplishment? Fulfillment? Vocation? Vacation?

2. Are you an idler? a busybody? a worrywart? a workaholic? What would have to change for you to see work as part of God's design?

INTRODUCTION TO THE CORINTHIAN CORRESPONDENCE

Paul's letters to the church at Corinth abound with energy and problems, reflecting the enthusiastic and problematic church to which he wrote. The difficulties, briefly summarized, are these:

1. The flip side of a great strength is a great weakness. People good at getting the job done often run slipshod over folk who get in the way. Men and women who dream great dreams are often poor at planning,

executing, and details. As we shall see, the Corinthians were strong in spiritual gifts. They were excited and energetic in their faith. But weaknesses of excitability and misuse of spiritual gifts threatened their very existence as members of the body of Christ. How can Paul harness their energies for a greater good? The lively interchange of reports and letters reflects this difficulty.

2. What we have is only one side of the interchange.

Corinthian "slogans" are found in 1 Corinthians 6:12; 7:1; 8:1. In these and other places, it is difficult for us to know where their comments (often maxims) end and Paul's begin. Paul refers to situations in the church that we are not able to reconstruct with certainty. Furthermore, he quotes from letters and reports he received that we do not possess. The church certainly knew what problems and teachings Paul was tackling; we cannot be so sure. Scholars can help us piece together the problem situations in Corinth, while the New Revised Standard Version puts quotation marks around phrases that came to Paul from the church. Keep in mind that, as usual, we cannot insist on certainty in these matters.

3. Even if we knew the specific situations and problems at Corinth, the question of Paul's advice to the Corinthians remains. Where does kerygma (proclamation of the gospel for all time) end and Paul's personal opinion begin? Should specific guidance concerning specific situations be treated as unique and distinctive advice, or as universal and applicable doctrine? Would Paul insist on slavish obedience to his practical guidance today? Can we discern the context and principles at work in Paul's teaching to the Corinthians, people who are like us in many ways but culturally removed from us by two millennia?

These problems come to the fore as we look at the Corinthian correspondence.

From Acts 18:1–18, we learn that Paul founded the church at Corinth following his customary pattern: he went first to the Jews, then to the Gentiles. He preached in the synagogue every Sabbath until he was driven out, then he took to house preaching at the home of Titius Justus. God-fearers (Greek converts to Judaism) and other Gentiles joined him there, along with some Jews and even the head of the synagogue, Crispus. Paul was brought before the proconsul Gallio for a trial (probably in A.D. 51). While Gallio dismissed the case as a Jewish, not a Roman, matter, Sosthenes (another ruler of the synagogue) was seized and beaten. After a year and a half in Corinth, Paul left and returned to Asia. A flurry of reports and letters ensued.

The church at Corinth was seriously divided. These divisions fell along party lines: the Cephas party, the Apollos party, the Paul party (1 Cor. 1:11), and those who followed the unnamed "superapostles" in 2 Corinthians 10—13. They fell along ethnic lines: Jews and Gentiles. They fell along developmental lines: the church was divided into the "weak" on one hand and the "strong" on the other. Finally, their enthusiastic reception of spiritual gifts led to further division; the gifted ones fought among themselves as to whose gift was the greatest.

The city itself fueled their excesses and divisions. Corinth was a bustling port city with plenty of first-century pleasure palaces. Transients and sailors were accommodated by brothels. "Sacred prostitution," a feature of the cults of Isis and Aphrodite found in Corinth and elsewhere, promoted extramarital relations. The sexual extreme of licentiousness carried over into the congregation, along with its opposite extreme, asceticism.

Set in an intemperate metropolis, plagued with internal strife, immature in both behavior and faith—one would not blame Paul for counting the Corinthian church as a lost cause. Instead, he worries over them as a father does his children (1 Cor. 4:15). He sees their dynamism, their enthusiasm, even their chaotic life together as potential strengths. Their pyrotechnics are at present so much wasted energy. What if the fireworks were focused? There would then be a steady flame, shining clear and bright.

A reconstruction of their interchange looks like this:

1. Paul sent Timothy to Corinth.
2. Paul wrote the church a letter (now lost), with instructions which they misunderstood.
3. Chloe's people brought Paul a report of divisions within the church.
4. Three men arrived with a letter from the Corinthians full of questions for Paul.
5. Paul wrote what is now 1 Corinthians from Ephesus, around A.D. 54.
6. Paul made a "painful" visit to Corinth around A.D. 56.
7. He sent Titus with a "severe" letter, what is now 2 Corinthians 10—13.
8. Titus met up with Paul in Macedonia. Titus was full of good news from the church. Paul then wrote yet another letter—the "letter of reconciliation"—which stands in the canon as 2 Corinthians 1—9.

The alert reader will notice that 2 Corinthians is split in two sections, with the last four chapters preceding (chronologically) the first nine. The study guide questions will follow this arrangement.

STUDY GUIDE FOR 1 CORINTHIANS

1. Read 1 Corinthians 1—4.
How does Paul describe the people of Corinth in 1:2?

_____

What do they possess (1:7)?_____
What is going on in Corinth (1:11–12)? What does this say about the Corinthians (3:1–4)?

_____

What is the message Paul preaches (1:23; 2:2)?

_____

What do some people think of this message (1:25)?

_____

Some groups within the church thought themselves uniquely endowed with knowledge. They formed an intellectual elite. They had power, knowledge, wisdom. What does Paul say about their "wisdom" in 1:17—2:5?

_____

From the passage you just read and 3:18–23, why do you think God is on the side of the "foolish" rather than the "wise"?

_____

What are ministers/priests/preachers, according to 4:1?

_____

Note the irony Paul uses in 4:8–13. What is the point of his scathing attack here?

_____

_____

2. Read 1 Corinthians 5—8.
What moral problem is referred to in 5:1? What is to be done about it (5:5)?

_____

What's another moral problem for Christians in Corinth (6:1), and what should they do with such problems (6:7)?

_____

What is yet another moral problem and Paul's teaching on it (6:15–16)?

_____

According to 6:17–20, what is fundamentally wrong with promiscuity?

_____

The opposite of promiscuity is "asceticism." What is the meaning of this term in a good dictionary?

_____

Evidently both these sexual extremes were practiced in the congregation. Note the Corinthian slogan in 7:1:

_____

What does Paul say about the following?
the relation of wife and husband (7:4)

_____

divorce (7:10–11)

_____

being single (7:25–28)

_____

What reasons does Paul give (7:25, 29) for this last piece of advice?

_____

What question is Paul addressing in 8:1 and 8:4?

_____

What should determine how the Corinthians use their freedom? See 8:9._____
The theme of chapter 8 is simply this: "Don't cause the weak to stumble." How does Paul amplify this theme here?

_____

3. Read 1 Corinthians 9—12.
What "rights" has Paul given up (9:4–7)?

_____

Why has Paul refused to exercise his rights as an apostle (9:12, 22)?

_____

What does 10:13 mean to you?

_____

_____

What should determine how Christians behave (10:23–24, 31–32)?

_____

_____

What issue does Paul deal with in 11:5?

_____

Paul's concern here is with propriety. It was considered unseemly for women to uncover their heads while praying. While proper decorum is the issue here, what does 11:11–12 say about the roles of men and women?

_____

What degrades their celebration of the Lord's Supper, according to 11:21?

_____

Name the spiritual gifts in 12:8–10.

_____

_____

_____

Where do these gifts come from, and what is their purpose (12:7)?

_____

What is the difference between equality and sameness? between diversity and discord?

_____

_____

Name the list of spiritual gifts in 12:28. Is the list hierarchical in order?

_____

_____

Do you think the lists (12:8–10 and 12:28) are meant to be exhaustive? Can you think of other spiritual gifts?

_____

_____

How does the metaphor of the *body* in 12:12–31 help Paul talk about:
A. the unity of the believers?

_____

B. the variety of gifts within the church?

_____

C. the fallacy of spiritual pride and elitism?

_____

With your own body as an example, illustrate the truth of 12:26.

_____

_____

4. Read 1 Corinthians 13—16.
What is the greatest spiritual gift (13:13)?_____
Paul describes the nature of love by using active verbs. List them here:

_____

_____

Power, knowledge, and wisdom were the principal virtues for the Greeks. What contrast does Paul make in 13:13 to this way of thinking?

_____

Where in chapter 13 does Paul speak to the pride of the Corinthians? Where does he speak to you?

_____

_____

See 14:5. Which is greater: speaking in tongues or prophesying (preaching)? Why?

_____

Gifts, then, are not individual bonuses to be enjoyed by the believer. They are to be directed toward a larger purpose, which is (14:12):

_____

How should women act in church (14:34–36)? What about women priests and ministers?

_____

_____

Paul mentions Prisca, Mary, Junia, Tryphaena, Tryphosa, and the deacon Phoebe in his letter to the Romans (Rom. 16). Why doesn't he tell these women to be quiet? Do you think the situation in the Corinthian church was different from that in Rome?

_____

_____

What do some Corinthians deny (15:12)?

_____

Who are those "who belong to Christ" and what will happen to them (15:22–23)?

_____

_____

Paul's analogy is drawn from nature in 15:35–38: the seed dies, the kernel bursts forth into a new and different form of life. Can you think of another analogy to make the same point?

The Greeks thought the idea of the resurrected body was absurd. The body and the material world were vile. The "soul" was detachable. At death the spark returns to the great flame, or the drop of water returns to the ocean, but good luck finding that spark or drop! The immortal soul sheds its evil dwelling place, the Greeks believed. (Of course, in doing so the individual personality is lost as well.) The implications of this thinking were injurious. If the body is not really part of us, then what we do with it doesn't matter. The extremes of either licentiousness (misusing, abusing the body) or asceticism (refusing, denying the body) follow.

What we do with the body *is* relevant, Paul argues throughout the letter. By the term "body," Paul means the entire self—flesh and blood and spirit in a psychosomatic unity. God is concerned with the whole of the created order. The physical and material world is important to God. And the entire self will be transformed by God.

What will resurrected bodies be like (15:44, 49)?

What does Paul order in 16:1–2?

How does this offer a pattern for Christian giving today?

Discussion Questions: 1 Corinthians

1. "Indeed, I am a Christian. Jesus really lived, really taught, and really died for my sins. But as for an 'afterlife', the thought is absurd. Jesus went to the grave dead as a doornail, and so will I. To think otherwise is clearly foolish." Using 1 Corinthians 15, show how Paul would respond to the statement above.

How do you respond to it?

2. Christ's union with the church is the key to Paul's argument in this letter. How do *factions* within the church dishonor this union? How is *impurity* in the church destructive of this union? How does identification with *idols* profane this union? How does *marriage* illustrate this union? How does the *Lord's Supper* emblemize this union? Finally, how does the *resurrection* consummate and crown this union?

1 CORINTHIANS 13 AND *THE ART OF LOVING*

I have no doubt that Paul would be pained to see the way his peevish "Women, keep silent in church!" has been used against half of the congregation in some churches today. His concern was building up the entire body of Christ, not ignoring half of it or demanding that it atrophy. One cannot visualize such impatient and impulsive words coming from Jesus. But Paul could not have imagined the negative repercussions these words would engender. Nor could he have imagined these scrappy letters to the Corinthians becoming Holy Scripture for a worldwide Christian church!

On the other hand, Paul would no doubt be pleased right now to see you reflecting on 1 Corinthians 13. He composed it with care, he choose the right words to fit his intention, and he has given us a timeless, classic portrait of *agapē* love.

In the twentieth century, another piece on love was written by Erich Fromm, which invites us to amplify the discussion in contemporary terms. Fromm was not writing as a theologian or even as a theist. Yet his ideas resonate with 1 Corinthians 13 in some striking ways.*

Love is an activity, not a passive affect; it is a "standing in," not a "falling for." In the most general way the active character of love can be described by stating that love is primarily *giving*, not receiving. . . . Giving is the highest expression of potency. In the very act of giving, I experience my strength, my wealth, my power. This experience of heightened vitality and potency fills me with joy. I experience myself as over-flowing, spending, alive, and hence as joyous. Giving is more joyous than receiving, not because it is a deprivation, but because in the act of giving lies the expression of my aliveness. [Pp. 22–23]

Beyond the element of giving, the active character of love becomes evident in the fact that it always implies certain basic elements, common to all forms of love. These are *care, responsibility, respect,* and *knowledge.* . . .

Love is the active concern for the life and the

---

*Excerpts that follow are taken from *The Art of Loving*, by Erich Fromm (New York: Harper & Row, 1956), 22–59.

growth of that which we love. . . . God explains to Jonah that the essence of love is to "labor" for something and "to make something grow," that love and labor are inseparable. One loves that for which one labors, and one labors for that which one loves.

Today responsibility is often meant to denote duty, something imposed upon one from the outside. But responsibility, in its true sense, is an entirely voluntary act; it is my response to the needs, expressed or unexpressed, of another human being. To be "responsible" means to be able and stand ready to "respond."

. . . Respect is not fear and awe; it denotes, in accordance with the root of the word (*respicere*= to look at), the ability to see a person as he is, to be aware of his unique individuality. Respect means the concern that the other person should grow and unfold as he is. Respect, thus, implies the absence of exploitation. I want the loved person to grow and unfold for his own sake, and in his own ways, and not for the purpose of serving me. [Pp. 26–28]

The longing to know ourselves and to know our fellow humans has been expressed in the Delphic motto "Know thyself." It is the mainspring of all psychology. But inasmuch as the desire is to know all of man, his innermost secret, the desire can never be fulfilled in knowledge of the ordinary kind, in knowledge only by thought. Even if we knew a thousand times more of ourselves, we would never reach bottom. We would still remain an enigma to ourselves, as our fellow humans would remain an enigma to us. The only way of full knowledge lies in the *act* of love: this act transcends thought, it transcends words. It is the daring plunge into the experience of union. [P. 31]

If it is a virtue to love my neighbor as a human being, it must be a virtue—and not a vice—to love myself, since I am a human being too. There is no concept of man in which I myself am not included. A doctrine which proclaims such an exclusion proves itself to be intrinsically contradictory. The idea expressed in the Biblical "Love thy neighbor as thyself!" implies that respect for one's own integrity and uniqueness, love for and understanding of one's own self, cannot be separated from respect and love and understanding of another individual. The love for my own self is inseparably connected with the love for any other being. [Pp. 58–59]

Discussion Questions: 1 Corinthians 13

1. List the seven characteristics of what love is, and the eight characteristics of what love is not, using 1 Corinthians 13:4–7.

2. Using the list of "love is . . ." characteristics, rewrite each to show what love could or should look like in your particular situation at home, work, school. Be specific.

3. Using Erich Fromm's ideas, write out another list describing the characteristics of love. How do Fromm's ideas compare and contrast with Paul's in 1 Corinthians 13? What concepts do you find most helpful? Why?

.

STUDY GUIDE FOR 2 CORINTHIANS

1. *Begin* your reading with the "severe letter" found now in 2 Corinthians 10—13.

Sometime after the Corinthian church received the letter now called 1 Corinthians, it became convinced that Paul was an apostle of weakness, preaching a gospel of weakness (2 Cor. 10:10). Meanwhile, the "superapostles" have come to Corinth. In 11:1–23, how does Paul characterize them? What spiritual and personal gifts do they appear to have, in contrast to Paul?

_____

_____

Ironically, Paul's refusal to accept financial support from the church is an issue. See 11:7–12; 12:13–17.

What problems have arisen in this regard?

_____

_____

In defense of his apostleship, Paul makes some remarkable autobiographical statements. List the *physical* hardships he catalogs in 11:24–29.

_____

_____

Who received the vision described in 12:1–6?

_____

How does he describe his *emotional* hardships in 12:7–10? While no firm decision is possible, what might you guess he is talking about here? Does 2 Cor. 1:8–11 help?

2. "When I am weak, then I am strong" (12:10). Discuss this paradox in light of what Paul says about Christ in 12:9 and 13:4.

A different kind of weakness is described in 11:20. What does it look like? What does Paul's caustic remark in 11:21 tell you about his attitude toward this type of weakness?

3. Now go to the beginning of 2 Corinthians. While Paul had threatened a painful visit in 12:20—13:10, he is now relieved to know such a visit is not necessary (2:1–4). He rejoices in Titus's report (7:13–16). He writes a "letter of reconciliation"—2 Corinthians 1—9. The tone of this letter is one of comfort and joy.

What has happened since his last letter (7:8–12)?

Paul speaks about *newness* in this letter. With the advent of the new covenant (3:6), all has changed (5:17). What is the newness he speaks of and how does it affect: the glory of God's ministry (2:14—3:11)?

our role in that ministry (3:12—4:6)?

our coping with the world, this life (4:7–18)?

our perspective (5:1–15)?

Look up "reconcile" in a good dictionary. Then augment this definition with what Paul says about reconciliation in 5:16–21. How does divine reconciliation take place?

What images does Paul present in 2:12—6:2 of our participation in this newness?

In light of Paul's suffering and endurance, what should the Corinthians do? What is Paul's hope for them (6:3—7:1)?

Paul's concern in 2 Corinthians 8; 9 is with the offering for the Jerusalem poor. What do these chapters tell you about giving and financial gifts? See especially 8:13–15 and 9:10–15.

Discussion Questions: Thessalonians and Corinthians

1. Compare the church at Thessalonica with the church at Corinth. What were the characteristics of each? What were the key problems for each as seen in Paul's correspondence with them?

2. Use 1 Thessalonians 4 and 1 Corinthians 15 together to show the key features of Paul's eschatology. At what points is he pretty clear and specific? At what points does his language denote that which is mysterious and unknowable?

3. While the doctrine of the Trinity was not nailed down until the Council of Constantinople in 381, Paul contributed to the understanding of "one God, three Persons." (In a discussion of the Trinity, one of my students used the metaphor of 3-in-1 Oil. The class found his remark helpful.) See 1 Corinthians 12:4–6 and 2 Corinthians 13:14. Then go to a library and find:

—either a theological dictionary to show the variety of ways this doctrine is understood

—or a history of the early church to show the controversies that provoked the crystallization of this doctrine.

CHAPTER 8

Letters to the Galatians and the Romans

INTRODUCTION TO GALATIANS

Picture a person who can run a marathon yet chooses to walk with a cane. Or imagine a person who can breathe freely choosing to hook up to a respirator. Ridiculous, absurd, or sad, you might think. This is the picture of the churches to which Paul writes the letter to the Galatians, the "charter of Christian freedom."

The Galatians were folk who had once run marathons and breathed fresh air. They knew the power of the Spirit. They had received the promise of new life in Christ. But something had happened. False teachers had arisen in the churches with a fearful and dangerous message. The Galatians were being told they were actually handicapped! These teachers, called "Judaizers," insisted that the promises of Jesus were not sufficient. The Galatians must now become Jews, submitting to torah (Jewish law) and to being circumcised. They had believed an inferior gospel; now it was time to practice the superior gospel. Then and only then could they count themselves true Christians. They must walk with canes and breathe with respirators. They were deluded if they thought otherwise.

Paul's contempt for these teachers is immense. He lays a curse on those who preach a false gospel (Gal. 1:9) and expresses a bitter wish that they would mutilate (butcher!) themselves (5:12). He fears that his preaching has been in vain, that he has lost the Galatian churches to those false teachers who would sabotage the freedom of the gospel which was already won for them in Christ. "You were running well; who prevented you from obeying the truth?" (5:7).

Paul's anxious concern for these churches, Gentile communities in central Asia Minor, is also striking. His spirited defense of his own authority as an apostle arises from his passionate concern for the Galatian believers. They are his "little children"; he suffers for them like a mother giving birth (4:19). If they revert to the Judaizers, they jettison the work Paul has done on their behalf. If they submit to circumcision and the torah, they abandon the gospel. How can Paul convince them? What can he say to get their attention and bring them around?

They are truly free and justified before God, not because of the works of the law, but because of the faith *of*

Christ (2:16: *pistis christou*, meaning both "faith in Christ" and "faith of Christ"). Their freedom has been won, in other words, not by what they must do, but by what Christ has already done. Paul demonstrates this teaching by referring the Galatians to the practices of Roman law. The terms of the law regarding inheritances would be known already to these churches. They deserve some explanation here.

Under Roman law, a *testator* assigned the *inheritance* to a *sole heir*. A *covenant*, or testament, was drawn up, which described the legacy. The covenant also gave the heir the right to designate beneficiaries who would share this legacy. This right was known as the *fidei commissum*. Through the *fidei commissum*, the sole heir could legally create other heirs of the testator.

The covenant, or testament, also allowed the testator to adopt an alien as a beneficiary so that in every sense that person became an heir. Further, the testator could designate tutors for the beneficiaries. The tutor would act as custodian and guardian until the death of the sole heir, at which time the inheritance would be shared. Once the heirs received the legacy, the tutor's role as guardian or custodian was terminated.

Keep these legal practices in mind as you read the central section of the letter, Galatians 3:26—4:7. Paul wants the churches to understand the *fidei commissum* as the faith of Christ, by which the sole heir (Christ) made them children of the testator: God. The torah was a tutor, but torah is no longer necessary. Through the *fidei commissum*, the legacy has been given to them. There is no need to rely on the tutor—torah—anymore! Once aliens, even slaves, they are now full-fledged heirs according to the promise—God's children. The faith *of* Jesus has accomplished this.

"For freedom Christ has set us free; stand firm, therefore, and do not submit again to a yoke of slavery" (5:1). In the following study guide, you will explore the meaning and nature of this freedom. Finally, you will read a piece with an entirely different perspective on freedom: an excerpt from Dostoyevsky's *The Brothers Karamazov*. In comparing and contrasting these perspectives, you will clarify your own understanding of Christian freedom and what it means to you.

Outline of Galatians

I. Paul's Authority as an Apostle: Galatians 1; 2
II. The Gospel of the Freedom in Christ: Biblical and Theological Arguments: chapters 3; 4

III. The Gospel of the Freedom in Christ: Ethical and Communal Implications of Life in the Spirit: chapters 5; 6

STUDY GUIDE FOR THE LETTER TO THE GALATIANS

1. The letter was written c. A.D. 55 to the churches in Asia Minor that Paul founded. Their members were ethnically Gentile, formerly pagan. The churches were probably those at Iconium, Lystra, and Derbe, cities where Paul and Barnabas preached the gospel in Acts 14:1–21. What do we know about the churches from this letter?

1:6 _____

3:2–3 _____

4:8–9 _____

4:12–20

_____

_____

5:4 _____

6:12–13 _____

2. The false teachers within the churches wish to undermine the gospel. What do they teach?

5:2, 10–12 _____

6:12–13 _____

Why do they teach this, according to 6:12–13?

_____

3. Paul's defense of himself as preacher and apostle of Christ.

The false teachers have insinuated that the gospel first preached to the Galatians by Paul was not authentic because Paul himself was not an authentic apostle. Paul counters with a remarkable autobiographical passage in 1:11—2:21.

How does Paul describe himself before his conversion (1:13–14)?

_____

_____

How does he characterize his conversion (1:11–12, 15–16)? To whom was he called to preach?

_____

_____

Three years after his conversion, Paul went to visit Cephas (Peter) in Jerusalem. While the church in Jerusalem did not know him, what was their opinion of him (1:18–24)?

_____

Fourteen years later, Paul went again to Jerusalem to meet with the pillars of the church. What happened this time (2:1–10)?

_____

_____

Still later, Paul met with Cephas (Peter) in Antioch. What picture of Peter and the Jerusalem church do you find in 2:11–13? How do you account for their inconsistency?

_____

_____

What picture does Paul paint of himself in 2:11, 14?

_____

Finally, why do you think Paul gives this account of controversy within the Jerusalem church? What is his relationship (if any) to that church?

_____

_____

4. Abraham and the heirs to the promise. Abraham was justified, or made right with God, through faith (Gen. 15:6). Indeed, torah could not justify him; torah did not come until centuries after Abraham, at the time of Moses (Gal. 3:17). Read 3:6–18. Who are Abraham's real descendants?

_____

5. The role of torah. What does Paul say about the works of torah in 2:15–16?

_____

If torah plays no role in being justified (or deemed righteous), why then was torah given by God? Use these verses for your answer:

3:19 _____

3:23–24 _____

6. The fulfillment of the promise. God promised a blessing to Abraham and his descendants, and that promise has come to fulfillment in Jesus. What happens when one is baptized according to 3:27–29?

_____

As heirs of the promise, what now is our status before God? See 4:1–7.

_____

7. Freedom versus slavery. What does the allegory of Hagar and Sarah in 4:21–31 tell you about the contrasts between slavery and freedom?

_____

Note that in 4:30 Paul quotes from Gen. 21:10–12, saying, "Drive out the slave and her child." Paul's use of this quote becomes, "Get rid of the people telling you to be slaves to torah!"

Write out and memorize Galatians 5:1.

_____

8. Life in the Spirit. First, make note of how Paul assures his audience that they have in fact received the Spirit in:

3:2, 5 _____

4:6, 29 _____

5:5 _____

What counts now is not circumcision (a work of torah), but faith working through love (5:6). Paul contrasts the "works of the flesh" with the "fruits of the Spirit" in 5:19–23. Make a chart with Paul's lists of vices and virtues as you read.

Works of the Flesh	Fruits of the Spirit
_____	_____
_____	_____
_____	_____

Now, how may the Galatians use their freedom from the demands of torah? What is the relationship between freedom (before God) and responsibility (for the neighbor)? See 5:13–14.

_____

9. The law of Christ is the law of love. Practically speaking, how are we to act according to the law of Christ? See 6:1–10 and write out the advice that you find most meaningful.

_____

Discussion Questions: Galatians

1. The letter to the Galatians is full of stark contrasts, of "either this or that." For example, Paul sees the contrast between flesh and spirit, death and life, slavery and freedom, torah and faith, license and liberty. Pick one pair of contrasts as your focal point, and use the letter to show the consequences of choosing one or the other.

2. Keeping torah was, for the Galatians, an attempt to be justified through obedience to the commandments. But through Christ, Paul argues, we are justified at the most fundamental level. Therefore, in terms of response, the analogy is this:

Obedience : torah : : faith : God's promise

Show how Paul works out this analogy in his letter to the Galatians. Keep in mind that *pistis Christou* may be translated either "faith of Christ" or "faith in Christ."

THE PROBLEM OF FREEDOM ("THE GRAND INQUISITOR")*

In Fyodor Dostoevsky's *The Brothers Karamazov,* in the chapter entitled "The Grand Inquisitor," Jesus has returned to earth. The site is Seville, during the Spanish Inquisition of the 1500s. Heretics are being burned by the Roman Catholic Church in the great *autos-da-fé*. Jesus is arrested by the Grand Inquisitor, who speaks to the prisoner about the temptations in the wilderness and Jesus' refusal to come down from the cross. Jesus remains silent throughout this speech.

"Judge Thyself who was right—Thou [Jesus] or he who questioned Thee then [Satan]? Remember the first question; its meaning, though not the exact words, was this: 'Thou wouldst go into the world, and art going with empty hands,

*The excerpt that follows is from Fyodor Dostoevsky's *The Brothers Karamazov,* trans. Constance Garnett, rev. Ralph E. Matlaw (New York: W. W. Norton & Co., 1976), 233–37.

with some promise of freedom which men in their simplicity and their natural unruliness cannot even understand, which they fear and dread—for nothing has ever been more insupportable for a man and a human society than freedom. But seest Thou these stones in this parched and barren wilderness? Turn them into bread, and mankind will run after Thee like a flock, grateful and obedient, though forever trembling, lest Thou withdraw Thy hand and deny them Thy bread.' But Thou wouldst not deprive man of freedom and didst reject the offer, thinking, what is that freedom worth, if obedience is bought with bread? Thou didst reply that man lives not by bread alone. . . .

"This is the significance of the first question in the wilderness, and this is what Thou hast rejected for the sake of that freedom which Thou hast exalted above everything. Yet in this question lies hid the great secret of this world. Choosing 'bread,' Thou wouldst have satisfied the universal and everlasting craving of humanity individually and together as one—to find someone to worship. So long as man remains free he strives for nothing so incessantly and so painfully as to find someone to worship. But man seeks to worship what is established beyond dispute, so that all men would agree at once to worship it. For these pitiful creatures are concerned not only to find what one or the other can worship, but to find something that all would believe in and worship; what is essential is that all may be *together* in it. This craving for *community* is the chief misery of every man individually and of all humanity from the beginning of time. For the sake of common worship they've slain each other with the sword. They have set up gods and challenged one another: 'Put away your gods and come and worship ours, or we will kill you and your gods!' And so it will be to the end of the world, even when gods disappear from the earth; they will fall down before idols just the same. Thou didst know, Thou couldst not but have known, this fundamental secret of human nature, but Thou didst reject the one infallible banner which was offered Thee to make all men bow down to Thee alone—the banner of earthly bread; and Thou hast rejected it for the sake of freedom and the bread of Heaven.

"Behold what Thou didst further. And all again in the name of freedom! I tell Thee that man is tormented by no greater anxiety than to find someone quickly to whom he can hand over that gift of freedom with which the ill-fated creature is born. But only one who can appease their conscience can take over their freedom. In bread there

was offered Thee an invincible banner; give bread, and man will worship Thee, for nothing is more certain than bread. But if someone else gains possession of his conscience—oh! then he will cast away Thy bread and follow after him who has ensnared his conscience. In that Thou wast right. For the secret of man's being is not only to live but to have something to live for. Without a stable conception of the object of life, man would not consent to go on living, and would rather destroy himself than remain on earth, though he had bread in abundance. That is true. But what happened? Instead of taking men's freedom from them, Thou didst make it greater than ever! Didst Thou forget that man prefers peace, and even death, to freedom of choice in the knowledge of good and evil? Nothing is more seductive for man than his freedom of conscience, but nothing is a greater cause of suffering. And behold, instead of giving a firm foundation for setting the conscience of man at rest forever, Thou didst choose all that is exceptional, vague and enigmatic; Thou didst choose what was utterly beyond the strength of men, acting as though Thou didst not love them at all—Thou who didst come to give Thy life for them! Instead of taking possession of men's freedom, Thou didst increase it, and burdened the spiritual kingdom of mankind with its sufferings forever. Thou didst desire man's free love, that he should follow Thee freely, enticed and taken captive by Thee. In place of the rigid ancient law, man must hereafter with free heart decide for himself what is good and what is evil, having only Thy image before him as his guide. But didst Thou not know he would at last reject even Thy image and Thy truth, if he is weighed down with the fearful burden of free choice? They will cry aloud at last that the truth is not in Thee, for they could not have been left in greater confusion and suffering than Thou hast caused, laying upon them so many cares and unanswerable problems.

" . . .Thou didst not come down from the Cross when they shouted to Thee, mocking and reviling Thee: 'Come down from the cross and we will believe that Thou art He.' Thou didst not come down, for again Thou wouldst not enslave man by a miracle, and didst crave faith given freely, not based on miracles.

"Thou didst crave for free love and not the base raptures of the slave before the might that has overawed him forever. But Thou didst think too highly of men therein, for they are slaves, of course, though rebellious by nature. Look round and judge; fifteen centuries have passed, look upon them. Whom hast Thou raised up to Thyself? I swear, man is weaker and baser by nature than Thou hast believed him! Can he, can he do what Thou didst? By showing him so much respect, Thou didst, as it were, cease to feel for him, for Thou didst ask far too much from him—Thou who hast loved him more than Thyself! Respecting him less, Thou wouldst have asked less of him. That would have been more like love, for his burden would have been lighter. . . . And so unrest, confusion and unhappiness—that is the present lot of man after Thou didst bear so much for his freedom!"

Discussion Questions: Freedom

1. For the Grand Inquisitor, humans are free, but this freedom is terrifying. Why is freedom feared? What would we rather have instead of freedom?

2. Contrast Paul's use of the word "freedom" with its usage in this excerpt. What are the characteristics of Christian freedom according to Galatians? Would Paul agree that humans prefer slavery to freedom? Why might this be so?

3. Finally, what is *your* understanding of Christian freedom? If you could speak to the Grand Inquisitor, what would you say? If Christ could speak to him, what do you think Christ would say?

INTRODUCTION TO ROMANS

Paul's letter to the Romans stands as the first among his letters because of its length, and as the premier epistle because of its place in the history of Christian thought. Those of us who are intimidated by "great books" approach this letter with fear and trembling. It is billed as "awe-inspiring," "magisterial," "dense," "theologically profound." Entire college courses are devoted to its study. Great tomes are written on its meaning. The giants of the Christian faith—Augustine, Martin Luther, Karl Barth—were inspired by its contents. In it Paul's monumental themes of grace, sin, justification, righteousness, and reconciliation are carefully argued and developed. I for one am overwhelmed by such a weighty and exalted text. What if I don't comprehend Romans in the way Paul intended? What if I miss the theological boat? Should I not wait to read it when I'm older and wiser?

I am heartened by the fact that Paul's audience, the church at Rome, knew neither Paul nor the scores of commentaries that have attached themselves, like barnacles on a boat, to the letter over the past twenty centuries. Clearly they thought it important: they preserved the letter. Probably it made a huge impact on them; the church at Rome went on to become (despite persecution) the preeminent church of the Western world. They were not encumbered with theological baggage and misconceptions, however. For them the words were fresh and new. Might we too read these words afresh? May we put aside notions of what we "ought" to receive from the letter and allow it to speak to us loud and clear?

As is the case with all the other study guides in this book, there are no "keys" for the "correct" or even "best" answers. The questions on Romans are invitations for your reflections, moderators in a panel discussion between you and the text. The resources you provide are a pencil, a dictionary, your time and energy. You need not suppose the work you do here is conclusive, but it does help you mark important milestones on your journey—a process of knowledge for some, of faith seeking understanding for others. The following information will set the stage for your reading.

We might imagine Paul sitting in a small room in Corinth. He is not alone. Evidence suggests that Paul's letters were group efforts, at least insofar as they were dictated to a scribe; probably the arguments were worked out in conversation with his companions. The year is around 57–58. Paul is making preparations for his next journey as he waits there in Corinth. He plans to go first to Jerusalem, bringing a gift from the Gentile churches, collections for the Jerusalem poor. Then he will go to Rome and points beyond, even as far as Spain. (We know that this plan foundered; Paul entered Rome not as a freeman, but under arrest after the Jerusalem visit.)

The Roman church was not founded by Paul; tradition holds that it was Peter's work. Its importance was immense. It was positioned in the capital of the empire and "all roads led to Rome." Paul supposed that the gospel would spread from this influential church westward, and he was correct. For these reasons Paul took great care in writing this letter, which follows many of the same themes as his earlier one to the Galatians. In fact, Galatians reads as a sort of rough draft, written in haste and in response to crisis. Romans has carefully measured arguments, which build on the Galatian letter but in a more systematic, well-organized, and theologically ambitious discourse.

Paul's great discovery was that the gospel of Jesus was not limited to its Jewish origins—that, in fact, it was universal in scope. Were it not for Paul, Christianity would have remained a Jewish sect, a Nazarene brand of Judaism. It would have required Gentiles to become Jews before entering the Christian church, and it would have eventually died on the vine. Jewish Christianity was, by its ethnic nature, exclusive. While it did not aim to undermine the universality of God's grace, the tendency of Jewish Christianity was to limit God to those covenant people to whom God was first made known. It was Paul's keen perception that showed the temporal nature of these limits, and the fact that with Christ the limits had faded away. Now the gospel was open to all peoples (as he wrote earlier, "There is no longer Jew or Greek, there is no longer slave or free, there is no longer male and female; for all of you are one in Christ Jesus," Gal. 3:28). This is because we are all justified—put in a right relationship with God—by faith. Here is the heart of Romans and of the entire gospel: justification *sola fide*, by faith alone.

Outline of Romans

I. Justification by Faith and Its Consequences: Romans 1—8
II. God's Righteousness Is Being Worked Out in the History of the Jews and the Gentiles: Romans 9—11
III. Ethical Implications of the New Life in Christ: Romans 12—15
(Rom. 16: a recommendation of Phoebe; perhaps a separate note intended for another church in Ephesus)

STUDY GUIDE FOR THE LETTER TO THE ROMANS

1. The greeting (1:1–7) and the thanksgiving (1:8–15). Jot down what these verses tell you about

Paul:_____

the church at Rome: _____

Jesus: _____

2. The thesis or theme of the letter. Read 1:16–17. The phrase "righteousness of God" can be read one of two ways: (1) It refers to God's justice, the fact that the holy God requires us to be righteous or morally right; or (2) it refers to God's mercy, the fact that the holy God establishes us to be in right relationship with God. Which of these readings best helps you understand Paul's thesis in 1:16–17?

_____

3. Faithless humanity and the power of sin: Romans 1:18—3:20.
How does humankind earn God's wrath? See 1:18–32.

_____

_____

_____

What do our *actions* have to do with God's wrath? See 2:5–11.

_____

_____

_____

Read 2:17—3:20. What, for Paul, is the value of being Jewish?

_____

_____

the value of circumcision?

_____

the value of torah (the law)?

_____

_____

Stop for a moment and reflect on what you have already read. In the argument of 1:18—3:20, how might you describe Paul's view of human nature?

_____

_____

_____

In this section, what does Paul say about the state of things for Jews and for Gentiles (Greeks)? In what ways are their situations similar?

_____

_____

_____

4. We are justified by faith alone: Romans 3:21—5:21. For each of the following terms, write out (1) a dictionary definition and (2) Paul's definition, as you infer it from the text.
A. Justification
(1)

_____

_____

(2)

_____

_____

B. Reconciliation
(1)

_____

_____
(2)

_____

_____

C. Grace
(1)

_____

_____
(2)

_____

_____

If righteousness comes *from God* (3:21–26), how does that affect the metaphor of God as judge?

_____

_____

If the righteousness from God is "apart from the law" (3:21), then what does Paul mean in 3:31 when he says, "Do we then overthrow the law by this faith? By no means! On the contrary, we uphold the law"?

_____

_____

In what ways is the timing of Abraham's being "counted righteous" important for Paul? See 4:4–12.

_____

_____

5. Sanctification, or life in the Spirit: Romans 6—8.
From your reading of 5:20–6:2, how are some people justifying the persistence of sin?

_____

_____

Explain what Paul means when he says that "all of us who have been baptized into Christ Jesus were *baptized into his death*" (6:2–4, emphasis added).

_____

_____

What does that "baptism into death" have to do with our being "dead to sin"? How are the two related?

_____

_____

If we are really *dead* to sin, how is it that we can still "let sin exercise dominion" in our bodies (6:11–14)?

_____

_____

Whereas believers were once "slaves of sin," Paul writes that believers now have become "slaves to

_____," which leads to

_____and whose end result is

_____. (6:15–23)
According to 7:1–6, how is a believer like a widowed woman?

_____

_____

In what ways is the existence of torah a good thing (7:7–20)?

_____

_____

On the other hand, what is the relationship between torah and sin?

_____

_____

If "I delight in the law of God in my inmost self," what is it about me that keeps me from doing good (7:14–25)? Is it (whatever "it" is) really part of me or not (7:20)?

_____

_____

See 8:1–3 on *freedom*. Those who are "in Christ Jesus" are freed from *what*?

_____

_____

The songwriter Bob Dylan wrote, "You've got to serve somebody." What are the choices of servitude, according to 8:5–11? If we choose to serve "the flesh," what happens? If we serve the Spirit, what follows?

_____

_____

_____

Explain your understanding of the differences between the "spirit of slavery" and the "spirit of adoption" (8:12–17).

_____

_____

Since we are "children" and "heirs" of God, we have a future that is good news. How does Paul describe this future (8:18–39)?

_____

_____

As *for now*, how are we comforted (8:26–39)?

_____

_____

After reading this section, (Romans 6—8), what is your understanding of sanctification, or life in the Spirit?

_____

_____

_____

6. The sovereignty of God: Romans 9—11. The transition from chapter 8 (nothing "will be able to separate us from the love of God in Christ") to chapter 9 ("I have great sorrow and unceasing anguish in my heart") is abrupt. What is Paul's concern in chapters 9—11?

_____

_____

Write out a dictionary definition of *sovereignty*.

_____

_____

Then show how Paul demonstrates God's sovereignty in 9:14–26.

_____

_____

_____

What does Paul say to those who consider God's choices unjust? How do *you* respond to this argument?

_____

_____

_____

How has Israel gone astray, and who is responsible for Israel's failure (9:30—10:21)?

_____

_____

What does Paul want for Israel? See 9:1–5, 10:1.

_____

For now, Christ is a stone over which Israel stumbles (9:30–33).
Yet the triumphant power and love of God will not allow Israel to fall. What does Paul say will happen in 11:1–2, 11–13, 25–32?

_____

_____

_____

Finally, Paul is overcome with awe in 11:33–36. What moves him from the "sorrow and anguish" of 9:2 to the hymn of praise in 11:33–36?

_____

_____

7. Life in the Christian Community; the pattern of Christ's life for others: Romans 12—15.
Read 12:1–8, then list the gifts of the Spirit within the community or "body of Christ."

_____

_____

_____

What does Paul say about revenge or retaliation in 12:9–21 and about judgment in 14:10–13?

_____

_____

How is Paul's confidence in Roman justice shown in 13:1–7?

_____

_____

Paul makes a distinction between those "weak" in faith and those who are "strong" in chapters 14 and 15:1–6. What should be the attitude of the strong toward the weak?

_____

_____

What does Paul say in this section about the model Christ provides?

_____

_____

_____

And so Paul demonstrates the movement from *faith alone* to life in the household of faith. Figure 8.1, "Paul's Argument in Romans," shows the relationship between the old covenant, which existed before Christ, and the new covenant, which comes with Christ.

Discussion Questions: Sin and Grace

You might have noticed that Paul does not use the word *sins* (plural), but the word *sin* (singular). The distinction is vital. While sins are attitudes, deeds, and thoughts that arise out of us, sin is the root and cause of these external manifestations. While sins are the symptoms, sin is the disease. And all of us exist in this

	Old Israel	**New Israel**
I. The "Righteousness of God"—Meaning?	God Demands Righteousness	God Declares Us to Be Righteous
II. The Means of Salvation	Human's Way: Obedience to Torah Makes Humans Righteous	God's Way: Justification by Faith Alone
III. The Character and Tone of the Covenant	Bondage, Slavery	Freedom, Liberations
IV. Function of Torah: (A) With Respect to God (B) With Respect to Other Human Beings	(A) To Save; to Justify Oneself (B) To Judge Others and the Self	(A) To Condemn, as Preparation for Faith (B) To Promote Unity, Edification, Reconciliation—"Build Up" the Body of Christ

Fig. 8.1 Paul's Argument in Romans

state of illness: all are in sin and have fallen short of the glory of God (Rom. 3:23).

While there is no substitute for the word *sin*, in reading Paul it is essential to rid ourselves of the notion that sins (misdoings, transgressions, errors) are what he is talking about. As Paul Tillich writes in our own time, sin is *separation*. It is our human condition, our very state of being. Sin is estrangement, alienation, division. This separation which is sin is manifested in three major ways: we are separated from God, from one another, and from ourselves. Paul's description of this last experience of sin is both personal and universal: "I do not understand my own actions. For I do not do what I want, but I do the very thing I hate. . . . The evil I do not want is what I do" (Rom. 7:15, 19). Why? Because of separation from self, because of sin "that dwells within me" (7:20).

Take one or more of the following passages from Romans and read aloud, using the word "separation" wherever you find the word "sin":

Romans 6:5–11
Romans 6:12–14
Romans 7:7–12
Romans 7:13–20
Romans 8:1–4

Reflect on what you have read. How does your perspective shift when you think of sin as separation? If sin is not what we *do* but what we essentially *are*, what difference does that make? If sin is the disease and sins are the symptoms, what then is the law? Why is torah, the law, useless as a cure for sin?

Finally, all that Paul has said about sin is weighted on the other side by the power of what he calls *grace*. "But where sin increased, grace abounded all the more, so that, just as sin exercised dominion in death, so grace might also exercise dominion through justification leading to eternal life through Jesus Christ our Lord" (Rom. 5:20–21). The Greek *charis* is translated "grace" or "free gift"; as the foil to sin/separation we may say *charis* is acceptance, reunion, reconciliation. Read these verses with that understanding in mind:

Romans 3:23–24
Romans 5:1–2
Romans 5:15–17

How does your thinking change when you understand grace as acceptance? What images or metaphors come to mind when you think of acceptance, reunion, reconciliation?

Sin is not simply a thing we do; grace is not simply a thing we have. Both have to do with our relationship to God. Both describe our very existence. Paradoxically, we live in separation, yet how much more do we live in reconciliation! This is the meaning of Paul's words, "where sin increased, grace abounded all the more."

A fitting conclusion for this discussion, and for Paul's argument on sin and grace in Romans, is found at the end of chapter 8: "For I am convinced that neither death, nor life, nor angels, nor rulers, nor things present, nor things to come, nor powers, nor height, nor depth, nor anything else in all creation, will be able to separate us from the love of God in Christ Jesus our Lord" (Rom. 8:38–39). With Christ, separation is overcome by reunion.

CHAPTER 9

The Prison Letters

INTRODUCTION TO THE PRISON LETTERS

The letters to the Colossians, Philemon, and the Philippians are treated as a group because of Paul's situation when he wrote them. He was under house arrest, supported in his ministry by the Philippian church, and waiting for release. He felt sure that he would be freed.

We know that such freedom was not to come for Paul if the site of imprisonment was Rome. There is much scholarly dispute over the provenance of the letters. Paul speaks of the praetorian guard and Caesar's household (not members of Caesar's personal family, but employees in the imperial civil service). These entities were found throughout the empire, however, not only in Rome. Ephesus in Asia Minor is put forth as a likely place for Paul's imprisonment for the following reasons:

1. Paul's close contact with the church at Colossae indicates rapid travel back and forth, not possible in the case of Roman imprisonment but certainly possible from Ephesus, only one hundred miles away. Likewise his communications with Philippi would have taken seven weeks from Rome, but only ten days from Ephesus.

2. Onesimus ran away from Colossae to join Paul, and Paul intends to send him back with the letter to Philemon. Again, the movement of this fugitive slave suggests Ephesus, a shorter and less hostile journey for an individual traveling in the empire.

3. Paul viewed Rome as a point on his way toward Spain, due west. However, in the prison letters he speaks of leaving imprisonment to visit the Philippians and the Colossians, in the east. Did he change his plans? Or was he not in Rome when he wrote the prison letters?

4. Two of Paul's friends sending greetings to Philemon were with him at Ephesus. Neither Timothy nor Aristarchus is mentioned in Acts as Paul's companion in Rome.

What do the letters actually say? Paul refers to multiple imprisonments in 2 Corinthians 11:23. The prison letters do not establish Paul's site at either Rome or Ephesus. They are clear only on the point of imprisonment, and we simply cannot know from whence Paul wrote.

However, the metaphor of prison functions in remarkable ways for Paul at the time, and for our understanding of the contents of these letters today. For Paul, the earthly and real circumstances of prison are the occasion for joy. Crisis becomes opportunity. Despite the chains, Paul is free in Christ, and he is thankful. His captivity (whether in Ephesus or in Rome) is secondary to the emancipation that is faith.

Reading the letters today, in particular the household code of Colossians and the treatment of slavery in Philemon, we might extend the metaphor of imprisonment. Paul was physically captive not only in space, but in historical time. His perspective was bound by Roman order and polity. The givens of Paul's world included not only prison, but society based on an extended patriarchal household and slavery. All were institutions that the Christian church inherited. Paul could no more have imagined another system (in which slavery was abolished, in which household systems were configured differently) than he could have imagined computerized Bibles. The empire and its practices provided the framework in which he wrote and thought.

The household code of Colossians 3:18—4:6 draws lines of submission and obedience from one household member to the next: slaves to masters, children to parents, wives to husbands. Some would say that hierarchies are implicit in the order of creation—that power is supposed to start from the top and flow down, from masters to slaves, from husbands to wives. In Colossians and Philemon, Paul is merely affirming what is.

But what about Galatians 3:28: "There is no longer Jew or Greek . . . slave or free . . . male and female; for all of you are one in Christ Jesus"? Here is the Magna Carta of reunion and reconciliation, the dissolution of societal (even natural) distinctions in the grace-ful nature of Christ Jesus. Why then, in the prison letters, did Paul send a slave back to his owner? Why does he tell wives to be subject to their husbands?

It was Paul's hope that Jesus would return soon, making earthly institutions such as slavery and marriage irrelevant. We also have an important clue in his argument: Paul's use of the word "fitting." Paul's advice in the household codes is the advice that any first-century moralist would give. It was the order of the day. Christians are not (yet) in a position to challenge this order; instead the world is watching, and unfitting behavior can only hurt the infant churches. Fitting, proper, and conventional behavior vis-à-vis the empire is necessary for their safety. Of course, persecution will come, because the gospel does not "fit" after all. Those who practice brotherly love will be deemed incestuous. Those who celebrate the Communion meal ("This is my body . . . this is my blood") will be declared cannibals. Those who bring male and female together in worship will be accused of unfitting orgies behind closed doors. Conventional behavior at home (Col. 3), the silencing of women in church (1 Cor. 14:34), even submission to the governing authorities (Rom. 13) did not protect the early church from its enemies as Paul had hoped.

Although he was imprisoned, Paul knew he was truly free in Christ. While he sought to accommodate the gospel to the prevailing order, the real freedom and unity in Christ that he preached would eventually prevail over that order. The keys of love and justice open prison doors. The good news cannot be confined to any one time, held captive in any one place, or subsumed to any existing social system.

STUDY GUIDE FOR COLOSSIANS

Colossae was a small town in the area of Asia Minor called Phrygia. Phrygians were fascinated with cults, notably the cult of the mother goddess Cybele, which originated there, and with the mystery religions. Magic competed with secret lore and cults competed with one another for spiritual excellence.

With the founding of a church at Colossae by Epaphras, the duel was between the Phrygian traditions, based on "elemental spirits of the universe," and the new teachings on Christ. Pagan (what is today called pre-Gnostic) teachers said Jesus was merely one of the elemental spirits (*stoicheia*)—there exists a hierarchy of spirits in which the fullness of mystery abides. These teachers insisted that Jesus-teaching was not enough. The church needed to progress from the simple gospel to the intricate teachings and ascetic practices that befitted the (elite) saved. With Epaphras in prison, what were the vulnerable Colossians to believe?

1. How does Paul describe his situation (1:24; 4:3, 18)?

_____

Who is Epaphras (1:3–8; 4:12–13)?

_____

See 2:1. Does Paul know the community personally?

_____

2. What kinds of things do the false teachers tell the Colossians to do in order to gain spiritual perfection?

2:16_____

2:18_____

2:20b–23_____

What would be the point of this asceticism and legalism?

_____

3. The false teaching was pre-Gnostic. It made salvation available to a spiritual elite, those who practiced and knew the "mysteries," which were unavailable to the rank and file. In contrast, how does Paul use the word "mystery" (*mysterion*) in 1:24—2:4? What limitations, if any, are placed on the mystery? What has happened to its hiddenness?

_____

_____

4. As Epaphras describes the church he founded to Paul, Paul sees that the real issue is the church's maturity before God. Its members feel they need to do more, to know more, to rise to spiritual heights. They seek perfection, thinking Christ is not enough. It must be "Christ and . . . ," not Christ alone. In his prayer for the faithful, what marks of maturity does Paul anticipate for them (1:9–14)?

_____

What will the mature church look like? Read 2:6–7 and draw a picture that captures these images.

5. The hymn to Christ, the Mystery of God. The remarkable christological passage of 1:15–20 is a treasure chest of ideas.

What is Christ's relation to God in 1:15a and 1:19?

_____

What is Christ's relation to the universe in 1:15b–17?

_____

What is Christ's relation to the church in 1:18?

_____

Who or what is reconciled (made right) by Christ in 1:20 (see also 1:21–22)?_____

How is the supremacy of Christ expressed in this hymn?

_____

_____

_____

6. Atonement refers to the saving work of Christ. How is this work described in 2:8–15?

_____

_____

What experience does the believer share with Christ?

_____

_____

What ideas in this passage are most meaningful to you?

_____

_____

7. Practical and ethical implications of the saving work of Christ. What does Paul say about:
the Christian's perspective on this world (3:1–4)?

_____

_____

the practices that must be "put away" (3:5–9)?

_____

_____

the new nature that must be "put on" (3:10–15)

_____

_____

What does the worshiping community practice according to 3:16–17?

_____

_____

See the household code of 3:18–4:1. Given the social arrangements of the first century, in what sense does Paul speak as a creature of his age?

_____

_____

Paul confirms that all these relationships are to be built around Christ. What difference does it make that he places all social arrangements under God?

_____

_____

STUDY GUIDE FOR PHILEMON

The shortest of Paul's letters was sent to Philemon, a slave owner in Colossae, along with the letter to the entire church. Tychichus was probably the bearer of both letters; he accompanies the fugitive slave Onesimus back to Colossae (Col. 4:7–9).

The institution of slavery was important to the Roman economic structure. Some six million slaves formed the base of the social pyramid, and provided skilled labor at little or no cost. The proportion of slaves to free people in the empire was about two to five. Revolts of disaffected slaves, such as that led by Spartacus, were frightening to the establishment. Slavery was enforced by laws punishing runaways (by death) and those who harbored them (with fines).

Legally, both Paul and Onesimus are guilty under Roman law. Personally, Paul has defrauded his friend Philemon by harboring the slave (who has, it appears, robbed his master). The situation calls for subtlety and diplomacy.

While Paul does not challenge the institution of slavery (he knows no other social arrangement), he tactfully asks for a radically different relation (as "brothers") between the master, Philemon, and his slave, Onesimus. Paul's persuasive powers are evident in every line of the little letter.

We don't know why Onesimus ran away, how he found Paul, or what he hoped for the future. We do know that once he found him in prison, Onesimus became like a son to Paul (v. 10) and was of such usefulness to him that Paul did not want to send him back (v. 13). Again, the situation is delicate. Paul's appeals to his friend push gently at the old fabric of legalized slavery and the new web of relationships made possible in Christ. Yet Paul seems sure that Philemon will not take the legal, easy way out, but will receive Onesimus back, this time as "a beloved brother" (v. 16).

The prison letters are dated somewhere between 56 and 61. Some fifty years later, Ignatius of Antioch wrote a letter to the bishop of Ephesus. In this letter Ignatius makes a play on the bishop's name ("useful") and refers to Philemon. Perhaps that bishop of Ephesus, named Onesimus, was the same person who ran to Paul for help years earlier and found freedom and empowerment in the gospel. It would make a fitting end to the story.

1. What picture do you have of Philemon after reading this letter, especially verses 1–2, 5, 7, and 17? (Note that the church at Colossae meets in Philemon's house.)

_____

_____

2. Onesimus means "useful" in Greek. What play on words does Paul use to persuade Philemon in verse 11?

_____

What picture do you have of Onesimus after reading this letter?

_____

3. What does Paul want Philemon to do (vv. 12–18)?

_____

_____

What do you think Paul is hinting in verse 21?

_____

4. What principle do you find in verse 16 that would eventually topple the institution of slavery altogether?

_____

_____

Discussion Questions

Why do you think Onesimus decided to return to Philemon? Could it have been something Paul said, or an experience he had? Use your imagination. Then read the parable of the prodigal son in Luke 15:11–32. How might the picture of reconciliation in this parable compare to the homecoming of Onesimus? Would it be similar or different? Why?

STUDY GUIDE FOR PHILIPPIANS

The descriptive word for this letter is "joyful." Paul is in chains, but the fruits of captivity are courage and confidence. As he reminds his beloved Philippian church, "Our citizenship is in heaven" (Phil. 3:20). In the letter Paul looks at this earth, this life, from heaven's point of view.

Luke's account of Paul's work in Philippi is one of the most dramatic and colorful chapters in the book of Acts. The mission begins with a heavenly vision in Acts 16:9. Paul is directed to set sail from Asia and go to Europe: "Come over to Macedonia and help us." First stop is Philippi. The story moves along quickly: Lydia received the gospel immediately, the slave girl was exorcised, Paul and Silas were beaten and thrown into prison. Their miraculous release, the conversion of the jailer, and the apologies they demanded (and got) from the Roman authorities make for splendid reading. See the account in Acts 16:11–40.

Given the turbulent beginnings, why is Paul so devoted to the Philippian church? For one, it is the first church he founded on European soil. For another, this church has supported him with gifts, financial assistance, and a partnership. In this support, the Philippians are unique (Phil. 4:15–16). In 2 Corinthians 8:2 Paul says of them, "Their abundant joy and their extreme poverty have overflowed in a wealth of generosity on their part." Furthermore, they sent the much-loved Epaphroditus to Paul in prison with still more gifts. While with Paul, Epaphroditus fell ill, news that brought great distress to the Philippian church (Phil. 2:25–30). On his recovery Epaphroditus is sent back home, carrying the warm letter to the church from Paul.

1. What are the sources of Paul's joy while in prison?

1:3–7_____

1:12–14_____

1:19–21_____

4:10_____

2. What does Paul's report from prison tell you about his situation, hopes, and morale?

1:12–14 (see also 4:22!)_____

1:23–26_____

2:24_____

4:11–13_____

When Paul says his desire is to depart (1:23), "departure" carries many images. Which of the following do you feel is closest to what he meant? (a) To pack up one's tent (b) To set sail (c) To set free a prisoner (d) To unyoke the oxen._____

3. How do you define "humility"? (a) Being a doormat, lacking in self-respect (b) Knowing your proper place in life (c) Using your strengths for the good of others (d) Other:

_____

How does Paul illustrate humility in 2:1–4?

_____

_____

_____

4. The hymn to Christ: Philippians 2:6–11.
How is Christ's self-emptying described in verses 6–8?

_____

_____

How is Christ's exaltation described in verses 9–11?

_____

_____

If you wish to dig deeper, go to the Suffering Servant psalm of Isaiah 52:13—53:12 and also Isaiah 45:23. What parallels do you find between the Hebrew scriptures and the hymn to Christ in Philippians?

_____

_____

5. How does Paul apply this hymn to Christian experience? Jesus is a model: he emptied himself in his service for others; he was filled up with grandeur by God. Paul describes this dynamic in his own life as well. See what he says about his losses and gains in 3:4–11:

_____

_____

_____

Paul speaks to the church about having "the same mind," in 2:2. What does this unity look like: Single-mindedness? Sameness? Conformity to one idea? Look at this exhortation in the context of 2:1–11 (note especially v. 5). Then describe what "being of the same mind" means in the Christian community.

_____

_____

_____

6. Opposition to Christ, Paul warns, takes basically two forms: legalism and licentiousness. What form is described in each passage?

3:2–4 _____

3:18–19 _____
What is the church's stance toward these opponents? See the athletic images in these verses:

1:27–30 _____

3:12–16 _____

7. Final appeals. Read 4:4–9.
What does Paul ask the church to do?

_____

_____

_____

Which verse appeals to you most? _____
Which exhortation do you find most difficult?

_____

What will be the fruits of Christian behavior?

_____

_____

Discussion Questions: The Prison Letters

1. "Work out your own salvation with fear and trembling; for it is God who is at work in you, enabling you both to will and to work for [God's] good pleasure" (Phil. 2:12–13).

Do you find this teaching logical or paradoxical? Who is doing the work here? Paul does not mean "work *for* your own salvation," but "see it through, follow it through to the end." What is the relationship between God's work and our own work?

2. The prison letters give us two complementary hymns to Christ. Paul stresses the *supremacy* of Christ in Colossians 1:15–20. He stresses the *humility* of Christ in Philippians 2:5–11. Taken together, we see that Jesus is supreme over all creation, yet this preeminence takes the form of the servant. On separate sheets of paper, write out each hymn in sense lines so you can see the structure of each. Then place the passages side by side. Where are the different emphases most apparent? What images guide and direct each hymn? Are there any terms or ideas you wish to explore? If so, use a Bible dictionary or a concordance to research these words. Finally, allow some time to reflect on the question: Who is Jesus Christ? Then try to formulate your own personal Christology. Artistic participants might paint a portrait; the rest of us will paint our picture in words.

ATONEMENT THEORIES

What did Christ do for us? Historically, the church has answered this question in a variety of ways. Theories of atonement (or redemption or reconciliation) are just that—theories—but underlying them are metaphors that can enrich and broaden your perspective on what the saving work of Christ means. The theories are not mutually exclusive. Rather, they present alternative forms of imagery that you might find helpful in answering for yourself the question, What did Christ do for us?

Figure 9.1, "Theories of the Atonement," presents three theories in schematic form.

The classical, or ransom, view was the dominant conception of atonement from the fourth through the eleventh centuries. It was put forth and developed by

Theories of the Atonement	I. Classical or Ransom View	II. Orthodox or Substitutionary View	III. Moral Influence View
Chief Problem for Humans	Enslavement to Sin and Death	Disobedience; Being Guilty	Fear of God and Our Inability to Respond to God
God's Response	To Defeat Those Powers Which Enslave	To Demand Justice, Satisfaction	To Provide the Embodiment of Love
Chief Actor in the Drama of Atonement	God	Christ	Humans
Christological Emphasis	The Resurrection and Christ's Triumph Over Death	The Crucifixion and Christ's Suffering	The Life and Teachings of Jesus; His Compassion
Key Terms	"Redemption" "Salvation"	"Justification"	"Conversion" "Regeneration"

Fig. 9.1 Theories of the Atonement

Irenaeus and Gregory of Nyssa. Its imagery depends on the ancient and medieval institutions of slavery, where persons could be freed from servitude if, and only if, the required price was paid. In the classical view, humanity has willingly given itself over to the powers of evil, incarnate in the devil. The devil was the slave owner who had the right to keep humanity in bondage. The ransom, or required price for freedom, was paid by God to the powers of evil. That ransom was God's son, Jesus. The resurrection broke the power of the demonic forces and freed humanity from enslavement to sin and death.

The orthodox, or substitutionary, view arose in the eleventh century with Anselm of Canterbury. Its images depend on the medieval institution of feudalism, where law and order rested on a strict code of honor. Instead of showing gratitude to their lord and creator, the liege, humanity, has disregarded God and disobeyed God's commands. The honor of God has been violated by human disobedience. However, God is no mere feudal lord; the gravity of the crime has been immense, as the stature of the Lord is immense. The only way to right the relationship was for the vassal (humanity) to make appropriate satisfaction (compensation) to the lord (God). But the dishonor was so great that humans, on their own, could not make restitution. The solution was for Christ to make the necessary satisfaction for humanity. Christ, the God-man, acts as the substitute for the human race. Satisfaction is paid to God on our behalf by Christ. Thus are we justified before God, and the proper relationship is restored.

The moral influence view also arose in the eleventh century, with Peter Abelard. (This scholar is also known in connection with Héloïse; theirs was a story of star-crossed love and lifelong commitment.) The human problem is our fear of God and our inability to respond to grace. Focusing on Jesus as the supreme manifestation of God's love, the moral influence view shows humanity moved and drawn to God by that love. Jesus' compassion kindles our hearts to be compassionate; his sacrificial love elicits a responding love. Here atonement is not a legal matter, and the categories of law and justice are not helpful. Jesus reaches out and draws us to God like a magnet. Our hearts are attracted by the embodiment of love found in Christ.

These views are all shaped by the experiences Christians had of the world, the social contexts in which they lived, and the prevailing institutions with which they were familiar. We think as creatures of our age. Theology speaks to us insofar as it speaks to our time and place. Thus the relationship between human experiences and biblical teaching is an ongoing process. Atonement theories must be dusted off, recast, formulated anew with each generation.

An important perspective on atonement is being formulated today by Christians who look at Christ's work for us, not in individual and spiritual terms, but in political ones. These Christians conceive of the salvation that Christ brings in terms of liberation from oppression. Liberation theology in its many forms (third-world, feminist, black) takes seriously Jesus' identification with the poor, the downtrodden, the powerless. The bondage they experience is manifested in social practices and political institutions. Those who suffer as Christ did find themselves empowered by Christ to work for societal change. The future is marked by God's justice and love.

Suggested Activities:

1. Read what a contemporary theologian has to say about atonement—what Christ's work means for us today. Use the categories in figure 9.1 to help you analyze what she or he says.

2. Explore one of the liberation theologies. What sort of language is used? How are key terms defined? Try to fill in the chart above from a liberation perspective.

3. Formulate your own theory of atonement. What do you think is the chief problem for us as humans? How would you describe God's response to this problem? Who is the chief actor in the drama of atonement? What aspects of Christology do you find most important here? Finally, what terms best describe for you the atoning work of Christ?

CHAPTER 10

Ephesians and the Pastoral Letters

INTRODUCTION TO THE PASTORAL LETTERS

No one says that New Testament scholarship is a simple exercise. The problems of authorship, intent, and historical context are nowhere more apparent than in the pastoral letters. The letters of 1 and 2 Timothy and Titus are known as the "pastoral" epistles because they deal with pastoral concerns, in particular with proper worship behavior and church leadership. In dealing with these issues, however, they raise a host of new issues for the contemporary reader.

The letters identify the author as Paul and the recipients as Paul's younger and close associates—Timothy and Titus. In 1 Timothy, Paul hopes to visit his "true son" soon; in 2 Timothy Paul is in chains, with no hope of release. Meanwhile the churches of Asia (the Roman province in western Asia Minor) have deserted him. Timothy is given instructions for dealing with the church at Ephesus while Titus is to establish church leadership on the island of Crete.

The church is patterned along the lines of the Roman household, with obedience and submission due to the paterfamilias. This model is carried over to the assembly, where the paterfamilias is the bishop and the various subgroups under his direction are given their proper duties. Paul writes these instructions so that "you may know how one ought to behave in the household of God" (1 Tim. 3:15). Finally, the letters deal with false teachers, who abuse the law (torah) and encourage ascetic practices; they must be countered or silenced.

Such is the data based on a quick read of the pastoral letters. But a closer reading indicates that the letters are not written by Paul. Before we pursue this argument, a few notes on New Testament authorship are in order.

1. Depending on the material, the modern reader reacts in various ways to pseudonymous authorship. Marian Evans used the pen name George Eliot; Samuel Clemens wrote under the name of Mark Twain. We have no problem with these pseudonyms. But if Marian Evans passed off her work as that of Mark Twain, we would call this a hoax, a forgery. A pen name is one thing, a deception another. What then is the author's intent in using a pseudonym?

2. Ghostwriting is a conventional practice today. We are familiar with corporate procedure where memos, letters, and reports are written by one person (or a committee) and signed by another. Similarly we know that politicians use speechwriters and researchers. The production of documents is one thing, their attribution another. Is the content consistent with the signatory's intent?

3. From a different historical perspective, it was common in antiquity for a writer to use the name of an honored predecessor. The writer's intent was not to deceive, nor to pull off a literary hoax, but to interpret the predecessor's teaching for a new time and context.

4. Questions of authorship are not the same as questions of authority. All twenty-seven books of the New Testament are recognized as canon, the scripture of the church. They have authority in spite of disputed claims of authorship.

The question for purposes of canonization, then, is not whether the document was written in Paul's own hand (after all, he used scribes for this laborious process). The question is whether the document is consistent with Christian doctrine and practice, that is, if the author writes "in the spirit of the apostle" or not. The pastoral letters are Pauline in that they represent Paul, the signatory, for an early second-century generation.

Let us return to the issue of authorship in the pastorals. What evidence does a close reading of these letters give us? How do these letters compare with the undisputed epistles (Romans, Galatians, 1 and 2 Corinthians, 1 and 2 Thessalonians, Philippians, Philemon)? How do these letters carry out the spirit of Paul's teaching?

Over a third of the words in the pastorals are not found in Paul's undisputed letters. Furthermore, 150 words are unique to the pastorals themselves, occurring nowhere else in the New Testament canon. Yet the greetings and closings of the letters include names of Paul's missionary companions. Summaries of Paul's teaching appear in fragments (1 Tim. 1:15–17; 2 Tim. 1:8–10; Titus 3:3–8), and a very Pauline last will and testament appears in 2 Tim. 4:6–8. The fragments and the moving farewell might be Paul's compositions, used by the author as reminders of what the church had received through the apostle.

Key words are interpreted differently in the pastorals. For Paul, "righteousness" denotes a new status in relation to God. In the pastorals, "righteousness" refers to a person's moral respectability and uprightness. Paul's emphasis on "faith, not works" is consistent in the undisputed letters, whereas good works appear to be ends in themselves in the pastorals, and "*the* faith" (emphasis added), a body of doctrine rather than a dynamic relationship, is to be upheld by true Christians. Bishops, elders, and deacons appear on the scene in the pastorals, replacing the apostles, prophets, and teachers of the Pauline epistles. In coping with heresy, Paul develops the kerygma in a creative response to false teachers, whereas the material in the pastorals typically contradicts, denounces, and ridicules them.

Paul shows that in Christ the old barriers that separated Jew and Greek, slave and free, male and female have been torn down. "All of you are one in Christ Jesus" (Gal. 3:28; also Rom. 10:12; 1 Cor. 12:13). Here is radical teaching indeed. But for the sake of church order and discipline, the distinctions between groups are preserved in the pastorals. Paul's emphasis on Christian freedom is missing; the word "freedom" does not appear at all in the pastorals. Women are to learn in silence, with full submission (1 Tim. 2:12); slaves are to submit to their masters (Titus 2:9). Women may attend public worship services, but they must be inconspicuous and they are not to preach or lead prayers. What has happened to "All of you are one in Christ Jesus"?

The question may be put in another way: What has happened between the time of Paul and the time of the pastorals? The organization of house churches in the mid-first century was fluid rather than fixed. But the author of the pastorals assumes a stable hierarchy in an organized worship setting. Ordained ministers must meet specific qualifications. Churches are now, in the early second century, dealing with a different set of problems than they faced in the first flush of Paul's mission work. They must defend the faith and strengthen their organization in order to survive. As you read, look for the ways pastors are told to keep the church healthy and strong in a later generation.

STUDY GUIDE FOR 1 AND 2 TIMOTHY, TITUS

1. The problem of heresy. Heresy denotes doctrine or practices contrary to generally accepted beliefs. In what ways are false teachers perverting the gospel?
1 Tim. 1:3–7

_____

_____

1 Tim. 4:1–3

_____

_____

I Tim. 6:3–5

_____

_____

2. Credentials for pastors. What should the church leadership look like in the second century, according to 1 Tim. 3:1–7?

_____

_____

_____

Evidently many "deacons" served under one bishop, or overseer. See 1 Tim. 3:8–13, especially verse 10. What kind of "test" do you think deacons were given?

_____

_____

3. Women in church. While Paul put restrictions on women's behavior in public worship, he insisted on their equality "in Christ" (see 1 Cor. 14:33ff.; compare Rom. 16:1). The pastorals take Paul's restrictions even farther. What is taught in 1 Tim. 2:9–15?

_____

_____

What is the basis for this teaching?

_____

Do you think these verses are meant to be applied to all women in all times and places, or do they apply only to a special problem with a special church? Why?

_____

_____

Use these same questions for the teaching on slaves in 1 Tim. 6:1–2.

What seems to be the problem with the widows in 5:3–16?

_____

_____

_____

4. Function of the church. The church must be orderly because it is the pillar and bulwark of the truth (1 Tim. 3:15). What instructions on worship are given in the following passages?
1 Tim. 2:1–9

_____

1 Tim. 5:17–22

_____

5. In 1 Timothy, the author reminds Timothy of the good faith, the good teaching, the good confession. What is the content of this teaching according to these verses?
1:15

_____

2:5–6

_____

3:16

_____

6. The letter called 2 Timothy is deeply personal and moving in tone. The author is in chains, awaiting his death and the heavenly kingdom (see 4:6–8). This is a last will and testament to a younger and beloved disciple. What is Timothy told to do, and why, in these passages?
2 Tim. 1:6–8

_____

2 Tim. 1:13–14

_____

2 Tim. 2:1–3

_____

2 Tim. 4:1–5

_____

7. On dealing with controversy.
What are the signs of the "last days," according to 2 Tim. 3:1–5?

_____

How does the advice in 3:5 compare with that in 2:25–26?

_____

What do you suppose these people are quarreling about in 2 Tim. 2:14–19?

_____

What is the role of sacred writings or scripture in 3:14–17?

_____

(Note that the author is talking about the Hebrew scriptures; the Christian canon was not set for another two hundred years.)
8. What three metaphors does the writer use to describe the commitment of the Christian in 2 Tim. 2:4–6?

_____

Looking back over the books of 1 and 2 Timothy, which metaphor do you think best applies to the writer? to Timothy? Why?

_____

9. The little letter of Titus is concerned with the formation of churches in Crete. Elders are to be appointed in every town (1:5). Titus is reminded of the qualifications church leaders should have, and the importance of sound doctrine. Here is an infant church in a land said to be full of "liars, vicious brutes, and lazy gluttons" (1:12). Adding to this uncivilized climate, churches face direct opposition. Opponents are Jewish rivals who uphold
1:10 _____
1:14 _____
1:15 _____
3:9 _____
10. What is the effect of these opponents? See Titus 1:11.

_____

11. What good deeds are required of these groups?
older men (2:2) _____
women (2:3) _____
younger women (2:4–5) _____
younger men (2:6) _____
slaves (2:9–10) _____
the churches in general (3:1–2) _____

12. How does the list of qualifications in Titus 1:6–9 compare with 1 Timothy 3:1–7? What does the addition of Titus 1:7 tell you?

_____

_____

_____

13. The environment in Crete was hostile and unruly. In contrast, how are Christians to behave? See 2:11–13 and 3:3–8.

_____

_____

_____

Discussion Questions: The Pastoral Letters

1. Compare Paul and the pastorals with regard to the relationship between faith and works, or between grace and ethics. Suggested passages:
Pauline letters: Romans 3:9–20; Romans 6:1–14; Romans 9:30–33; Galatians 2:15–21; Galatians 5:1–6
Pastorals: 1 Timothy 4:6–8; 1 Timothy 2:15; 2 Timothy 2:19–21; 2 Timothy 3:14–17; Titus 2:11–14; Titus 3:1–8.

2. The books of the New Testament speak with different voices and witness to different traditions. What are the major emphases of the pastoral letters? Why do you think such matters as church doctrine and structure are stressed here and not elsewhere?

3. The letters to Timothy could be subtitled "Instruction for a Young Preacher." "Don't let anyone look down on you because you are young," Timothy is advised. Look back over what you have read, especially 1 Timothy 4:11–16; 2 Timothy 1:3–7; 2 Timothy 2:22. If you were a young preacher, what advice would mean the most to you?

INTRODUCTION TO EPHESIANS

This magnificent New Testament book is Pauline in that it owes much to Paul's theology and writings, but it is unique in that the author is a theologian in his own right. Dated around A.D. 90, Ephesians witnesses to the influence of Paul after his martyrdom. In the book we may trace developments of Paul's thought as well as many distinctive contributions coming from what must surely be Paul's best student.

Originally the salutation read simply "To the saints" (Eph. 1:1). In the fourth century, "at Ephesus" was added, possibly because the letter circulated through Asia Minor and ended up there. No mention is made of specific problems or individuals in Ephesus. The letter to the Ephesians is really a letter "to whom it may concern," or better, a treatise for churches everywhere. Meditation and prayer best describe its format as the author reflects on the great themes of theology (or the nature of God) and ecclesiology (or the nature of the church). Ephesians is close in style to Colossians, duplicating many words and themes but reworking them in a new context. While Colossians is concerned with Christ, Lord of all creation, Ephesians is concerned with Christ's body, the church. The agent of unity and the manifestation of God's plan for humanity is to be found in the universal church.

Outline of Ephesians

I. Theological Affirmation: The Unity of All Things in Christ: Ephesians 1—3.
II. Ethical Teaching: The Practical Consequences of Unity in Christ: Ephesians 4—6.

STUDY GUIDE FOR EPHESIANS

1. Ephesians opens with a prayer of blessing in 1:3–14. Here we find the major themes that will be developed in the writing. "We" refers to the Jews; "you" refers to the Gentiles. What is God's plan for the entire world (1:10)?

Through whom is this plan realized (1:7)?

What is the first sign or seal of God's plan (1:13–14)?

2. Read the thanksgiving passage of 1:15–23. What does the author want the readers to know about God's power among them?

3. Write out and memorize the great teaching on salvation found in 2:8–9.

4. The relationship between Jew and Gentile. Note that torah and the Temple, gifts from God, had actually functioned in history as dividing walls between God's chosen people and everyone else. Human hostility had taken God's gifts and made them something God never intended they become: agents of separation and rivalry. See 2:11–22. Before Christ came, our problem was one of alienation from God and from one another. What was the model of alienation (2:11–12)?

What has happened to the old distinction between Jew and Gentile?

What is the new human type created by God in Christ?

Is this new creation a future hope or a present reality? See 3:1–6. What then is "the mystery of Christ"?

5. Ecclesiology, or doctrine of the church. What does God intend to do through the church? See 3:10–12.

What three figures does the author use to describe the church? How well do you think these analogies "work," and why?
1:22–23

2:19–22

5:23–33

6. The Trinitarian emphasis of Ephesians. While the doctrine of the Trinity (one God, three Persons) was not explicitly formulated until the Council of Nicaea in A.D. 325, the author of Ephesians uses Trinitarian language to show that the church (1) has been called by God, (2) has been redeemed and forgiven through Christ, and (3) is directed by the divine, indwelling Spirit. Read the following verses, then write what they have to say about each Person in the Trinity: Eph. 1:5, 12, 13; 2:18–22; 3:14–17.
A. God:

B. Christ:

C. Holy Spirit:

7. Because there is one Spirit, one Lord, one God, the teaching material that begins in chapter 4 stresses the unity of the church. What is the difference between the unity that already exists (4:3–6) and that which is yet to come (4:13–16)?

What are the various gifts found in 4:8–13? What is their purpose?

8. Put off the old self; put on the new. Reading 4:17—5:21, list the old, hostile attitudes and behaviors that must be put aside. Then list the characteristics of the new life that must be put on. How do these two lists compare?

_____

_____

_____

_____

9. Ephesians 5:21—6:9 closely resembles the household code in Colossians 3:18—4:1. However, the Ephesians material uses marriage to make a point about the church. What is this distinctive teaching?

_____

_____

How does 5:21 apply to all the relationships here? How could this household code be misused apart from this context?

_____

_____

10. God's plan for the fullness of time is to unite all things in heaven and on earth in God (1:10). The symbol of that plan is the church; the seal is the Holy Spirit. But as Paul writes in 2 Cor. 10:3–4, "Indeed, we live as human beings, but we do not wage war according to human standards: for the weapons of our warfare are not merely human, but they have divine power to destroy strongholds." Ephesians describes this warfare in cosmic terms. On a separate piece of paper, draw a picture of the Christian warrior after reading 6:10–18. Label the six pieces of armor and write out the marching orders.

Discussion Questions: Ephesians

1. What does a mature Christian look like? How would you describe a person who is growing up "in every way . . . into Christ"?

2. Discuss several ways in which the teachings in Ephesians can be useful in the modern "ecumenical movement" (1) on a worldwide level; (2) on the national level; (3) on your own local level.

CHAPTER 11

Hebrews

INTRODUCTION TO HEBREWS

The book of Hebrews is a favorite of mine because it is in itself a study on the Old Testament, or the Hebrew scriptures. To read Hebrews is to remind New Testament students of our roots in Jewish history, theology, and understanding of the covenant. Not knowing (or caring) about the Hebrew backdrop to the New Testament is like dismissing one's family tree.

Unfortunately, many contemporary Christians are ignorant of these roots. Like Marcion, a religious leader in Rome c. A.D. 140–160, they feel that the Old Testament God is miles away from the New Testament God, and that the Old Testament canon is passé. Marcionite Christianity was condemned by the early church fathers, notably Irenaeus, who insisted that the Christian faith was continuous with the Hebrew scriptures. Why? Jesus claimed that continuity, for one thing. Secondly, there are not two Gods, one of creation (Old Testament) and one of salvation (New Testament), but one God who is author of all. Third, the Old Testament prophets are not to be dismissed; they were inspired by the same God who sent the Son to the world for us. To reject the Old Testament is to jettison belief in the Creator and the goodness of creation, to undermine the historical value of the prophets and covenant history, and to ignore, even scorn, Jesus' understanding of himself.

However, there are many who neglect the Old Testament, not out of some misguided conviction as Marcion, but simply because they lack the training and background to read these scriptures for meaning. The material appears foreign, the quantity overwhelming. For these the book of Hebrews and a bit of patience can serve as a primer for Old Testament studies. Be prepared to flip back and forth between Hebrews and the Torah, or first five books of the Old Testament. Be prepared to study some prophetic teachings and to enter the mysterious world of sacrificial liturgy. In doing so you will *see* the continuity between the Old Testament and the New Testament, *learn* much in the way of Old Testament history, and *trace* the unfolding of Old Testament themes in New Testament thought.

Based on the closing remarks in Hebrews 13:18–25, in which the author asks for the prayers of the congregation "so that I may be restored to you very soon" (13:19), Hebrews is commonly called a letter. Up to that point, however, the book has the character of a carefully reasoned treatise rather than a letter. The author writes not as a historian, church leader, or even as an evangelist, but as a theologian. The author ranks (along with Paul) as one of the first theologians of the Christian faith.

The book is unique to the New Testament canon in that one major thesis is developed and sustained throughout the entire document. What keeps the argument vital are two concerns: the Old Testament is the key to understanding the work of Christ, and the church (in Rome?) is in a crisis situation. Whether Hebrews was written to Christians who had undergone persecution in the past or Christians who might face it in the near future is impossible to ascertain. Perhaps both cases are true. The emperors Nero (in the 60s) and Domitian (in the 90s) both persecuted Roman Christians. The book is commonly dated c. 80–90. Its authorship, for those who insist on this information, "is known to God alone" (Origen first said this). We know the author only by his eloquence and concern, and by the author's excellent training in scripture (that is, the Old Testament). In studying this book, may we become more eloquent and concerned, as well as trained in Hebrew scripture!

Outline of Hebrews

I. Jesus as Son of God Speaks from God to Humans: Hebrews 1:1—4:13

II. Jesus as High Priest Speaks to God on Behalf of Believers: 4:14—10:19

III. Go Forward in the New and Living Way Pioneered by Jesus: 10:19—13:25

A QUICK OLD TESTAMENT SURVEY AS SEEN IN HEBREWS

DIRECTIONS: Match the Old Testament material with the appropriate passage from Hebrews. The list of citations from Hebrews appears at the end of this section. If you wish to dig deeper, read the Old Testament citations too.

_____The Lord God created male and female in the image of God, giving them dominion (lordship and stewardship) over the rest of creation. (Gen. 1:26–31; Ps. 8.)

_____God called Abraham from Ur in Sumer, thereby "creating" the first patriarch of the chosen people. God's covenant with Abraham was threefold: God would make a mighty nation from his offspring, they would inherit the Promised Land (Canaan, or Israel), and through him all the nations of the earth would be blessed. Incidentally, Abraham was ninety-nine years old when he was told he would have an heir! (Gen. 12:1–3; 17:1–8; 21:1–7.)

_____ Abraham met a mysterious priest-king of Salem (Jerusalem) named Melchizedek. Nothing is known of him other than his designation as priest of "God Most High." The *first* priest mentioned in the Old Testament, he blessed Abraham and Abraham gave him a tenth of all he owned. (Gen. 14:18–20; Ps. 110:4.)

_____ Seven hundred years after Abraham was told he would be the father of a nation, we find this nation enslaved in Egypt. Around 1290 B.C., Moses is designated their leader, and out of Egypt they go (the exodus). Moses was unique in all of Old Testament history; he was the only one whom the Lord knew face to face. (Ex. 3:7–12; Ex. 14; Deut. 34:10–12.)

_____The terms of the covenant made with the Hebrews under Moses were simple: God said, in effect, "If you obey my voice, you will be my people" (Ex. 19:3–6). Obeying God's voice meant obeying God's torah, or law. The Mosaic covenant was ratified in a rather messy ceremony: once the people agreed to be obedient to the law, oxen were sacrificed and their blood was thrown all over the altar and on the people themselves. Why? Blood is the sign of life. The covenant gave the Hebrews life as God's people. The splattering of blood established the covenant community between God and the Hebrews. (Ex. 24:3–8.)

_____Once out of Egypt, however, the Hebrews were an ornery lot. They repeatedly complained and grumbled about their sojourn in the wilderness. Finally they rebelled against Moses and made plans to return to Egypt. For this, they spent another forty years wandering in the desert, so that it was a new generation who entered the Promised Land. The old, rebellious generation died off in the wilderness. (Ex. 17:1–7; Num. 14:1–35.)

_____While in the wilderness, the Lord instructed the Hebrews to make a Tabernacle, or a portable tent of meeting. Inside the Tabernacle a curtain separated the Holy Place from the most sacred space in the Tabernacle, called the Holy of Holies. Only the high priest could enter this space. The Holy of Holies housed some sacred objects: the *mercy seat* sat atop the *ark of the covenant*, wherein was placed a jar of manna (from the wanderings), Aaron's rod (confirming his priesthood), and the tablets of stone (Decalogue, or Ten Commandments). The presence of God dwelt most especially in that space defined by the mercy seat. (Ex. 40.)

_____ Moses and his older brother, Aaron, were from the tribe of Levi, Levi being one of the twelve sons of Jacob (Jacob was also known as "Israel"). Aaron and his descendants were designated the high priests of the Israelites, and given the tribe of Levi as helpers. Thus we have the Levitical priesthood, and the book of Leviticus, which details their duties. (Ex. 28:1; Num. 1:47–54.)

_____The Mosaic covenant and torah were received by Moses on Mount Sinai (also called Mount Horeb), somewhere on the southern tip of the Sinai peninsula between Egypt and Israel. Mount Sinai, while safe for Moses, was a place of deadly holiness; anyone who approached it was to be killed. Smoke, fire, and earthquakes on the mount were the signs of God's presence there. (Ex. 19:10–23.)

_____ In that priestly handbook called Leviticus, the word "blood" appears over forty times in connection with sacrifices. Why was the shedding of blood so important in making atonement with God? In the exact retribution teaching of "eye for eye, tooth for tooth, life for life," sin against God required as payment no less than the shedding of one's blood, the seat of life. Fortunately provision was made for *substitutionary* sacrifice. An animal was killed instead of the sinner, with the sinner laying hands first on the animal to symbolize identification with the slain. Blood of the animal acted then as a covering for sin. It blotted out the transgression. Such was the ancient idea of atonement, or reconciliation with God. It should also be noted that no sacrifices could be made for deliberate sins, only those made unwittingly. (Num. 15:22–31; Lev. 1.)

———————————————————Yom Kippur, the Day of Atonement, is described in Leviticus as the most important day in the liturgical calendar. After laying hands on the scapegoat, the high priest would send the goat into the wilderness, thus bearing away the sins of the entire congregation. With Yom Kippur, atonement (forgiveness and reconciliation) was made for all Israel once a year. Great shouts of thanksgiving accompanied the release of the goat as the slate was wiped clean—a fresh start was made possible! (Lev. 16.)

———————————————————Over six hundred years after the conquest of Canaan, the Israelites experienced a crisis of great magnitude. Nebuchadnezzar invaded the Southern Kingdom of Judah in 586 B.C., destroyed the Temple and most of Jerusalem, and deported the king and leading citizens to Babylon. The Babylonian Captivity marks the lowest point in Old Testament history. But it was to these captives that the great prophet Jeremiah addressed his Book of Consolation (Jer. 30—31). Therein he foretells the coming days when the Lord will make a "new covenant" with God's people—one based not on human obedience, as the Mosaic covenant was, but on divine forgiveness. It will be marked by a change of heart, and it will be everlasting. In calling scripture written after Jesus' resurrection the "New Testament," the church affirms its belief that the new covenant of Jeremiah has been actualized. (See especially Jer. 31:31–34 and 32:37–41.)

Citations found in Hebrews that "match" the items above:

1. Hebrews 1:1–8.
2. Hebrews 3:1–6.
3. Hebrews 3:7–19.
4. Hebrews 5:1–4 and 7:11.
5. Hebrews 6:13–15.
6. Hebrews 7:1–10.
7. Hebrews 8:6–13.
8. Hebrews 9:1–5 and 10:19–21.
9. Hebrews 9:6–7.
10. Hebrews 9:11–14 and 10:11.
11. Hebrews 9:18–22.
12. Hebrews 12:18–24.

STUDY GUIDE FOR HEBREWS

Now that you have a sense of the Old Testament background of the book, let us examine the message. The writer concludes, "I appeal to you, brothers and sisters, bear with my word of exhortation, for I have written to you briefly" (13:22). What audience was being addressed? What exhortations does the author feel must be made? And on what basis does the author formulate the argument?

1. The audience was a community that recognized the importance of Moses and the priesthood. They had a good grasp of Hebrew scriptures and the imagery of Jewish worship. However, the community was experiencing difficulty. Briefly summarize the dangers they faced according to these verses:

2:1 _____

3:12 _____

4:11, 14 _____

5:11–14 _____

10:23–25, 35–36 _____

In contrast to their present apathy and spiritual laziness, the author reminds them of an earlier time when they showed great confidence. See 10:32–34. How would you describe this earlier time?

_____

_____

2. The author's style is distinctive in its use of exposition ("Since God or Christ has done this . . . ") and exhortation ("Therefore let us do this . . . "). For example, read and briefly summarize the arguments in these passages:

A. exposition of 1:1–4 _____

  exhortation of 2:1–4 _____

B. exposition of 3:1–6 _____

  exhortation of 3:7–15 _____

C. exposition of 4:14–15 _____

  exhortation of 4:16 _____

D. exposition of 10:11–18 _____

  exhortation of 10:19–22 _____

3. The Greek philosopher Plato (fifth century B.C.) understood two spheres of existence: the material (or earthly) world, characterized by change and corruption, and the spiritual (or heavenly) world, characterized by perfection and incorruptibility. For Plato, the latter is the real world of forms, ideas, the Good. The earthly realm is but a shadow, a muddled and muddied reflection of true reality. For example, earthly love, no matter how pure, is at best only a reflection of Perfect Love, an eternal form, or prototype. The author of Hebrews similarly thinks in terms of two spheres of existence. See and summarize the Platonic thinking in:

8:5 _____

10:1 _____

The author, however puts a special twist on this Platonic outlook. In Hebrews, the contrast is not so much between *heavenly* and *earthly* things, but between the *old* and the *new* things. The past is the type for the present; Moses and Melchizedek prefigure the work of Christ.

A. How does Jesus compare to Moses? See 3:1–6.

_____

_____

B. How does Jesus resemble Melchizedek with respect to:
the extent (in time) of their priesthoods (6:20; 7:3)?

_____

the means by which they became priests (7:15–16, 20–22; 5:10)?

_____

C. How is the blood of Christ superior to the blood of animal sacrifices (9:13–14; 10:4)?

_____

D. How is the atonement made by Christ superior to Yom Kippur (the annual Day of Atonement) (9:12; 10:14)?

_____

E. How is Jesus superior to the high priesthood (7:11, 23–28; 9:24–26)?

_____

_____

4. "High priest" is the dominant title for Christ in chapters 7—10. This title shows Christ's uniqueness: there can be only one high priest at any given time. However, the author also argues that Christ was in

every way "like us," that is, human. See and summarize the humanness of Jesus in these verses:

4:15 _____

5:7 _____

12:3 _____

Then read the important passage in 2:10–18. Why is it essential that Jesus was one of us? What is the connection between what happened in Christ and what is to happen in ourselves?

_____

_____

Finally, see the titles for Christ found only in Hebrews:

2:10 _____

6:20 _____

12:2 _____

What metaphors or images come to mind as you reflect on these titles? Draw one of these pictures in the margin or on a separate sheet of paper.

5. For a discussion of Hebrews 11, see the next section, on "The Great Cloud of Witnesses."

6. The author gives some specific advice to his audience about how they are to treat one another. What is the advice given in these passages?

12:15 _____

12:25 _____

13:1 _____

13:4 _____

13:5 _____

13:7 _____

13:17 _____

7. The author also gives some specific advice to his audience about how they are to treat others—those who are not (yet) in the congregation. What is the advice given in these passages?

12:14 _____

13:2 _____

13:3 _____

13:9 _____

13:16 _____

Summary: Jesus Christ, the great high priest, is the mediator of the new covenant. Jesus is the one, sufficient sacrifice for sin, having made atonement for all in a concrete, unrepeatable historical deed. Jesus learned obedience to God and sympathy for us through the things he suffered. "Jesus Christ is the same yesterday and today and forever" (13:8).

Therefore, "let us run with perseverance the race that is set before us" (12:1), encouraging one another and cultivating Christian virtues. The closing benediction is a fitting end to your study. "Now may the God of peace, who brought back from the dead our Lord Jesus, the great shepherd of the sheep, by the blood of the eternal covenant, make you complete in everything good so that you may do his will, working among us that which is pleasing in his sight, through Jesus Christ, to whom be the glory forever and ever. Amen" (13:20–21).

THE GREAT CLOUD OF WITNESSES: HEBREWS 11

This chapter is traditionally known as the "roll call of the heroes of faith." Again we return to the Hebrew scriptures for a mini-lesson on these personalities. Go to the scripture references if you wish to dig deeper.

Hebrews 11:4. Abel and Cain, first sons of the primeval first family, both offered sacrifices to God. The Genesis record does not tell us why God chose or "preferred" Abel's sacrifice over brother Cain's. The first murder, the horror of fratricide, is the real focus of the story. Thus began the spread of sin throughout the earth. (Gen. 4:1–16.)

Hebrews 11:5. Enoch is listed as one of the descendants of Adam and Eve in Genesis 5, in the "book of the generations" (5:1, RSV). He is six generations removed from Adam and the great-grandfather of Noah. While nothing is recorded about his life, of his death it is written simply that "he was no more, because God took him." In other words, he never actually died! (Gen. 5:21–24.)

Hebrews 11:7. Noah lived at a time when "the wickedness of humankind was great in the earth," but he was favored by God. He built an ark and survived the great flood, together with his family and two "of every living thing, of all flesh." After the flood God set a "bow in the clouds" as a promise never again to flood the earth, but the story ends as it began: "the inclination of the human heart is [still!] evil from youth" (Gen. 8:21; see 6:5, 19).

Hebrews 11:8–12. Abraham, as we have already noted, was the first patriarch of the chosen people. Rather than dealing with the whole earth as in Genesis 1—11, God chose instead to focus on an individual in Genesis 12 and work through him and his descendants. One of God's promises is enacted as Abraham ("one as good as dead") and Sarah have a son, Isaac, late in life. From Isaac came Jacob, and from Jacob twelve sons, from whom the twelve tribes of Israel are descended. (Gen. 12—17.)

Hebrews 11:17–19. Abraham's faith was tested when he was told to take the heir to the promise, his only son Isaac, and offer him as a sacrifice to God. Just as the boy was about to be killed, the Lord's angel intervened and Abraham was blessed for not withholding his only son from God. This strange story is given a twist in the book of Hebrews: Abraham figured that God *could* raise a person from the dead, and God *would* do so in order to fulfill his first promise (Isaac being heir to the promise).

Hebrews 11:20. Isaac grew up, married Rebekah, and the couple had twins: Esau and Jacob. Esau was favored by his father, while Jacob was his mother's favorite. When Isaac was old and blind, he called in Esau to receive the blessing. Rebekah and Jacob tricked him, substituting Jacob in Esau's place. The blessing passed on to Jacob (later renamed "Israel"), with Esau (the father of the Edomites near Israel) receiving a lesser blessing instead. (Gen. 27.)

Hebrews 11:21. Jacob dies in Egypt, his family having settled there in the land of Goshen to escape the famine back in Canaan. Before he died, Jacob adopted his two grandsons: Ephraim and Manasseh. In adopting them he made them full-fledged heirs to the promise. These two became powerful tribes in Israel. (Gen. 48.)

Hebrews 11:22. Jacob and his clan found safe haven from the famine in Egypt because of Joseph, his favorite son. Fed up with Joseph's status, his brothers sold him to slave traders, who brought him to Egypt. In a stunning reversal of misfortune, Joseph eventually became prime minister to the pharaoh. As he told his brothers, "Though you intended to do harm to me, God intended it for good, in order to preserve a numerous people, as [God] is doing today" (Gen. 50:20). He went on to foretell the exodus from Egypt, which would occur over four hundred years later, saying "God will . . . bring you up out of this land to the land that he swore to Abraham, to Isaac, and to Jacob." (Gen. 50:22–26.)

Hebrews 11:23. Moses was born during the time of a decree from the Egyptian pharaoh stating that all male Hebrew babies were to be thrown into the Nile. Respecting the letter of the law but subverting its intent, Moses' mother, Jochebed, took her three-month-old baby and put him in a basket, then placed the basket strategically among the reeds of the Nile at just the place where the pharaoh's daughter went to bathe. Thus the boy was found by a sympathetic caretaker and raised in the pharaoh's household (Ex. 2:1–10).

Hebrews 11:24–28. Moses' years in the pharaoh's household are hidden from us; when we next see him he is full grown and taking a tour of the labor camps in which his people worked. (How did he know his identity as a Hebrew? Perhaps it was from his mother, who was taken by the pharaoh's daughter as nursemaid for Moses when she found him at the Nile.) Moses saw an Egyptian beating a Hebrew in the labor camp, and killed the Egyptian. Subsequently he fled Egypt to escape punishment, settling for a while in Midian. It was there, on Mount Horeb (Sinai), that he was called by God. Returning to Egypt, he confronted the pharaoh with the demand to "let my people go." Ten plagues later, after the death of the firstborn Egyptian males, the pharaoh did just that. The blood of the lamb on the doorpost signaled the destroyer to "pass over" the Hebrew households during this last plague. (Ex. 2:11–15; 3; 5:1; 12.)

Hebrews 11:29. The "faith" of the people here was preceded by their panic when they were pursued by the Egyptians to a sea of reeds (*yam suph*, often mistranslated "Red Sea"). "It would have been better for us to serve the Egyptians than to die in the wilderness." (Ex. 14:12). However, the waters were parted by the Lord, and they crossed over on dry ground, safe and sound. The waters returned to engulf the hostile Egyptian army. The exodus from Egypt completed, the Hebrews went forth, bound for the Promised Land. (Ex. 14.)

Hebrews 11:30–31. Forty years later, the Hebrews once again crossed over a body of water, this time the Jordan River. They entered the Promised Land from the east and camped on the plains of Jericho. Joshua (their leader now that Moses was dead) had already sent spies to Jericho to get the lay of the land. The spies found safekeeping in the house of Rahab, a prostitute. She cleverly hid the spies from the king of Jericho, professed her faith in "the LORD your God," and obtained a promise that she and her household would be spared destruction when the Hebrews attacked. When the walls of Jericho fell with a shout, the spies brought out Rahab and all her household. "Her family has lived in Israel ever since. For she hid the messengers whom Joshua sent to spy out Jericho" (Josh. 6:25). (See also Josh. 2 and 6:1–24.)

Others are mentioned in Hebrews 11:32–38, a few named and many unnamed. What we have here is a "great . . . cloud of witnesses" (12:1), folk who surround us and look upon us from their posts in the past. They encourage us to "run with perseverance the race that is set before us" (12:1), the race that they too ran, the race that was first finished by Christ.

These heroes of faith are not so much role models as they are witnesses to *our* faith. It is as if (using the metaphor of the race again) they are jogging in place, watching and waiting for us to make it to the finish line, cheering us on. It is then that the heroes will come "home" to finish. As the author writes, "Yet all these, though they were commended for their faith, did not receive what was promised, since God had provided something better so that they would not, *apart from us,* be made perfect" (11:39–40, emphasis added). They are not made perfect, whole, complete, without us! The great roll call of heroes is not finished until our names are called too. And so we see that the past is continuous with the present. While we might ignore its heroes, they will by no means ignore us. And your Old Testament lessons take on a whole different perspective!

CHAPTER 12

The General Letters and the Revelation to John

INTRODUCTION TO THE GENERAL LETTERS

About the only thing the seven "general letters" of 1, 2, and 3 John, 1 and 2 Peter, Jude, and James have in common is that they are known to us by an author's name rather than a specific church's name (e.g., Romans, Galatians). Since the fourth century A.D., the church has grouped these letters as "general" or "catholic" (universal) epistles, because they are addressed to Christians in general. The letters of John were treated in chapter 5 along with the Gospel of John. The four other general letters are examined in this chapter.

Identifying the author of each letter is problematic. There are at least five different men in the New Testament named James, but the author of the epistle identifies himself simply as "James, a servant of God and of the Lord Jesus Christ." The early church associated the letter with the brother of Jesus and head of the Jerusalem church, but this link is by no means certain. The writer's familiarity with other New Testament documents suggests a date c. 100. We know nothing whatsoever about Jude, except that he identifies himself as a brother of James (Jude 1), and again the question arises, which James? Because the issues in Jude (and 2 Peter, which quotes from Jude) reflect a well-established church, Jude is dated c. 125. The letters of 1 and 2 Peter appear to come from different pens, or perhaps different students of Peter, based on their distinctly different styles of Greek. The author of 2 Peter is writing in the middle of the second century, long after the death of the apostles and at a time when Paul's letters have been collected and regarded as scripture. The author of 1 Peter speaks of Rome as "Babylon," an association made after the destruction of Jerusalem in A.D. 70. These references weigh against authorship by the apostle Peter, who was martyred in the mid-60s. However, some scholars hold that Peter had Silvanus send out the letter from Rome just before he was martyred. Most date 1 Peter around A.D. 96.

Letters are written because some problem needs to be addressed; there is a reason for a letter. There is also a reason for inclusion of the letter in the New Testament canon. While the latter is harder to ascertain, especially in the letters of 3 John and Jude, we will be looking for what these letters tried to accomplish at the time. Finally, we will look for what these letters say to us today.

STUDY GUIDE FOR JAMES

While this document is called a letter, the form reads like a sermon. After the greeting of 1:1, the author does not return to an epistolary (letter) format. Instead he makes short notes on a variety of subjects to show that what one *says* needs to be consistent with what one *does*. James is scathing when he writes about the plays for power that fly in the face of ethics. He insists instead on love for the have-nots of this world.

Martin Luther, the Protestant reformer, called James "an epistle of straw" because of its lack of any real theological discourse (it makes only two references to Jesus Christ). Luther did admit, however, that it is good in that it "sternly declares the law of God." As you read, look for this law of God and its practical implications.

1. On partiality and favoritism. Read 2:1–13. Evidently the church had succumbed to the age-old tendency of institutional behavior: the rich and mighty were given special honor and consideration.

Make a mental sketch or draw a picture of the scene described in 2:2–3.

How does the author describe wealthy (and calloused) folk in the following verses?

1:9–11_____

2:6_____

4:13–14_____

5:1–6_____

God shows a different kind of partiality. Whose side is God on according to these verses?

2:5 _____

4:6 _____

What is the "royal law" that his readers must really fulfill (2:8)?

_____

2. On faith and works. Read 2:14–26. Paul wrote that we are saved by "faith alone," blasting apart the notion that Gentiles might win salvation for themselves by fulfilling the Jewish torah. James writes to folk who have no intention of fulfilling the law at all. The problem James sees is that Paul's teaching has been distorted to mean that "faith" (verbal assent) alone is all that counts. They talk the talk; James insists they also walk the walk. What does he say about the relationship between faith and works in these verses?

2:17 (key verse) _____

2:14–16 _____

2:26 _____

1:22–25 _____

3:13 _____

James focuses the discourse not on works in general, but on works of mercy and caring. Describe these works in the following verses:

1:27 (which also gives James's famous definition of religion)

_____

2:15–16 (again) _____

2:25 (Rahab first appears in Josh. 2) _____

3. On right speech. Read 3:1–12. What images does James give in this passage to show the power of the tongue (or the words we speak)?

_____

_____

What ethical advice does he then give in

1:19–20 _____

1:26 _____

4:11–12 _____

5:9 _____

5:12 _____

Prayer is a proper and powerful use of speech. Show the effects of prayer in these verses:

1:5 _____

5:13–16

_____

4. On worldliness. After reading 3:13–18 and 4:1–10, what do you think James meant by "friendship with the world" and that which is "earthly"?

_____

_____

In contrast, what does "wisdom from above" look like?

_____

_____

Discussion Questions: James

1. Read the last verse of James, then discuss: What are some ways "wandering from the truth" has been described in this document? What has James said to try to bring the wanderers back?

2. If James were the only letter in the New Testament canon, what points of teaching and theology would you miss?

3. If James were dropped from the New Testament canon, what points of ethics and practice would you miss?

STUDY GUIDE FOR 1 PETER

First Peter follows the classic letter format, thus:
I. Greeting: 1 Peter 1:1–2
II. Thanksgiving: 1:3–9
III. Body of the Letter:
   A. Theological reflection on holiness (1:10—2:10)
   B. Exhortations on practice and ethics (2:11—5:11)
IV. Closing: 5:12–14

1. The audience. The churches of Pontus, Galatia, Cappadocia, Asia, and Bithynia (modern Turkey) are the recipients of this letter (1:1). They are Gentiles, converts to Christianity in a pagan world. What have they become in God's eyes? See 2:9–10.

_____

The author describes them as aliens (exiles, strangers, sojourners) in 1:1 and 2:11. How are they treated by their neighbors now?

2:12 _____

4:3–4 _____

4:12 _____

4:14 _____

5:9 _____

Are they being persecuted physically? mentally? Both? Give reasons for your answer:

_____

2. The posture of Christians with respect to one another. As resident aliens, set apart from the culture that surrounds them, how are the believers to treat one another?

1:22 _____

2:1 _____

3:8 _____

4:8–11

_____

_____

5:5 _____

What special instruction does the author have for the elders (officials) in these churches? See 5:1–3.

_____

_____

3. The posture of Christians with respect to the social order. The believers, characterized by their love for one another and their separation from the world, must nevertheless live in the world. For all its hostility, the present social order is the one with which they must work.

With regard to the state (here, the Roman Empire), how should they behave and why? See 2:13–17.

_____

_____

_____

With regard to the institution of slavery, a given in that day and age, how should Christian slaves (in pagan households) behave, and why? See 2:18–25.

_____

_____

Finally, with regard to the household, how should Christian wives (with pagan husbands) behave, and why? See 3:1–6.

_____

_____

The church, then, includes women and slaves who, on one hand, have shown their disregard for custom. The established order says they should worship the gods of their masters and husbands; this they no longer do. However, Peter does not recommend going the next step and defying the conventional systems in order to change them for the better.

4. As resident aliens, the believers suffer (in their households and in public). Why does the author advocate non-violence on their part? See these verses:

2:12 _____

2:21–23 (especially v. 23) _____
3:9–12

_____

_____

3:13–16 (especially v. 16) _____

How much longer will they have to suffer? Consider these verses:

4:7 _____

4:13 _____

5:10 _____

5. Finally, these aliens and exiles are to have hope. What is the foundation of this hope? See these verses:

1:3 _____

1:13 _____

1:21 _____

Discussion Questions: 1 Peter

1. What does the image of "resident aliens" mean to you? Does this image pertain to the institutional church today? to individual Christians? Why or why not?

2. To be holy is to be set apart by God. Why would the holiness of the Christian community in Peter's day provoke such harassment and hostility?

3. In a time of persecution (either overt or covert), Peter's advice to citizens, slaves, and wives is to submit to those in charge. Do you share Peter's positive attitude toward authority figures? Why or why not? Does Peter's attitude arise out of practical concerns (to stay alive) or theological conviction (this is how God wants it to be)?

STUDY GUIDE FOR 2 PETER

The problem identified here is a different one from that in 1 Peter. While 1 Peter's churches must figure how to live in a hostile world, 2 Peter's church is plagued by false teachers within the community. The author makes reference in 1:16–18 to his presence at Jesus' transfiguration and identifies himself as Simon Peter. Yet he knows "all [Paul's] letters" (3:16) and refers to them as scripture. The content reflects not the primitive church, but a church in its second or third generation (whose ancestors have died—3:4).

1. Chapter 2 is a polemic (aggressive attack) against false teachers with destructive opinions. Whether or not Peter is actually the author, the apostle's impulsive and hotheaded style is certainly reflected in this polemic! Read chapter 2 aloud. In what particularly colorful ways are these teachers described? What terms and images apply? What motivates them?

_____

_____

_____

_____

2. The teachers scoff at the church's belief in the second coming of Christ. If this is God's promise, and it has not been fulfilled, then it stands to reason that God's other promises will not be fulfilled. What does the author say instead about the promises of God?

1:3–4 _____

3:3–7 _____

3:13 _____

What does he say about the judgment of God in 2:4–10?

_____

_____

Finally, what does he say about God's timing versus human timing? See 3:8–10.

_____

_____

3. Read 2 Peter 1:5–7. Put these verses in a form other than prose: a flowchart, diagram, building blocks, picture.

STUDY GUIDE FOR JUDE

Much of the short little document of Jude is duplicated in 2 Peter 2. Most scholars think that Jude was written first. It is a colorful and angry polemic against false teachers. We do not know exactly what they teach; instead we know of their immoral practices.

The references to Cain and Korah indicate their enviousness and greed. In what other ways are they described?

_____

_____

_____

What is the difference between Paul's use of the word "faith" and its usage in verse 3 ("the faith")?

_____

_____

Finally, write out and memorize the beautiful doxology (good words) found in the last two verses of Jude.

_____

_____

_____

_____

INTRODUCTION TO REVELATION

The Revelation to John is the New Testament's representative in the category called apocalyptic literature, much as Daniel 7—12 is the premier apocalyptic piece of the Old Testament. Other books contain apocalyptic passages (as in 2 Thessalonians and chapter 13 of Mark), but Revelation is apocalyptic through and through.

The rules of this genre are fairly simple. Apocalyptic

literally "lays bare" the future for a seer, or visionary, in this case John the Elder (no relation to John the evangelist). It arises during times of persecution, here probably that of Domitian, around A.D. 95. It insists that change is coming, but that change would never be caused by human agents. What is necessary is no less than an act of God. God will vanquish the enemy, Christ will come again, and a new age will be inaugurated. Apocalyptic insists that things will get worse before they get better. But once God begins to act, God is unstoppable.

The problem John the Elder faced (as did all apocalyptic writers) was twofold. He had received a vision, and, like the "wheels within wheels" vision of Ezekiel 1, this vision is exceedingly difficult to put in words. Second, after attempting to translate the images into verbal pictures, there's the danger of this piece falling into the wrong hands and causing still further persecution. Therefore apocalyptic literature uses codes. Colors, numbers, beasts, and aliases abound. All of these "stand for" something else, which the churches would understand while the authorities would not. In fact, fascination with these codes and what they signify has extended far beyond the writer's time and situation, producing fantastic and embarrassing predictions of the coming end of time. Put it this way: if you have to sit down and figure out the code, the encoded message was not meant for you. John the Elder's readers knew perfectly well what he meant with his numbers and animals; those on the outside did not.

In one sense, Revelation was not meant to be read by us. It was written for a specific audience (the seven churches on a mail route) undergoing intense persecution (due to their refusal to conform to the Roman emperor's edicts). Clearly we are not them; our circumstances are not theirs. But in another sense the message is timeless and meant for churches anywhere and everywhere. John the Elder used no code when he wrote out of this conviction: God is sovereign, appearances notwithstanding, and God's goal for history is more glorious than one could ever imagine (or any thinker could ever plan out!).

Two extreme views exist among interpreters of Revelation. (1) One extreme sees apocalyptic literature as prophecy turned senile—unintelligible and basically worthless. Furthermore, they add, the literal words did not become literally true. So Revelation is simply erroneous. (2) The other extreme analyzes every jot and tittle of the document, searching for contemporary parallels (the "beast" equals not Rome but the Third Reich, the Soviet Union, an upcoming evil empire). The document is simply a foreign puzzle, which can (indeed must) be deciphered. The literal words will, perhaps soon, become literally true.

Actually both extremes arise out of the same analytical mindset. One rejects Revelation as being incapable of analysis while the other tackles it as being a great theological cryptogram. Both are stuck in rational ruts. Both seek to control the content of the text. Neither allows for the text as experience.

We are closest to the spirit of the text when we see it interpreted in art, hear it sung in music, or encounter it in the liturgy of the church. In classrooms, teachers are finding that Revelation is best "taught" by reading it aloud, stopping for explanation only occasionally, allowing the force of the writing to be experienced as it is heard. John the Elder might say, "Now *that's* what I had in mind!" (see 1:3).

You will find a few explanatory notes for each chapter. Read them either before or after you read the text, but make sure you do read the text aloud, or hear it read to you. Discussion questions follow at the end for those who insist on using their analytical skills.

NOTES ON REVELATION

Chapter 1. John is writing from his exile on the island of Patmos, a rocky island in the Aegean Sea. The seven churches he addresses are in western Asia Minor (modern Turkey). "Death" and "Hades" are synonymous, both reflecting the Hebrew idea of Sheol, or the place of deep sleep for all who have died.

All numbers are numinous, some more so than others. One is the number for God. Three stands for heaven and perfection. Four is the number for the earth (the four corners, the four winds). Seven is the number of completeness (the combination of three plus four, of heaven and earth). Colors have symbolic value too. White is the color of victory and joy. Alpha and Omega are the first and last letters of the Greek alphabet.

Chapters 2 and 3. Each of the seven churches is given a message that includes (1) acknowledgment of the church's persecution, (2) evaluation of the church's response, and (3) a promise of what the church will receive if it holds fast. The Nicolaitans taught that Christians may eat food sacrificed to idols and practice immorality. Jezebel was probably a Nicolaitan; the code name used for this woman is that of Ahab's wife. She was the queen in Elijah's time who supported the prophets of Baal in Israel.

Chapters 4 and 5. The rainbow reminds us of the sign of God's everlasting covenant with the whole creation after the Flood (Gen. 9:8ff.). Twenty-four is the sum of the twelve tribes of Israel plus the twelve apostles. The "four creatures" recall Ezekiel 1; the "Holy, holy, holy" chant recalls Isaiah 6. Jesus is called both the Lion, the animal of victory, and the Lamb, the beast of sacrifice.

Chapter 6. The four horsemen of the apocalypse are known by their colors: white for conquest, red for war, black for famine, pale green (or livid) for death.

Chapter 7. The number 144,000 (12 x 12,000) is the number used to symbolize the complete household of faith. Their beautiful hymn is echoed in the poetic proclamation of 21:3–4. The Lamb is also the shepherd.

Chapter 8. A half hour of silence precedes the blowing of the trumpets. The trumpet, or the ram's horn *shofar*, was used to announce God's judgment in the Old Testament. Recall the plagues in Egypt before the exodus. Wormwood is a bitter drug.

Chapter 9. Note that both the locusts and the horses (200,000,000 of them!) are transformed into fantastic monsters who are instruments of God's wrath. Both the Hebrew and Greek names for the angel of the bottomless pit mean "destruction." Nevertheless, idolatry remains.

Chapter 10. John consumes the scroll as did the prophet Ezekiel (Ezek. 2:8; 3:1–3).

Chapter 11. The two witnesses resemble Elijah, who had power over drought, and Moses, who set the plagues in motion in Egypt (v. 6). Two witnesses were required in court for valid testimony. Perhaps John is referring to the witness of the church to the gospel of Christ. Three and one half years (1,260 days) is an incomplete number, half of seven or the number of completion.

Chapter 12. The woman clothed with the sun is, like Israel, mother of both the Messiah (the firstborn) and the church (the rest of her offspring). The red (deadly, bloody) dragon is the devil. Michael is the patron of Israel.

Chapter 13. The beast from the sea (the vast Roman empire) is incited by the dragon to uphold idolatry (including, but not necessarily limited to, emperor worship) and persecute the saints. The beast from the earth is a false prophet. John is probably referring to the Emperor Nero, but he is simply called 666, or "evil, evil, evil." (The number six symbolizes that which is inferior, incomplete, bad.) Nero died in A.D. 64, but many in the empire believed that he would return to life and rule again.

Chapter 14. In the Old Testament, one of the rules for the Israelites who fought in holy war was that they abstain from sexual intercourse. These 144,000 are forever chaste; they exceed the standard of purity required by the Old Testament holy wars. The final ingathering for judgment is made in verses 18–20.

Chapters 15 and 16. Even after these fearful plagues, humans still curse God. The place name Harmagedon [Armageddon] refers to the hill of Megiddo in Palestine, where Israel won important battles.

Chapter 17. The earthly beast of chapter 13 is ridden by the whore, "Babylon," or the city of Rome. Both Rome and Babylon conquered Jerusalem and destroyed the Temple. As the woman clothed with the sun gave birth to the saints, this woman gives birth to the earth's abominations. Her beast of burden is full of blasphemous names—divine titles given to Roman emperors. Remember the myth about Nero: once alive, now dead, believed to come again.

Chapter 18. Babylon is condemned for her sorcery, her idolatry, her persecution of the church, and her enormous and disproportionate wealth. Those who mourn her passing are the ones who grow rich off her: kings, merchants, mariners.

Chapter 19. For verse 6, think of Handel's "Hallelujah Chorus"! The great wedding is between Christ and the church. God's triumph will be celebrated with a great feast, the marriage supper of the Lamb and the bride. The rider of the white horse is of course Christ, "Faithful and True, . . . King of kings and Lord of lords." His robe is dipped in blood: the blood of the crucifixion and of the martyrs. The final battle is told with remarkable brevity (vv. 19–21).

Chapter 20. Satan is bound for "a thousand years"— an uncountable period—while the martyrs will be resurrected with Christ. A second battle will occur when Satan is loosed from his prison, ending with Satan joining the two other beasts in a fiery lake. Finally, even Death itself dies and is cast into the lake of fire. Evil is destroyed completely.

Revelation 20:1–6 has been a subject of controversy since the second century A.D. While Irenaeus and other church fathers argued for a literal reign of Christ on earth for a thousand years, Origen and Augustine argued for a figurative and symbolic reading of verses 1–6. The two viewpoints persist today. Those who look for a second coming of Christ, followed by a thousand-year reign with the saints, are called "premillennialists" (Christ's return before, "pre," the millennium or thousand years). The Anglican, Orthodox, Roman Catholic, and mainstream Protestant churches see the thousand-year period as symbolic.

Chapter 21. The new Jerusalem is described as the bride of Christ. The speaker in verses 5–8 is God. The city is represented as a cube, another symbol of perfection. The pearls, gold, and precious stones indicate nothing less than sheer beauty. The new Jerusalem has no need for a temple, or the sun, or gates that shut.

Chapter 22. Holy Scripture begins with Eden in Genesis, and finishes with Eden in Revelation. This time, however, none will hide from the Lord as did Adam and Eve. Instead, all shall worship and "see his face." This time no evil is permitted, not even a snake, for the Tempter is gone. This time we stand beside a tree, the tree of life. The revelation ends with eager anticipation of this future: *Maranatha*, "Come, Lord Jesus!"

Discussion Questions: Revelation

1. If you wish to learn more about the ways in which chapter 20 and the "thousand years" have been interpreted, go to a library and research these terms: Millennialism, Eschatology, Dispensationalism, Second Coming. Theological dictionaries are helpful. You may wish to explore your particular church's tradition. Look up these terms in the index of a text on your church's beliefs.

2. Compare Revelation with 1 Peter as to purpose, tone, and content. Answer these questions for each document:
A. Why do Christians have cause to rejoice?
B. What metaphors are used for Christ and his activity?
C. What appeals are made to believers?
D. What is the attitude toward civil authority?
E. What is the attitude toward suffering?
F. What strategy should believers follow in dealing with the state?

If you were suffering persecution, which book (Revelation or 1 Peter) would be more helpful to you? Why?

SCENES FROM DÜRER'S "APOCALYPSE"

The Revelation to John, with its dynamic images of fire and brimstone on one hand and beatific vision on the other, has prompted the creative energies of artists down through the ages. The German artist Albrecht Dürer (1471–1528) was one of those who was inspired by Revelation. His "Apocalypse" series, fifteen woodcuts first published in 1498, is one of the best known representations of the book in the Western world. Woodcuts #1, 4, 7, and 15 (Figs. 12.1–12.4) will give you an idea of what Dürer "saw" as he read John's words.[1]

#1 (Fig. 12.1): The series begins with this woodcut showing the first of John's many visions. The Lord appears to John in terrifying majesty. Seven candlesticks light the sky; seven stars are held in the Lord's right hand. John falls at his feet in awe. (Rev. 1.)

#4 (Fig. 12.2): The fourth print of the series is one of Dürer's most famous woodcuts. The four horsemen (viewed from right to left) stand for Conquest, War, Famine, and Death. Under the presence of an angel, the three powerful horses trample men and women. Death's bony nag treads upon a bishop falling into the jaws of the dragon of Hades. (Rev. 6.)

#7 (Fig. 12.3): Many of the disasters climaxing the Apocalypse are crowded into this single woodcut. As God watches and angels blow trumpets, a pair of giant hands plunge a mountain into the sea.

A star falls, ships are wrecked, fires and locusts ravage the earth. Just below center, an eagle screeches the German words "Woe, woe, woe." (Rev. 8.)

#15 (Fig. 12.4): In the final woodcut of the series, evil is overcome. An angel with a key imprisons Satan in a pit that is fitted with a lock and key. Another angel shows John the way to the new Jerusalem, where the righteous will live in peace. For the architecture of this new Jerusalem, Dürer used as a model his own town of Nuremberg in Germany. (Rev. 20:1–3; chap. 21.)

WAYS OF BEING RELIGIOUS IN THE NEW TESTAMENT

The New Testament gives us not one but four Gospels, or portraits of Jesus. It also gives us a variety of letters and writings with widely different audiences and emphases. All are firmly anchored in the kerygma: Christ has died, Christ is risen, Christ will come again. But with that anchor firmly in place, the ships of the New Testament documents sail wide and far, tacking here, putting up sails there, and navigating the seas as best they can.

[1]These four reproductions, plates 30, 32, 36 and 46 are from *Albrecht Dürer: Master Printmaker*, ed. Boston Museum Fine Arts staff (New York: Hacker Art Books, 1987).

Fig. 12.1 Scenes from Dürer's "Apocalypse" #1

Fig. 12.2 Scenes from Dürer's "Apocalypse" #4

Fig. 12.3 Scenes from Dürer's "Apocalypse" #7

Fig. 12.4 Scenes from Dürer's "Apocalypse" #15

The variety of perspectives in the New Testament is deliberate. There is no "harmony of the Gospels" or summary of the epistles. Different voices speak loud and clear. They offer ways of being and seeing appropriate to folk in specific circumstances. In your own journey, you will find certain documents speaking to you and affecting you more profoundly than others. The variety is there, sometimes as a corrective to a heavy-handed emphasis on

one perspective at the expense of the many, sometimes as a help in clarifying our response to the good news and strengthening us as sojourners.

The chart in figure 12.5 is based on material found in Norman Perrin's *The New Testament: An Introduction* (New York: Harcourt Brace Jovanovich, 1974), 305–8. The format and any lack of subtleties are my own, with apologies to Perrin.

Chief Concern:	Despair with the world as it is, hope for its coming end	Need for Atonement—being cleansed and redeemed	The world and life are ordered by God; thus, seek out this order	A sacred person and his life—a sacred time	The glory and power of Christ and Christ's concern for us
Christology; Role of Jesus	Redeemer who will destroy and remake, judge and redeem, when he comes again	He does that which the law can't do, and which persons can't do for themselves: justification	Revealer of truth; bearer of verbal revelation	Model for what it means to be religious	Descending/Ascending Redeemer, who gives life to those who believe
What It Means to be Religious	To believe in and prepare for the imminent destruction of the world; to be caught up in the drama of history hurrying to its close	To live the life of power and freedom rather than the life of guilt and fear, and to accept justification as a gift	To obey the revealed truth; to organize one's life on the basis of obedience	To imitate Jesus: to care for the outcasts and the neighbor, to manifest the love of Christ in human relations	To contemplate the glory of Christ and of Christ's oneness with God, then to find the self at one with Christ in mystical union
Central Element	The end of time (beginning of a new age)	The cross (the sign of reconciliation and overcoming the power of evil)	The church (the means by which we attain obedience)	The Spirit (which enables us to exhibit qualities of Christ)	The cross (the sign of victory and glory)
New Testament Sources	Apocalyptic	Paul's Letters	Matthew	Luke/Acts	John

Fig. 12.5 Ways of Being Religious in the New Testament

CHAPTER 13

What Does It Mean to Me?

The articles and exercises in this chapter may be used at the beginning of your study, to set the stage for a close reading of the New Testament. Or they may be used at the conclusion of your study as a way to reflect on what you have read and, more specifically, on what you think about what you have read.

RELIGIOUS EXPERIENCE: ITS BASIS AND CHARACTERISTICS

Religious experience brings us into contact with what is most real about ourselves and about God. The experience is not irrational, momentary, or sentimental, nor is it esoteric, removed from this life. It is holistic; it involves the whole person.

The experience of the Holy is characterized by:

1. a revelation of the power and force of God
2. the establishment of humans as creatures of God
3. intensity
4. the discovery of what is most real in one's person
5. a call to action

The New Testament citations that follow will help you identify some of these characteristics. Look them up and either quote or summarize in the space provided.

I. The Basis of Religious Experience: Resurrection Accounts
   A. The women find the empty tomb.
Mark 16:1–8

_____

_____

Matthew 28:1–8

_____

_____

_____

Luke 24:1–11

_____

_____

_____

John 20:1–10

_____

_____

_____

Note the elements of surprise (fright, astonishment, fear, amazement) and command (come, see, go).
   B. The resurrected Lord appears to his followers.
Matthew 28:9–20

_____

_____

_____

Luke 24:13–49

_____

_____

_____

John 20:11—21:25

_____

_____

_____

Note the emphasis on the realness of Jesus as well as his sudden and unexpected appearances. He gives the apostles proof of his life; he then gives them a mission to the world.
   C. The resurrected Lord appears to Paul.

1 Corinthians 15:3–8

_____

_____

Galatians 1:15–16

_____

_____

Then see the accounts of Paul's conversion experience in:
Acts 9:3–8

_____

_____

_____

Acts 22:6–11

_____

_____

Acts 26:12–18

_____

_____

Note that this is an ineffable experience for Paul, one that cannot be dealt with in ordinary terms. Paul also saw the risen Christ as the one who *questions* ("Why do you persecute me?") and the one who *commands* ("Get up and go!").

II. The Basis of Religious Experience: the Holy Spirit and the Living Lord
　　A. Confession of belief in the resurrection is rooted in possession of the Holy Spirit.
Acts 2:1–4

_____

_____

John 20:22

_____

Luke 24:49

_____

1 Corinthians 12:3

_____

The Spirit gives the power to proclaim and to believe.
　　B. The Spirit is not impersonal, but is the life-giving presence of the risen Lord.
2 Corinthians 3:17–18

_____

_____

1 Corinthians 2:12

_____

1 Corinthians 15:45

_____

Romans 8:11

_____

_____

　　C. Jesus will come again in fullness of power to deliver the world to the kingdom of God.
1 Corinthians 15:24–28

_____

_____

Hebrews 9:27–28

_____

_____

Therefore, Jesus is not only alive, but is Lord. Jesus is not a figure of the past, but living and active, present in the sacraments and working through the church. His aliveness radically affects the existence of the individual.

Keep in mind that we find a *variety* of religious experience in the New Testament. The community experience is not qualitatively the same for all members. Although its basis remains constant, the experience itself varies from person to person.

Discussion Questions: Religious Experience

Of the five characteristics of religious experience listed at the beginning of this section, which do you see most clearly in the New Testament? Which do you see most clearly in your own experience? What other qualities and features of religious experience do you wish to add to the list?

PREPARING YOUR SPIRITUAL AUTOBIOGRAPHY

There is something about a good story that touches our hearts, clarifies our own experience of living, and connects us to others. The gospel is story, after all, and hearing it well is the point of New Testament studies.

The gospel invites us to enter into a rich, dynamic experience (the "kingdom") and see the world in a different way. God's story becomes our story.

When we reflect on the past events of our lives, we

make connections between those events and our present. In a very real way, we enlarge our lives, make them bigger, by seeing ourselves not simply as one point on a time line (that is, in the present) but as a series of points on a continuum that stretches back into the past and forward into the future. It is helpful to learn ways to tell our stories to ourselves and to others. This exercise in preparing a spiritual autobiography will give you suggestions as to how to begin.

A small group setting is ideal for the telling of your story, and instructions for this setting are included. Whether or not you actually present your autobiography (or a part of it) to another person or a group, use a journal to record your thoughts and feelings. Putting yourself on paper is part of the experience of storytelling. This does not mean, once you have finished, that you have captured your autobiography once and for all. As many times as I have prepared this exercise, I have never told it the same way twice. Emphases and insights change with time and with different perspectives. The distinction must first be made between two German words for "history":

(1) *Historie* denotes data, the facts, events listed without commentary (e.g., "I was born in Atlanta, the oldest child of three . . . ")

(2) *Geschichte* denotes the meaning of events, the interpretation of data (e.g., "Since I was the oldest child, I felt or knew that . . . ")

Geschichte, or interpreted history, is your aim in preparing your autobiography. The temptation is to list a string of notable events (*Historie*) with no examination of why these events are important, or what their effect has been on you. The hard part, and ultimately the fun part, is to push beyond "the facts" to their significance, specifically the connection between the data and your own spiritual development. Group members have the responsibility of listening and making connections with what you say; they also need to gently guide you (through questions) to get at the significance of the data you give to the group.

Method 1: Dyads

Pick two events, two people, and two ideas that have been meaningful to you. Compare and contrast the pairs to describe them more clearly. Tell the ways in which these dyads have changed you or affected you.

Method 2: Stepping-Stones

In chronological order, and limiting yourself to no more than eight items, list the major stepping-stones in your life. One way to look at a stepping-stone is as a turning point: a time when life was heading one way, then took a turn in a different direction. Try to isolate each stepping-stone in terms of time and place and meaning. The reason for the limit of eight is to keep you from giving your group a jumble of events without meaning (or *Historie*).

Method 3: Past and Future Windows

Pick any three items from the middle column below. Tell about your past, using the items you chose and lots of stories and descriptive material. Your aim is not to tell your entire story, but simply to open a few windows into the past and tell your group what you see. Then do the same for the future, again picking items that capture your imagination. Your future story will of course be creative and fanciful. Have fun with this, but again try to paint word pictures that the group can understand.

PAST		FUTURE
influential	Person	you see in yourself
evocative	Place	you'd like to create
turning point	Experience	you will bring about
formative	Idea	you will live by
impact	Book	you'd like to write

THE EXPERIENCE OF CHRISTIANITY

I saw a cartoon recently that showed two Roman soldiers standing at the foot of the cross. One said to the other, "Don't worry; this will all be forgotten a hundred years from now." The fact that you are reading this now says something about the irony of seemingly insignificant beginnings. Indeed, the inception of Christianity was obscure: it was launched with the ignominious death of its founder and was at first a movement of unlearned men and women. Its chief appeal was to slaves, the outcasts, the poor. Within three centuries it became the religion of an empire. Twenty centuries later its adherents number some one and a half billion (1989 *Encyclopaedia Britannica Book of the Year*). How do we account for this?

The success of Christianity cannot be explained by social, political, or economic factors. Nor can it be explained by the purity of its ethic and teaching. What is key is Christianity's claim to have actualized good news to all persons. The power of the faith, and the reality of its experience, must be examined.

This study guide will direct you to New Testament passages on the experience of Christianity. Read and

take notes on the features that impress you, or summarize the verses.

I. Glimpses of the Early Church
   A. Shared possessions and gifts
      Acts 4:32–37

      _____

      _____

         2 Corinthians 9 (all)

      _____

      _____

      _____

         Acts 2:41–46

      _____

      _____

   B. Persistence of the believers, zealous for the faith
      Acts 7, on Stephen

      _____

      _____

         2 Corinthians 11:22–33, on Paul

      _____

      _____

   C. Earliest church hymns
      Philippians 2:5–11

      _____

      _____

         Colossians 1:15–20

      _____

      _____

II. Christianity's Claim for the Whole World
    A. "Disciples of all nations"
       Acts 1:8

      _____

         Matthew 28:19

      _____

    B. Victory won
       1 Corinthians 3:21–23

      _____

      _____

         1 John 5:4–5

      _____

      _____

    C. God's purpose for the world made manifest in
       the church

         Romans 6:17–18

      _____

         Ephesians 3:10–11

      _____

      _____

III. How the Christians Could Make Such Claims for
     the Faith
     Their claims are based on their salvation *from*:
     A. The powers of destruction and death
        Romans 8:37–39

      _____

      _____

         Ephesians 2:1–2

      _____

      _____

         Colossians 1:13–14

      _____

      _____

     B. The law and bondage
        Romans 6:15–23

      _____

      _____

         Galatians 3:23—4:7

      _____

      _____

     C. Fear
        Romans 8:14–16

      _____

      _____

         Hebrews 2:14–15

      _____

IV. How Their Claims Are Made Manifest
    A. Freedom
       1 Corinthians 6:12

      _____

         Romans 8:2

      _____

         Galatians 5:13

      _____

    B. Boldness of speech

John 18:20

_____

2 Corinthians 3:12

_____

C. Joy
  1 Peter 4:15–16

_____

_____

Philippians 4:4–7

_____

D. Endurance of suffering
  Hebrews 12:1–4

_____

_____

2 Corinthians 1:3–5

_____

_____

James 1:2–4

_____

_____

1 Peter 4:12–14

_____

_____

E. Fellowship in love
  1 John 1:3

_____

1 John 4:7–12

_____

_____

Philippians 2:1–4

_____

_____

Christianity brought newness in an age of antiquity worship. It proclaimed teaching that was accessible to all. Finally it affirmed that God is at work, already, in the deliverance of the believer.

V. The New Thing Brought About by Jesus
  A. New covenant
    1 Corinthians 11:25

_____

2 Corinthians 3:7–9

_____

B. New life, new creation
  Romans 6:4

_____

Ephesians 4:22–24

_____

_____

2 Corinthians 5:17

_____

_____

C. "Wisdom," thought to be accessible only to the elite, now available to all persons
  1 Corinthians 1:30

_____

1 Corinthians 1:17–24

_____

_____

Ephesians 1:9–10

_____

Colossians 1: 9–10

_____

James 3:17

_____

VI. Conviction of God's Present Activity, and God's Final Deliverance
  1 Corinthians 1:4–9

_____

_____

Romans 6:1–5

_____

_____

1 Thessalonians 4:13–14

_____

_____

Acts 1:10–11

_____

Mark 13:24–27

_____

_____

Romans 5:9–10

_____

_____

2 Corinthians 6:2

_____

Discussion Questions:
The Experience of Christianity

1. Faith is an active commitment to a way of life. The core of faith is experience and reflection on the meanings of this experience. But what specifically is the *content* of this faith for Christians? Using the records of first-century Christianity found in the passages you have just read, identify the *basis* of Christian religious experience and highlight the *claims* of these believers.

2. If you were living in the Roman Empire in the first century, what New Testament passages above would capture your attention?

3. From these New Testament readings, what statements and claims are most meaningful to you right now? Why?

WRITING YOUR CREDO

"Now faith is the assurance of things hoped for, the conviction of things not seen" (Heb. 11:1).

"I believe; help my unbelief!" (Mark 9:24).

"*Credo ut intelligam*" (I believe in order to understand) (Anselm of Canterbury).

The Latin word *credo* means "I believe." Christianity is a creedal religion because from the beginning it has called humans to declarations of faith. Faith seeks understanding; it must be spoken and made intelligible. Faith seeks to be understood; it must be communicated and thereby serve as a connection between the believer and others, between the believer and God.

Faith is not limited to reason, but as humans we know that the commitment called faith needs to be thought through and expressed with some clarity. It is part of loving God with the whole person: the mind as well as the heart and the soul. This is a process, not a once-and-for-all product. Thus the credo you write today may not be the one you write ten years hence. Writing your credo not only clarifies faith but becomes itself the means of deeper commitment, of deeper understanding. Your credo, then, does not mark the end point of your journey, but is a signpost along the road.

The best-known Christian creed, used in both Western and Eastern churches, is the Nicene Creed. It has a three-part structure reflecting the Trinitarian understandings of the early church. It was introduced at the Council of Nicaea (A.D. 325) and finally formulated at the Council of Constantinople (381). The following translation is from *The Book of Common Prayer* (1979) of the Episcopal Church.

We believe in one God,
   the Father, the Almighty,
   maker of heaven and earth,
   of all that is, seen and unseen.
We believe in one Lord, Jesus Christ,
the only Son of God,
eternally begotten of the Father,
God from God, Light from Light,
true God from true God,
begotten, not made,
of one Being with the Father.
Through him all things were made.
For us and for our salvation
   he came down from heaven:
by the power of the Holy Spirit
   he became incarnate from the Virgin Mary,
   and was made man.
For our sake he was crucified under Pontius Pilate;
   he suffered death and was buried.
   On the third day he rose again
      in accordance with the Scriptures;
   he ascended into heaven
      and is seated at the right hand of the Father.
He will come again in glory to judge the living and
the dead,
   and his kingdom will have no end.
We believe in the Holy Spirit, the Lord, the giver of life,
   who proceeds from the Father and the Son.
   With the Father and the Son he is worshiped and
   glorified.
   He has spoken through the Prophets.
   We believe in one holy catholic and apostolic Church.
   We acknowledge one baptism for the forgiveness of
   sins.
   We look for the resurrection of the dead,
      and the life of the world to come.

In formulating your own creed, pay as much or as little attention to the one above as you wish. Begin "I believe in" or "I believe that" and continue from there. Suggested length is one page handwritten.

EXCLUSIVISM, INCLUSIVISM, OR PLURALISM?

Before you read the excerpt that follows, sit for a moment with a pencil and paper. Think of a metaphor or image that expresses for you the relationship between the religious traditions of the world: Christianity, Judaism, Islam, Buddhism, Hinduism, Confucianism, Taoism. Complete this sentence: The world's religions are like . . . .

What picture comes to mind? Write out a description, or draw the picture. If you are stuck, here are some possible metaphors to consider. Think of a mountain, a path, a family, a tree, a race, a ladder, a library. Do any of these images help you express the relationship between the various religions of the world? If so, pick one and describe how it works. If not, think of another.

When you have finished with this exercise, read the following excerpt from *Faith, Religion, and Theology.** Then answer the questions at the end.

The traditional understanding of how to understand the uniqueness of Jesus in relation to other faiths can be called the *exclusivist* model. This attitude characterized most of the history of the church, roughly from the fourth to the seventeenth centuries. It viewed Jesus as the one and only Savior and the Christian church as the one and only true religion. Therefore, as the ancient saying put it, "There is no salvation outside the church." Since Jesus is the only Savior and since he is to be found only in the church, everyone outside the church was going to have a rough time knowing God and making it to heaven. Though there have been some exceptions to this attitude, it has characterized the way most Christians look on followers of other faiths; it also provided the motivation for such great missionaries as Francis Xavier, who traveled to foreign lands in order to baptize as many souls as possible to save them from hell.

But gradually, as more and more of the "New World" became known to the old world of Europe, and as Christians became aware of the millions of people who through no fault of their own had never known Christ, they had to ask themselves how a God of love could pack off so many people to hell just because they hadn't been born

*The pages that follow, until the Discussion Questions, are reprinted from *Faith, Religion & Theology,* copyright 1990 by Brennan Hill, Paul Knitter, and William Madges, published by Twenty-Third Publications, P.O. Box 180, Mystic, CT 06355.

in Europe. There developed a new model for understanding the uniqueness of Jesus and other religions, that of *inclusivism.* . . . While it holds to Jesus as the only, or at least the clearest, way of finding salvation, it believes that the saving presence of Jesus and his Spirit can operate beyond the visible church and can be found in other religions, even though adherents to those religions do not recognize it.

For this inclusivist model, there is much value in other religions, and it calls upon Christians to recognize this value and to dialogue with other believers. But in the end, these other religions are to be included in Christ and his church, for Christ remains the final and the normative expression of God's will for all peoples. The value and the truth found in other faiths is there in order to prepare them for recognizing God's final and full revelation in Jesus. So, while this model affirms the presence of God in all religions, it insists that this presence is found fully and finally only in Jesus.

In recent years, some Christians and Christian theologians have been raising questions about this inclusivist model, whether it really allows for authentic dialogue and whether it is really consistent with what Jesus thought of himself. They are therefore exploring a new model for understanding the uniqueness of Jesus in relation to other religions. It has been called the *pluralist* model. These theologians want to continue to affirm the uniqueness and distinctiveness of Jesus as the Savior for all persons, but they want to be open to the possibility that Jesus may not be the only Savior for all persons. They want to recognize the possibility that God may be working in and through other religions and religious figures in a way similar to God's working in Jesus and Christianity. They suggest that Christians may have as much to learn from other religions as other religions can learn from Christianity.

. . . How does it [the pluralist model] square with what the Bible says? Theologians who follow the pluralist model would want to sharpen that question and ask how it squares with what Jesus said. Admittedly, it's not always easy to know precisely what Jesus said, since so many of his words were "interpreted" by the gospel writers. Still, most of the experts on the New Testament would agree that the heart of Jesus' message—what he was most concerned about—was not himself but what he called "the kingdom of God." This was

Jesus' passion and the focus of his preaching; he wanted people to believe in and start working for the kingdom of God. This kingdom, as the scholars tell us, was both the future kingdom of heaven and a kingdom of love and justice and unity to be realized here on earth. This was what Jesus was all about, preaching and working for this kingdom, especially for those who needed it most: the poor, the sick, the outcasts of society.

After his death and resurrection, the followers of Jesus shifted the focus of their preaching from the kingdom to Jesus; they did so not simply to extol Jesus, but because they felt that preaching about Jesus was the best way to work for the kingdom. Still, the early Christian church became "Jesus-centered." While there were good reasons for this shift, we must remember that Jesus himself was "kingdom-centered." What was most important for him was not that people praised him above all others, but that they believed his message and worked for a society of love and justice. . . .

For pluralist theologians, this means that being faithful to Jesus today does not require Christians to hold him up as the only or the best or to put down other religious figures like Buddha or Muhammad; rather, being a faithful follower of Jesus means mainly to live his message of love and justice in one's life, to work for the kingdom of God. And if this can be done together with followers of Buddha and Muhammad, so much the better. After all, Jesus also said that "Those who are not against us, are with us" (Luke 9:50).

And yet we also have powerful statements in the Bible that do use the word or idea *only* when speaking of Jesus: "only begotten Son of God... No other name . . . only mediator between God and humanity . . . once and for all. . . . " That kind of language is pretty clear. To which the pluralist theologians would respond, It's clear if taken literally; not so clear if taken in its context. They point out that the language about Jesus in the New Testament is a special kind of language; we do it a great disservice, and end up abusing it, when we try to turn it into a type of language it was not intended to be. According to Krister Stendahl, former dean of the Harvard Divinity School, statements about Jesus such as "only-begotten Son" or "no other name" are examples of what he calls "confessional" or "love language." It's the kind of language people use when they are excited about or in love with someone else; it's meant to express what they feel about that person and how they are committed to him or her. Such language

is not meant to provide theological or philosophical definitions of who that person is.

. . . So, when the early Christians proclaimed that Jesus was the only mediator between God and humanity, they were stating how much this man had affected their lives and how he could also affect the lives of others; they were calling others to take Jesus as seriously as they had and to experience the healing and the energy in him that they had encountered. The main thing they wanted to say was that God was really present in Jesus for them and for all people. In their situation of deep feeling and excitement, in order to say really, they used words like "only" and "not other," just as spouses express the reality and depth of their love for each other by saying "only you."

The primary intent of all this "one and only" language about Jesus in the New Testament, therefore, was to say something positive about Jesus, not to say something negative about others. It was to extol Jesus as the presence of God, not to exclude or put down other people in whom God might also be present. Therefore, pluralist theologians conclude, for Christians today to use such statements as "There is salvation in no other name" as a means to put down Buddha or Muhammad is to abuse this language. Again, this means that one can be fully committed to Jesus and at the same time be open to and appreciative of Buddha.

Whether this pluralist model is an acceptable Christian model and whether Christians can understand the uniqueness of Jesus differently than they have in the past are questions that still have to be decided. Perhaps the best way of deciding them is for Christians to engage in dialogue with other religions as openly and honestly as they can. In dialogue, they will know Jesus more clearly.

Discussion Questions

1. Briefly define the three models discussed above: exclusivism, inclusivism, pluralism.

2. What are the strengths and weaknesses of each model?

3. The pluralist model is clearly the focus of the writing. Is the pluralist model an acceptable model for Christians? Why or why not?

4. Go back to your metaphor or picture. Does it express exclusivism, inclusivism, or pluralism? What does your metaphor tell you about your beliefs? Does the metaphor imply or belie what you really think?

Appendix: Writing Creatively About New Testament Characters

CREATIVE WRITING USING A BIBLICAL PERSONALITY

You do not have to be a professional writer to enter imaginatively into the world of the New Testament. We are created in the image of God (Gen. 1:27), the Author of life, which indicates to me that every one of us has the creative spark inside—the urge and ability to become authors ourselves. If you keep a journal, and I recommend journal writing to any student of the New Testament, you will find yourself reflecting not only on the great themes of theology and Christology but on what religious experience means for you. You might also reflect on what the encounter with Christ meant for persons mentioned in the New Testament.

In my years of teaching I have read many remarkable short stories written by young people who have reflected on New Testament personalities using a few simple guidelines. The instructions are given below, followed by an example of a student's writing. The models I used in the classroom came from Frederick Buechner's *Peculiar Treasures: A Biblical Who's Who* (New York: Harper & Row, 1979). Buechner's use of contemporary allusions and settings made an unmistakable impact on these young authors.

You are encouraged to try your hand at writing your own short story. Have fun!

INSTRUCTIONS:

1. Pick a personality and one episode or narrative involving this person. Possibilities are listed below.

2. Read closely all the New Testament literature concerning this personality. Be thorough.

3. In choosing a personality, pick an episode in which a dramatic change occurred or might have occurred.

4. Decide whether you wish to write in the first person (from the character's perspective) or the third person (from an omniscient narrator's perspective).

5. Write an imaginative story, using contemporary language, in which you include either

(a) the events, actions, thoughts leading *up to* and including the biblical episode, or

(b) the biblical episode and the events, actions, thoughts *following* this episode.

Anachronisms are fine. Do not worry about keeping a historical distance from the action. Wherever possible, *show* your character's thoughts and feelings; do not *tell* them.

Personalities in the Synoptic Gospels

(Parallels are listed on the same line; a new episode is listed on a different line.)

Barabbas: Mark 15:6–15
Herod the Great: Matthew 2:1–16
John the Baptizer: Matthew 3:1–17; Mark 1:4–11; Luke 3:1–22
Joseph: Matthew 1:18–25
    Matthew 2:13–23
    Luke 2:41–51
Judas Iscariot: Matthew 26:14–16; Mark 14:10–11; Luke 22:3–6
    Matthew 26:47–50; Mark 14:43–50; Luke 22:47–48
    Matthew 27:3–10
Pontius Pilate: Matthew 27:15–26; Mark 15:1–15; Luke 23:1–25
Zacchaeus: Luke 19:1–10
the paralytic: Mark 2:1–12; Matthew 9:1–8; Luke 5:17–26
the Gerasene demoniac: Matthew 8:28–34; Mark 5:1–19; Luke 8:26–39
the woman with hemorrhage: Mark 5:25–34
Herod Antipas: Matthew 14:1–12; Mark 6:14–29; Luke 9:7–9
the Syrophoenician woman: Mark 7:24–30; Matthew 15:21–28
Joseph of Arimathea: Matthew 27: 57–60; Mark 15:42–46; Luke 23:50–56
the rich young ruler: Matthew 19:16–30; Mark 10:17–31; Luke 18:18–30
the woman with ointment: Matthew 26:6–13; Mark 14:3–9; Luke 7:36–50
Mary Magdalene: Matthew 28:1–10; Mark 16:1–11; Luke 24:1–11
Zechariah: Luke 1:5–23
    Luke 1:57–80
Elizabeth: Luke 1:5–7, 24–25
Mary: Luke 1:26–38
    Luke 1:39–56
    Luke 2:41–51
Simeon: Luke 2:22–35
Centurion slave owner: Matthew 8:5–13; Luke 7:1–10
the lawyer: Luke 10:25–37

Martha: Luke 10:38–42
the poor widow: Luke 21:1–4; Mark 12:41–44
the thief on the cross: Luke 23:39–43
Cleopas: Luke 24:13–35
Peter: Matthew 4:18–22; Luke 5:1–11; Mark 1:16–20
    Matthew 16:13–23; Mark 8:27–33; Luke 9:18–22
    Matthew 17:1–8; Mark 9:2–8; Luke 9:28–36
    Matthew 26:69–75; Mark 14:26–31, 53–54, 66–72;
Luke 22:31–34, 54–62

Personalities in John's Gospel

Mary (wedding at Cana): John 2:1–12
Nicodemus: John 3:1–15 (see also 19:38–42)
Samaritan woman at the well: John 4:7–29
woman caught in adultery: John 8:1–11
Lazarus (or his sisters, Mary and Martha): John 11:1–44
Peter at the Last Supper: John 13:1–10
Peter and the resurrected Christ: John 21:1–19

Personalities in Acts of the Apostles

Peter at Pentecost: Acts 2:1–42
Ananias and Sapphira: Acts 5:1–11
Stephen: Acts 6:8—7:60
Simon Magus: Acts 8:9–24
Philip and the Ethiopian eunuch: Acts 8:26–39
Ananias in Damascus: Acts 9:10–19
Tabitha (Dorcas): Acts 9:36–43
Cornelius: Acts 10
Rhoda; Peter's escape from prison: Acts 12:1–17
Lydia: Acts 16:11–15
the Philippian jailer: Acts 16:25–34
Eutychus: Acts 20:7–12
Herod Agrippa: Acts 25:13—26:32
Publius on Malta: Acts 28:1–10

STUDENT ESSAY: "AS SEEN FROM A CROSS"

(I wish to thank my former student Ellen Shippen for allowing me to use her short story here.)

As I heard the horrible clank of the door shutting between me and the jailer, the reality of the cell and pain and death finally hit me. If I had just not been so overcome by the beauty and value of that gold, I would not be here. If I had just dropped the gold and run like the other men, they never would have caught me. But then I could sit here all day and think of what-ifs and still not get anywhere. Why me?

An icy shudder went through me as I remembered that hand grab my shoulder and fling me around face to face with the meanest looking soldier I ever saw. The gold coins spilled onto the deck, rolling toward his sandaled feet. Terrified, I stood there, unable to move or say a word. Then he laughed haughtily and called out, still looking straight into my eyes, "Hey, boys, we caught ourselves a live one with his hand in the cookie jar. We'll have ourselves a grand time with this one."

Then I looked around to see that the ship was empty of everyone but Roman soldiers.

"I guess one's better than none," another soldier said. "Those others are all gone—See?" He pointed to the small ship a little way off. "But I would like to see, just once, a man crucified who I caught with my own hands."

"Well, your turn will come. Come on. Help me with this one."

Crucified! My heart sank. Of course they're going to crucify me. The other pirates had warned me of this before, but I never thought it would happen to me. Now it has, I thought. Now it has. My body went limp as the soldiers dragged me to jail. I didn't try to fight. Fighting would have made the soldiers hit me harder than they did. Hot, dusty, and numb, I landed on the hard floor of the jail.

The metallic slam of the door broke my thoughtless state, taking me back to the events of the day.

The day had started out the same way it had for the past seven years. I awoke to the rocking of the boat and to the sound of the breakfast bell. I ate some bread and had a little water, then began my job helping in the kitchen. The other men busied themselves with their jobs while the captain and first mate made plans and gave orders. These were the tedious times. They were bad, but the good times were so good that these times didn't matter. The memory of the good times made me smile. It was because of this glory and adventure that I had decided to become a pirate in the first place.

I can hear my parents' voices at the dinner table right now.

"Dysmas, your grades came today. Your father and I are disappointed, son."

"Yes. Why can't you be more like your brother? Ed makes fine marks and he's also captain of the swim team. He doesn't waste his time, but all you seem to care about is hanging out with those no-good friends of yours. Why don't you apply yourself more?"

"I'm sorry I'm such a failure to you and Mom, Dad,"

I'd retort. "I guess you really got stuck when you had me."

Then I'd go out to the street where the rest of my friends usually were and we'd grab a jug of wine and try to find some fun. We'd steal apples off neighbors' trees, laugh at the beggars, and taunt women. These pranks were fun but what I really liked was being included.

Occasionally we'd go down to the dock and sit and fantasize about being pirates.

"Just think how great it would be—just a ship on the sea. No more of this crummy town," someone said.

"Yeah, and no parents to bug you," I put in.

"All those exotic, beautiful places. Spain, Italy, Greece. And all those exciting battles. No boredom like there is here."

"And all that partying—all the bounty—silks, silver, gold . . . GOLD. Let me tell you guys, gold is really worth dying for."

I looked around the cell. It was dark except for the beams of evening light that shone through the small window in the middle of one wall. In the corner opposite me was another prisoner snoring furiously on a bench just like the one on which I sat. He was the rough type. His hair and beard were snarled. He was big and muscular and looked as if he were just a few years older than I. I thought, He looks like he could eat me alive, but then what would it matter? I'm going to die tomorrow anyway. Hold on now. What happened? I'm going to be nailed to a cross tomorrow and no one cares. No one.

Oh, I wish at least Mom and Dad were here so I could see them one last time. I left on such a hateful note they were probably glad I went. Couldn't I just see them one last time to tell them I love them, and that I'm sorry for all the pain I caused them? I wish I'd listened to them. They were so right. Irony. I guess I really am a failure after all. Oh, I wish they were here so I could know someone in this lonely world might not want me to die.

I felt the tears welling up and for once I did not try to hold them back. I cried silently for a long time out of fear, regret, and guilt.

I must have fallen asleep because when I woke up it was morning. The other prisoner, who was snoring loudly when I arrived, was now standing up, looking out the window at the big crowds in the street.

"What's all the commotion about?"

"Tomorrow's Passover, man. How long have you been asleep, anyway?" he grumbled.

"Oh, that's right."

"Rotten world. All of those stupid people running around like ants so afraid they might not have enough food for one day; like it's the end of the world. Well, it is for you and me, Bud. Ain't that a joke? They're supposed to let one prisoner out because of the Passover,

but with the big arrest and with Barabbas around, you think anybody's going to remember a couple of nothings like us? Nah. We'll get it like the rest of the crooks."

"Wait a minute." I was hurt by his insult but decided that it was too late to worry about hurt feelings. "What big arrest and who's this guy Barabbas? Why is he so popular?"

"Man, where have you been? Haven't you heard of Jesus of Nazareth?"

"No. Gimme a break. I'm from out of town."

"Well, he's the one they call the Son of God, the Messiah, King of the Jews. They said he works great miracles—making the blind see and the lame walk. And he constantly preaches the good news of the Lord."

I was amazed. No man could ever profess to be the Son of God. Never, not on any of my trips around the Mediterranean, had I heard of anything like this.

"Tell me more. Do you believe he's the Son of God?"

"How should I know? He could be as he says or he could be a complete lunatic who's a pretty good magician on the side. Who knows? But I can tell you this: if he is the king of the Jews, he certainly is a disappointment. What a weakling!"

I kept after him with questions, but I tried not to be too pushy, knowing he was tired and miserable. Still I managed to get out of him some interesting stories he had heard. They gave me something to ponder.

"Now then, you say, one prisoner is to be released and it will be Jesus or who else?"

"Barabbas. He's the Jew who started that rebellion against the Romans. So, of course, you can see how the Jews would side with him. You and me don't stand a chance. Pilate will let Barabbas out and we'll be crucified. Who knows what they'll do with Jesus. Hey, ya want some? It's good to have a friend here and there."

He handed me a full jug of wine and I gladly took a swig.

"Thanks, I needed that," I said, wiping my mouth on my sleeve. Then I watched as he chugged down the entire jug and passed out in the corner. I sat there with my face in my hands.

I was disturbed by the jailer, who turned the key and pushed open the door.

"Get out here!" he shouted, but I stayed there on the bench, frozen in terror. I glanced quickly across the cell. The other prisoner hadn't waked up yet. Then the soldiers came into the cell and dragged us out, onto the street. There in the street in the center of a crowd was a young man who had been whipped mercilessly. It brought tears to my eyes to look at him. The other criminal, still drunk, nudged me. "That, my dear fellow, is Jesus Christ."

I was stunned. This man who had simply preached about God deserves this? I tried to look more closely at him, but then a swift kick knocked me down before a huge piece of wood.

"Carry it!" they screamed.

We, the other crook and I, picked up our crosses and waited. We stood there for a long time while the soldiers entertained themselves with Jesus. They put a long purple robe on him and wove a "crown" out of thorn and mashed it onto his head. So much abuse heaped on such a quiet man, I thought.

It hurt me to look at him, so I tried to look away. Then the soldiers pushed us forward. Keeping my eyes on the ground, I stumbled through the wall of howling people as the soldiers brutally drove us through the gates. Like a pack of wolves, the people closed the gap and followed us as we started up the hill. It seemed I'd barely reached the top when they grabbed me from behind. They threw the cross down under me and tied the ropes around me. Before I had time to think, I felt the cold iron against my skin and the fierce slam of the hammer nailing my hands and feet. Then they raised me up and hoisted the cross into its stand.

Practically unconscious from the pain, I looked around. My head spun. I saw the cross there next to mine and the people all around it. Women were weeping; a few men stood in silence. Some were praying, but most were screaming angrily. The soldiers were drinking and the priests, like cheerleaders, were getting the crowd to shout louder and more fiercely at Jesus. Then I heard the most amazing thing from Jesus' lips. In the midst of all the hatefulness he said very softly, "Father, forgive them, for they know not what they do."

He was, incredibly, asking forgiveness for these savage people who had nailed him to a cross.

I looked up to read the sign above his head, and as I had expected, it read "Jesus of Nazareth, King of the Jews." This helpless man was the king of the Jews. The crowd below was still heaping insult after insult on him. They laughed, mocked, and spat on him.

The agony and shame were too much for my fellow prisoner. He shouted miserably, writhing in pain, "I thought you said you were the Christ! Save yourself and us!"

I had wondered this myself, but when I heard it spoken, the taunt sounded hollow and echoed in my ears. Jesus was so calm and peaceful. He looked intently at the other man on the cross, then turned and looked at me. His eyes seemed to reach into my very soul, and all of my selfishness, lies, and petty jealousies were exposed. This look turned me completely around. I believed with all my heart that he really was who he claimed to be. I had to defend this good man.

"Don't you fear God since you are under the same sentence? We are getting what we deserve but this man has done nothing wrong." I turned to look at Jesus again. His eyes shone. He really seemed to care. I said, "Jesus, remember me when you come into your kingdom." He answered me, "I tell you the truth. Today you will be with me in paradise."

With those words my soul was released and for once I truly relaxed in perfect freedom. The agony continued, but it was a small price to pay to die beside the Christ.

Bibliography

Aland, Kurt, ed. *Synopsis of the Four Gospels.* New York: United Bible Societies, 1970.

Bauman, Edward W. *An Introduction to the New Testament.* Philadelphia: Westminster Press, 1961.

Bonhoeffer, Dietrich. *Ethics.* New York: Macmillan Publishing Co., 1978.

Buechner, Frederick. *Peculiar Treasures: A Biblical Who's Who.* San Francisco: Harper & Row, 1979.

Francis, Fred O., and J. Paul Sampley, eds. *Pauline Parallels.* Philadelphia: Fortress Press, 1984.

Harvey, Van A. *A Handbook of Theological Terms.* New York: Macmillan Publishing Co., 1964.

Hill, Brennan R., Paul Knitter, and William Madges. *Faith, Religion, and Theology: A Contemporary Introduction.* Mystic, Conn.: Twenty-Third Publications, 1992.

Johnson, Luke T. *The Writings of the New Testament: An Introduction.* Philadelphia: Fortress Press, 1986.

Laymon, Charles M., ed. *The Interpreter's One-Volume Commentary on the Bible.* Nashville: Abingdon Press, 1984.

Leon-Dufour, Xavier. *Dictionary of the New Testament.* Translated by Terrence Prendergast. San Francisco: Harper & Row, 1980.

Morrison, Clinton. *An Analytical Concordance to the Revised Standard Version of the New Testament.* Philadelphia: Westminster Press, 1979.

Newsom, Carol A., and Sharon H. Ringe, eds. *The Women's Bible Commentary.* Louisville, Ky.: Westminster/John Knox Press, 1992.

The NIV Serendipity Bible for Study Groups. Grand Rapids: Zondervan Publishing House, 1989.

Throckmorton, Burton, ed. *Gospel Parallels: A Synopsis of the First Three Gospels.* New York: Thomas Nelson & Sons, 1957.

Tyson, Joseph B. *The New Testament and Early Christianity.* New York: Macmillan Publishing Co., 1984.

Wink, Walter, *Transforming Bible Study.* Nashville: Abingdon Press, 1989.

Young, Robert. *Young's Analytical Concordance to the Bible.* Grand Rapids: Wm. B. Eerdmans Publishing Co., 1975.

Printed in the United States
218698BV00001B/18/A

9 780664 254841